Ethics: The Basics

Updated and revised, *Ethics: The Basics, Second Edition* introduces students to a rich variety of ethical concepts, principles, theories, and traditions while providing them with the conceptual tools necessary to think critically about ethical issues.

Presented in a convenient, reader-friendly format, chapters lay out the foundation of the discipline while introducing a series of living ethical traditions—each with its own associated set of ethical concepts and principles. Major questions and core ideas are considered from the perspective of different historically-influenced philosophical approaches to ethics, including virtue, natural law, social contract, utilitarian, deontological, and care ethics. In addition, the volume reviews several western and non-western ethical traditions, along with selected religious interpretations of ethical principles, and includes a variety of supplementary materials to reinforce concepts and aid in comprehension.

Retaining all of the core elements and features that have earned *Ethics: The Basics* its place as one of the most popular and accessible texts for introductory ethics courses, Mizzoni has also added several new features to this edition, including a series of boxed inserts highlighting various concepts and arguments, problems, and meticulously-curated lists of related online resources. *Ethics: The Basics, Second Edition* provides students with a solid foundation of fundamental principles, along with the valuable critical-thinking skills necessary to navigate the moral quandaries of today's complex world.

Ethics
The Basics

Second Edition

John Mizzoni

WILEY Blackwell

This second edition first published 2017

Edition history: John Wiley & Sons Ltd (1e, 2010)

Registered Offices
John Wiley & Sons, Inc., 111 River Street, Hoboken, NJ 07030, USA
John Wiley & Sons Ltd, The Atrium, Southern Gate, Chichester, West Sussex, PO19 8SQ, UK

Editorial Office
350 Main Street, Malden, MA 02148-5020, USA

For details of our global editorial offices, customer services, and more information about Wiley products visit us at www.wiley.com.

Wiley also publishes its books in a variety of electronic formats and by print-on-demand. Some content that appears in standard print versions of this book may not be available in other formats.

Library of Congress Cataloging-in-Publication data applied for

Paperback ISBN: 9781119150688

Cover Image: Holly Mindrip/unsplash.com
Cover Design: Dennis Mizzoni and Wiley

Set in 10/13pt Palatino LT Std by SPi Global, Pondicherry, India

10 9 8 7 6 5 4 3 2 1

Contents

Ethics Self-Orientation

I. The General Nature of Ethics

Read each of the statements below and score it with a number between 0 and 10, with 0 being "totally disagree" and 10 being "totally agree."

1. ____ There are some universal ethical values.
2. ____ We can't just ask if something is good/evil/right/wrong; we must always ask, `good/evil/right/wrong *where, when,* and *for whom?'*
3. ____ Right/wrong is always a function of a society's beliefs and no more than that.
4. ____ There aren't any universal ethical values.
5. ____ Ethical values and principles have a deeper source than simply a society's collective beliefs.
6. ____ There are some unchanging ethical standards, some things are just good and other things are just evil.

Scoring for the General Nature of Ethics

A	B
1. ___	2. ____
5. ____	3. ____
6. ____	4. ____

____ + 40 − ____ = ____________

Total Total *General Nature of Ethics Total*

If your *General Nature of Ethics Total* score is between 50 and 70, you seem to believe in Ethical Universalism.

If your *General Nature of Ethics Total* score is between 10 and 50, you seem to believe in Ethical Relativism.

II. Practical Ethics: How do you think you should decide whether what you are doing is ethical or not?

Read each of the statements below and score it with a number between 0 and 10, with 0 being "totally disagree" and 10 being "totally agree."

1. ____ I should make sure I am not doing a bad action hoping that good will come out of it.
2. ____ I should look to see whether I am caring for those with whom I am in close relationship.
3. ____ I should look to see if I am destroying human goods or values.
4. ____ I should look to see how deeply rooted in care my action is.
5. ____ I should look to see that I am acting in accord with human nature.
6. ____ I should look to what kind of person I want to be.
7. ____ I should ask whether it would be reasonable and rational for someone to agree to follow this moral rule.
8. ____ I should attend to the needs of those it is in my power to help.
9. ____ I should look at my action and make sure it is respectful of persons and their rights.
10. ____ I should look to see what outcome my action will have on all who will be affected by it.
11. ____ I should look to see if others are also willing to agree to follow this moral rule.
12. ____ I should ask `what kind of person would do this?'
13. ____ I should look to see whether I am preserving human goods and values.
14. ____ I should check whether what I am about to do will bring about the greatest happiness for the greatest number.
15. ____ I should look to see what my duties are, and not focus on the outcome of my action.
16. ____ I should attend to the rules that are necessary for social living.
17. ____ I should ask `what character trait am I exhibiting if I do this?'

18. ____ I should look to see if my motive is to seek goodness for goodness's sake.
19. ____ I should look to make sure that the end will justify the means.
20. ____ I should think about how I would like to be remembered.
21. ____ I should examine if my action will have the best consequences for all concerned.

Scoring for Practical Ethics

In each of the following six boxes, add up the scores you gave for the questions in Part II.

Utilitarian Ethics	**Deontological Ethics**	**Virtue Ethics**
10. _____	1. _____	6. _____
14. _____	9. _____	12. _____
19. _____	15. _____	17. _____
21. _____	18. _____	20. _____
Total: _____	Total: _____	Total: _____
If your score is 30 or more, you seem to follow Utilitarian Ethics.	*If your score is 30 or more, you seem to follow Deontological ethics.*	*If your score is 30 or more, you seem to follow Virtue Ethics.*
If your score is close to 0, you disagree with Utilitarian Ethics.	*If your score is close to 0, you disagree with Deontological ethics.*	*If your score is close to 0, you disagree with Virtue Ethics.*

Natural Law Ethics	**Social Contract Ethics**	**Care Ethics**
3. _____	7. _____	2. _____
5. _____	11. _____	4. _____
13. _____	16. _____	8. _____
Total: _____	Total: _____	Total: _____
If your score is 20 or more, you seem to follow Natural Law Ethics.	*If your score is 20 or more, you seem to follow Social Contract Ethics.*	*If your score is 20 or more, you seem to follow Care Ethics.*
If your score is close to 0, you disagree with Natural Law Ethics.	*If your score is close to 0, you disagree with Social Contract Ethics.*	*If your score is close to 0, you disagree with Care Ethics.*

Introduction

Let's begin with a few ethical questions. Do murderers, because of their actions, deserve the death penalty? Is executing murderers morally justified because it will likely have more good consequences for society than sentencing them to life in prison?

A pregnant woman who drinks alcoholic beverages while pregnant stands the chance that her baby will be born with hearing and vision problems, motor-skill problems, language-use problems, or memory or attention problems. Is it morally permissible – is it ethically right – for a woman to drink alcohol while pregnant? We need some way to assess the importance of the risks involved.

How would we begin to answer ethical questions like these? Are there ethical standards we can use to help us answer ethical questions? If so, where do these ethical standards come from? Do ethical standards come from one's society? Do they come from God or religion? Are they in some way derived from rationality and logic? Perhaps ethical standards are derived from human nature that has been designed by God. Or maybe ethical standards somehow sprang from our human nature that has been shaped by millions of years of evolution.

Each of these questions about ethical standards is closely related, yet slightly different. One way to sum up what they all have in common is to say that they are concerned with the origins of ethics. As we will see in this book, people have attempted to formulate and support answers to these philosophical questions about ethics for many centuries, stretching far back into antiquity. Philosophers, in addition to thinking about such questions and attempting to formulate answers to them, are known for their skill in grouping questions together as a first step in

Ethics: The Basics, Second Edition. John Mizzoni.

organizing our thoughts on these issues. As a way of organizing the above cluster of questions, we can describe the cluster as *the philosophical problem of the origins of ethics*.

Solving the problem and fully answering its questions would involve providing a well-developed account of where ethical standards come from. Someone might claim that philosophical questions do not have answers and therefore philosophical problems cannot be solved. But that couldn't be the case in this situation; for each of us surely uses ethical standards (at least some of the time), and these ethical standards surely came from somewhere! Where did they come from? Solving this problem might be an exceedingly difficult task, but why would it be *impossible* to solve? The challenge is in providing a convincing and well-supported case for where ethical standards actually come from. And even if we have a well-supported case, experience tells us that we might still be wrong! The difficulty, then, is not that there are no answers to these philosophical questions about ethics, but that it is hard to be sure which answers are the correct answers.

There are other philosophical problems in ethics related to the philosophical problem of the origins of ethics; that is, there are other philosophical questions about ethics that can be thematically clustered. For instance, do we always learn ethics from others, or are there ethical standards somehow prepackaged inside our hearts and minds? If we always learn ethics from others, and ethical standards are wholly derived from one's society, then doesn't that imply that all ethical standards are relative, since each society is different and has its own unique history? And, on the other hand, if ethical standards come from our individual hearts and minds, doesn't that also imply that ethical standards are relative, since each individual person is different and unique?

Thinking about the close relationship between ethics and society might prompt us to wonder what life would be like and how human beings would behave if they didn't live in civilized society. Would ethical standards apply to these people? How would these people become aware of ethical standards and principles? This particular cluster of questions that centers on the issue of whether ethics is always a direct function of society can be considered *the philosophical problem of relativism*. This is a philosophical problem of ethics that is all the more pressing as globalization advances, that is, as global interactions of societies become more extensive.

In attempting to answer questions about the origins of ethics and the seeming relativity of ethics, many thinkers have had to closely examine human nature. But what is human nature? The difficulty in answering this question ushers in yet another philosophical problem close to the heart of ethics: *the philosophical problem of human nature*. One way to begin to get a handle on this problem is to focus on human characteristics. Which characteristics are essential to being a human person? Rationality? Emotional intelligence? Made in the image of God? Do men and women have different essential characteristics? If men and women have different characteristics, would that mean they use different ethical standards? Is there, then, such a thing as a feminist ethics, as opposed to a masculine ethics?

Another important dimension of human nature that bears upon ethics is the question of whether human beings are selfish creatures who act only to benefit themselves. Is it the case that when people help others in need, for instance, they are truly motivated by genuine concern for others? Or are they calculating how they themselves will need help in the future? Are human beings social creatures who genuinely care for the well-being of others? For many centuries, thinkers have pursued answers to this cluster of questions that forms the philosophical problem of human nature; the same is true for the problem of the origins of ethics, and the problem of relativism.

Aside from these three rather *theoretical* problems of ethics, there is a more basic and fundamental ethical problem, one that we face all the time (and it is the philosophical problem of ethics that occupies most of this book). The problem is captured in the following question: How should I determine the right thing to do? Or, more broadly expressed, how should I live my life? What counts as a life lived well? What kind of person should I become? We will call this *the problem of conduct*. As opposed to the three previous ethical problems mentioned, this one is very practical. The answers to the questions at the core of this problem will require us to take action: it is a philosophical problem about what we should *do*.

Just to give you some idea of the immense range of solutions to this fundamental ethical problem, consider some of the following philosophical questions that are relevant. The questions themselves provide clues to how different people have attempted to solve *the problem of conduct*.

Is ethics about doing one's duty, being responsible; or is ethics about being happy and working toward making others happy? Is ethics about doing what's best for me? Am I responsible for the person I am, the choices I make, the characteristics I possess, and the happiness I attain? What is happiness? Does happiness have to do with pleasure or spirituality? Can human beings really achieve happiness in this life, or is an afterlife needed for complete human happiness and fulfillment? How is ethics informed by religion? Is the golden rule a Christian ethical principle? How is ethics informed by science? How is ethics shaped by society? How might ethics be derived from rationality? If ethics is derived from rationality, does that mean that only rational beings count, morally speaking? Or are non-rational beings worthy of respect, too? What are rights? Are they something all humans possess, or do only rational beings possess them?

In attempting to solve the *philosophical problem of conduct*, in this book we will consider an extensive assortment of ethical concepts, principles, theories, and traditions. I introduce you, the reader, to a range of ethical concepts, ethical principles, ethical theories, and ethical traditions that you can consider as you attempt to solve this problem for yourself. You are living a life right now, so you have no choice but to attempt to deal with the problem and answer the following questions, How should I live my life? What counts as a life lived well? What kind of person should I become? What makes an action morally right or wrong? And how should I determine the right thing to do? In this book, what I am offering is a framework to help you organize a truly bewildering array of philosophical questions about ethics. Part of the framework I offer is the fourfold distinction between ethical concepts, principles, theories, and traditions.

Let's take a further look at the framework. Ethical concepts are the most basic building blocks of ethics. An introduction to ethics will involve becoming familiar with a range of concepts such as virtue, rights, duty, happiness, freedom, etc. Next come principles. An introduction to ethics will gather together basic ethical principles that most people have heard of, like the golden rule, or the principle "the end does not justify the means." But an introduction to ethics will also include lesser-known principles, such as the principle of utility and the categorical imperative.

The ethical theories and traditions discussed will range from those first formulated in ancient Greece over 2,000 years ago, to those first formulated in the twentieth century. We can think of an ethical *theory* as an attempt to pull together a collection of ethical concepts and principles into a coherent whole in order to answer an ethical question or solve an ethical problem. An ethical *tradition*, by contrast, is a theory that has taken on a life of its own. An ethical tradition has a theoretical center that passes from generation to generation but it also stays alive through the actions and practices of actual people. An ethical tradition is a living theory, not merely an abstract theory in a theoretician's mind. We ourselves, for instance, probably conduct our lives within the broad outlines of a particular ethical tradition. We may not readily be able to articulate the details of this ethical tradition or the ethical theory that underlies it, but it is surely there nonetheless.

Part of the difference between an ethical theory and an ethical tradition is that over time a theory may be changed and modified. For instance, the virtue ethics approach of Confucius is different from Aristotle's virtue ethics approach, which is different from a Christian virtue ethics. Similarly, the utilitarian ethical approach of Bentham in the 1700s is different from Mill's utilitarian ethical approach in the 1800s, which is different from Singer's utilitarian ethical approach in the 1900s; so there is not *one* utilitarian or virtue theory, but rather, there is a utilitarian ethical tradition and a virtue ethics tradition.

Ethics is a field that not only looks at ethical and moral ideals that we *should* have, but also examines actual codes of conduct that people do indeed follow and use, whether consciously or unconsciously. Some ethical codes of conduct are written out and some are orally or socially transmitted. Which ethical concepts and principles do *you* routinely lean on when you are thinking about whether something is morally right or wrong? Are you presupposing a certain ethical theory or ethical tradition without even realizing it? This book will help you identify your ethical orientation: the ethical concepts, principles, and theories you use and the ethical tradition to which you belong. As a first (rough) start to this process, complete the Ethics Self Orientation exercise that appears before this Introduction.

Because this book is only an introduction to several core philosophical problems in ethics, its aim is not to convince you to agree with the solutions that the author personally favors. You will have to work out the solutions for yourself. The book provides most of the necessary conceptual tools you will need for this project, but it will be up to you to put the tools to work.

The ethics of capital punishment and the ethics of fetal alcohol syndrome are but two of the vast numbers of concrete ethical issues we can work on with these tools. In the context of discussing ethical concepts, principles, theories, and traditions we will engage with various ethical issues. These issues range from life and death issues like abortion, euthanasia, suicide, and animal ethics, to issues of justice like punishment, civil disobedience, and racism, to issues of character, to public policy issues. This is not a book about ethical issues, however; it is a book that simply provides an ethical framework. You can use the framework to help you think about a few core philosophical problems in ethics, or simply use it to aid you in thinking about ethical issues. Readers can use this ethical framework to think through ethical issues that are important to them, issues that may or may not be discussed in this book.

What makes this book unique is that it attempts to lay out clearly and simply a rich collection of ethical concepts, principles, theories, and traditions that are in use in today's society. A brief introduction like this can be helpful to students who wish to engage in productive discourse about ethical issues in our society.

This book is a product of many years of teaching ethics to undergraduates. Today, there are introductory ethics books in print that include too much material and quickly move beyond the introductory level. This book, however, is genuinely introductory. Undergraduate students should be able not only to read and understand this book, but to master the ethics material in the book. There are plenty of introductory ethics books that claim to offer tools for students to do ethics themselves. But if the students cannot understand and master the tools, how can they possibly *use* them? The material in this book is meant to be mastered by undergraduate students so that they can apply it to their own thinking about ethics.

Summary of Philosophical Problems about Ethics

This book discusses three theoretical problems of ethics and one practical problem of ethics. The theoretical problems are: (1) *the problem of the origins of ethics*, (2) *the problem of relativism*, and (3) *the problem of human nature*. Various thinkers have suggested different solutions (or answers) to these problems.

(1) As a solution to the problem of the origins of ethics we will look at: Ethical Relativism and Ethical Universalism (Chapter 1), Virtue Ethics (Chapter 2), Natural Law Ethics (Chapter 3), Social Contract Ethics (Chapter 4), Utilitarian Ethics (Chapter 5), Deontological Ethics (Chapter 6), Divine Command Ethics (Chapter 6), and Care Ethics (Chapter 7).
(2) As solutions to the problem of relativism we will primarily look at Ethical Relativism and Ethical Universalism (Chapter 1). These two theories, though, can take on many different forms. As we will see,

we could have a virtue-based ethical relativism, for instance, or a utilitarian-based universalism.

(3) Solutions to the problem of human nature are offered in various ethical traditions: Universal Ethics, Relative Ethics, Virtue Ethics, Natural Law Ethics, Social Contract Ethics, Utilitarian Ethics, Deontological Ethics, and Care Ethics. Although each of these ethical traditions deals with the problem of human nature, their solutions are not always fully developed.

(4) As solutions to the fourth, practical, problem of ethics discussed, *the problem of conduct*, we will look at Virtue Ethics, Natural Law Ethics, Social Contract Ethics, Utilitarian Ethics, Deontological Ethics, and Care Ethics.

As you can tell, the theories and traditions considered in this book usually provide answers and solutions not only to one ethical problem, but often more than one. Take Social Contract Ethics, for example. It offers solutions to all four ethical problems. The same is true for Virtue Ethics, Natural Law Ethics, Utilitarian Ethics, Deontological Ethics, and Care Ethics. The fact that one theory can offer a solution to four different ethical problems is an indication of the theory's depth, breadth, power, and plausibility.

Though we will work with four different philosophical problems about ethics, the central theme of the book focuses on the most pressing practical ethical problem each of us faces, *the problem of conduct*.

Chapter 1

Relative Ethics or Universal Ethics?

Iqbal is a boy, seven years of age, who must work 12 hours a day weaving rugs. In his culture child labor is customary. Around the world, in fact, there are millions of children who work to earn money instead of going to school. A recent report numbered child laborers, between five and 14 years of age, at over 200 million.

In some cultures, in order to protect young women from sexual advances of boys and men, they undergo at puberty the process of "breast ironing," a cultural practice in which their breasts are pounded and massaged in order to make them disappear.

It is not a strong concern in some cultures that adults have heterosexual sex with young teens and children; and in other cultures, it is customary for men to have sexual relations with younger boys.

One last example of this kind. In order to preserve their chastity and honor, in some cultures girls from seven to thirteen years of age have their clitoris surgically removed – it is known as female circumcision. Opponents of the practice call it female genital mutilation.

Are these practices ethical? What makes a cultural practice or social norm ethical or unethical?

Everyone is familiar with philosophizing about where ethical rules and standards come from. At one time or another we have all asked the questions, What makes something right or wrong? and Where does right and wrong come from?

Ethics: The Basics, Second Edition. John Mizzoni.

1.1 Relative Ethics

These may seem to be very broad ethical questions, yet the existence of child labor, breast ironing, female circumcision, and divergent sexual practices make them very real questions – and in some cases, where children's lives are at stake, quite urgent. People have thought about and struggled with these kinds of questions about the origins of ethics for many centuries. When one faces these hard questions, thinks about the philosophical problem of the origins of ethics, and becomes aware of the great variety of human customs the world over, it becomes tempting to say that right and wrong are just a matter of opinion, since what is regarded as right or wrong in one culture may not be seen in the same way in another culture. Right and wrong seem culturally relative. Also, some practices that were once regarded as right, either a century ago or 20 years ago, are nowadays regarded as wrong. Ethical standards seem to change, and there is so much disagreement between cultural practices that *ethical relativism*, the view that right and wrong are always relative, seems justified (see Figure 1.1).

Those who defend the idea that ethics is relative emphasize the differences among our ethical judgments and the differences among various ethical traditions. Some relativists call these cultural and ethical traditions *folkways*. This is a helpful concept for understanding ethical relativism because it highlights that the ways and customs are simply developed by average people (folk) over long periods of time. Here is how the twentieth-century social scientist William G. Sumner describes the folkways:

> The folkways...are not creations of human purpose and wit. They are like products of natural forces which men unconsciously set in operation, or they are like the instinctive ways of animals, which are developed out of experience, which reach a final form of maximum adaptation to an interest,

Figure 1.1

1. In culture A, we observe arranged marriages.
2. In culture B, we observe polygamous marriages.
3. In culture C, we observe self-arranged marriages.

---

4. Therefore, marriage is all relative.

> which are handed down by tradition and admit of no exception or variation, yet change to meet new conditions, still within the same limited methods, and without rational reflection or purpose. From this it results that all the life of human beings, in all ages and stages of culture, is primarily controlled by a vast mass of folkways handed down from the earliest existence of the race. (Sumner 1906: 19–20)

Folkways: The concept that customs are developed by average people (folk) over long periods of time.

Something is right, an ethical relativist will say, if it is consistent with a given society's folkways and wrong if it goes against a society's folkways. Relative ethics will say that in cultures where female circumcision has taken place for centuries, it is right to continue to circumcise young girls, and wrong to attempt to change this tradition.

Relativists believe that ethical differences between cultures are irreconcilable. On their view, irreconcilable differences are actually quite predictable because each society today has its own unique history and it is out of this history that a society's ethical values and standards have been forged. Around the globe, each society has its own unique history; consequently, each society has its own unique set of ethical standards. Relativists would say that if there are any *agreements* between cultures on ethical values, standards, or issues, we should not place any importance on that accidental fact, because, after all, the true nature of ethics is relative, and the origin of ethics lies in each society's unique history.

1.2 Universal Ethics

Not everyone, though, is content with the relativist's rather skeptical answer to the question about the ultimate nature and origin of ethics. Instead of a relativist answer to the question, plenty of people have asserted that *not everything* is relative. A critic of relativism will say that not everything in ethics is relative, because some aspects of ethics are universal. Those who hold this view are called *ethical universalists*. In contrast to the ethical relativist who claims that all ethics is relative, the universalists contend that there are *at least some* ethical values, standards, or principles that are *not* relative. And this somewhat modest claim is all that a universalist needs to challenge the relativist's generalization that all ethics is relative. An easy way to grasp what universalists are talking about is to consider the concept of universal human rights. The *Universal Declaration of Human Rights* was created in 1948 by the United Nations General Assembly. It has inspired close to 100 bills of rights for new nations. People who believe in universal human rights hold ethical universalism: they believe there are certain rights that all human beings have, no matter what culture or society they belong to. An ethical relativist will deny this, and maintain that rights are meaningful only within a particular cultural tradition, not in a universal sense.

1.3 Cultural Relativism or Ethical Relativism?

In order to achieve a bit more clarity on the issue of relativism, we must consider the difference between *cultural* relativism and *ethical* relativism. *Cultural relativism* is the observation that, as a matter of fact, different cultures have different practices, standards, and values. Child labor, breast ironing, divergent sexual practices, and female circumcision are examples of practices that are customary in some cultures and would be seen as ethical in those cultures. In other cultures, however, such practices are not customary, and are seen as unethical. If we took the time to study different cultures, as anthropologists and other social scientists do, we would see that there is no shortage of examples such as these. As the anthropologist Ruth Benedict has put it: "The diversity of cultures can be endlessly documented" (1934: 45).

As examples, consider wife and child battering, polygamy, cannibalism, or infanticide. There are some cultures (subcultures at least) that endorse these practices as morally acceptable. Western culture, by contrast, regards these practices as immoral and illegal. It seems to be true, therefore, just as a matter of fact, that different cultures have different ethical standards on at least some matters. By comparing different cultures, we can easily see differences between them, not just on ethical matters, but on many different levels.

> *Cultural Relativism*: The theory that, as a matter of fact, different cultures have different practices, standards, and values.

What we need to notice about *ethical* relativism, in contrast with *cultural* relativism, is that ethical relativism makes a much stronger and more controversial claim about the nature of ethics. *Ethical relativism* is the view that *all* ethical standards are relative, to the degree that there are no permanent, universal, objective values or standards. This view, though, cannot be justified by simply comparing different cultures and noticing the differences between them. The ethical relativist's claim goes beyond observation and predicts that all ethical standards, even the ones we have not yet observed, will always be relative. More simply put, *ethical relativism* is an ethical theory, hence its name. *Cultural relativism* is not an ethical theory, it is simply the view that cultures differ and display much diversity.

1.4 Cultural Relativism and Universal Ethics

A universalist will respond to ethical relativism by pointing out that very general basic values – not specific moral rules or codes – are recognized, at least implicitly, to some extent in all societies. Even though on the surface, in particular actions or mores, there seems to be unavoidable disagreement, a universalist will observe that there are general values that provide the foundations of ethics (see Figure 1.2). One ambition, then, for the universalists who wish to immerse themselves in cultural studies, is not only to attempt to understand and appreciate other cultures' perspectives and experiences, but to detect what common ground – common values – are shared by the different cultures. Certainly there is cultural difference on how these values are manifested, but according to universalism, the values themselves represent more than arbitrary social conventions.

An ethical universalist, then, can agree that there are cultural differences and that cultures display diversity. But universalists will also claim that only some social practices are merely conventional; they hold that not all practices are merely conventional. Thus universalists

Figure 1.2

1. In culture A, we observe arranged marriages.
2. In culture B, we observe polygamous marriages.
3. In culture C, we observe self-arranged marriages.

---

4. Therefore, many cultures value marriage.

Figure 1.3

Possible combinations:
- Cultural relativism & ethical relativism
- Cultural relativism & ethical universalism

will explain that it is possible to believe that both ethical universalism and cultural relativism are true (see Figure 1.3).

Although ethical universalism is conceptually consistent with cultural relativism, this point can sometimes be overlooked, since social scientists from the first half of the twentieth century who carried out extensive research into different cultures and societies have contributed to the linking in our minds of ethical relativism and cultural relativism. The distinction between cultural relativism and ethical relativism is an important one. Everyone agrees with cultural relativism, even universalists, but not everyone agrees with ethical relativism. Ethical relativism is a theory about the ultimate nature of ethics, cultural relativism is only a theory about cultural diversity.

1.5 Ethics and Human Nature

We do find some scientists and philosophers of biology who explicitly oppose ethical relativism; they deny ethical relativism because they assert that humans have a biological nature carried by their genes that cultures cannot obliterate but can only adjust to their unique circumstances. As the philosopher of science Michael Ruse puts it:

> … the Darwinian's position does not plunge him/her into wholesale ethical relativism … Against this, the Darwinian recognizes that there are indeed differences from society to society, and also within societies, particularly across time. However, these are readily (and surely properly) explained in the way that most moral theorists would explain them, as secondary, modified consequences of shared primary moral imperatives. (Ruse 1998: 255)

Most theologians also distance themselves from ethical relativism. About the social sciences that sometimes tend toward relativism, the late Pope John Paul II described them as, "theories which misuse scientific research about the human person." "Arguing from the great variety of customs, behaviour patterns and institutions present in humanity," he said, "these theories end up, if not with an outright denial of universal human values, at least with a relativistic conception of morality" (1993: 49). Theologians can deny ethical relativism for monotheistic reasons, for instance. There is one God, they'll say, so it makes sense that there would be universal ethical standards that are in harmony with God's intentions.

The belief in a common human nature is not merely an assumption, but a belief rooted in observation. There is no doubt that social scientists in the nineteenth and twentieth centuries emphasized differences between cultures and gave support to cultural and ethical relativism. But in the last quarter of the twentieth century, the human sciences have been swinging the pendulum to the side that observes shared deep structures concerning ethics and human nature. (This is not unrelated to the major advances in understanding the human genome.) In many sciences today (like evolutionary psychology) there is the perception that there are universal human traits having to do with human language, human facial expressions, the way the human mind works, human food preferences, etc. Evolutionists say that over millions of years these traits have been put into place by the process of natural selection. (It is true that theologians will offer a different account of how these traits have been put into place: they might say they are directly put into place by God, or perhaps indirectly by God via human evolution.) But the main point is that nowadays the view that we can observe common human traits comes from many fields, and it is not merely an unsupportable assumption made by ethical universalists.

1.6 Ethics and Human Rationality

Another way universalists have supported their case for ethical universalism is by pointing to universal features of human rationality. These universalists seek to deny ethical relativism by asserting that humans have a rational nature that is not shaped by their cultural surroundings, but rather, is part of their human nature. Just as there are rules of logic and rational thinking that are universal, some ethical universalists say that there are ethical rules that are universal.

In this view, not only is it believed that there are rules of thought, that is, rules that humans follow when they think, but that there are also *good* rules of thought, that is, rules that humans *should* follow when they are thinking. What makes them good, we might say, is that they give reliable results to the people who follow them. Some universalists, then, believe not only that there are ethical rules that humans follow (some of which were acquired solely because of the unique culture in which they were raised), but that there are good ethical rules that people *should* follow when they are living. Again, we might say that what makes them good ethical rules is that they give reliable results (happiness, success, flourishing) to the people who follow them. To explain how it is that people arrive at similar rules, the ethical rationalist will say it is because of our universal rationality.

1.7 Relative Ethics or Universal Ethics?

Ever since antiquity, ethical relativism, as providing the best account of the ultimate nature of ethics, has gone in and out of favor among moral theorists. And just as long as there have been ethical relativists, there have been ethical universalists. On the whole, though, ethical relativism has spent the most time out of favor.

A universalist will ask, having reflected about our experiences and identified common values, experiences, and emotions (respect, friendship, love, fear, etc.): Does it make sense to conclude that all human values are relative to the degree that there are no permanent, universal, objective values or standards? The universalist will say No, for the motives, actions, emotions, and relationships that we see in other cultures and societies will often have a counterpart in our own lives; and this should tell us that there are shared human values, if not on the surface then at least below the surface. Universalists will assert that ethical relativism is an exaggeration and the only truth in relativism is cultural relativism, because there is no doubt that we see differences among different cultures.

In reading about different marriage rituals in different cultures, for example, we may infer that every society has different ideas about marriage and leave it at that (it's all relative!). The universalist says that if we look hard enough, however, we can bring to the surface the deeper shared values that our cultural and societal differences can often, but not always, obscure. In the case of marriage rituals, to stop at a relativistic conclusion would be to ignore the potential for a deeper probing into the values of relationship, cooperation, love, and companionship, some dimensions of human beings that have deeper roots than ethical relativists would have us think. The subset of features of who and what we are that are not culture-bound can range from basic human needs and values like those discussed by social scientists and evolutionary biologists, to those discussed by theologians.

One of the attractions of ethical relativism is that people believe it is a call for tolerance. Relativists (whether cultural or ethical) emphasize that there are differences between human ways of life and there doesn't seem to be one way of life that is *the* right way of living. It seems, then, that relativism would imply that we should tolerate other people who have different ways of living than we do.

We have to be careful here, though. A surface reading of ethical relativism tells us we ought to be tolerant of different ethical values and standards than ours. But if we look closely at what ethical relativism tells us, namely that right and wrong are relative, then whether we should be tolerant of others is *also* relative. The point of ethical relativism is, "When in Rome do as the Romans do." If we come from a cultural tradition that values tolerance then we should be tolerant, but if we come from a cultural tradition that *does not* value tolerance, then – to be consistent ethical relativists – we have no reason to be tolerant, for it is not part of our ethical values and standards.

A similar point can be made with human rights. An ethical relativist need not put a high priority on rights, for under the framework of ethical relativism, whether we value human rights is a matter of a culture's ethical tradition. As we saw above, this is not the view of ethical universalism. Universal human rights have a natural fit in an ethical universalist framework, not a relativist framework.

The same is true about tolerance. Even though, on the face of it, tolerance seems to have a natural fit with ethical relativism, upon closer examination it makes more sense to say that if one believes that tolerance is an important value no matter what culture we are talking about, we are actually endorsing ethical universalism. To assert that one always must be tolerant of others could not possibly be an ethical relativist's claim, for they say that ethics is relative. To assert that one *always* must be tolerant of others is assuming that tolerance is a universal guideline that must always be followed.

Instead of describing tolerance as a value or a guideline, it is more appropriate to describe it as a virtue. We will continue to touch on the issue of relative ethics and universal ethics in the next chapter, which focuses on virtue ethics.

1.8 Conclusion

This chapter has dealt with three philosophical problems in ethics: the philosophical problem of the origins of ethics, the philosophical problem of relativism, and the philosophical problem of human nature.

Briefly, the theories of relative ethics and universal ethics each offer a different solution to the origins of ethics problem. Ethical relativists see ethics as of purely social origins, wholly dependent on society. Universal ethics denies this, and simply claims that not all ethical standards and values are relative. Where ethical relativism is most commonly supported by considerations of social anthropology, ethical universalism has been supported in a variety of ways: some ethical universalists say ethical universals have their origin in human nature, human biology, human rationality, or God. Fully solving the problem of the origins of ethics and fully answering its questions would involve providing a well-developed account of where ethical standards come from.

This chapter has also dealt with the philosophical problem of relativism. Again, relative ethics and universal ethics offer different solutions to this problem. For ethical relativists, the great variety of human customs the world over, the disagreement between cultures and eras, and how ethical standards change over time, provide evidence that right and wrong are *always* relative. The universalist solution to the problem of relativism, by contrast, is to distinguish between cultural relativism and ethical relativism and claim that the only truth in relativism is cultural relativism – there are observable differences between cultures on ethical standards. Even though it accepts cultural relativism, the universalist solution points to underlying shared transcultural (universal) values that they assert cast doubt on the ethical relativist's claim that right and wrong is *always* relative. Fully solving the problem of relativism and fully answering its questions would involve providing a well-developed account concerning the existence and status of universal ethical values and principles.

Lastly, this chapter has also dealt briefly with the philosophical problem of human nature. Ethical relativism will emphasize how human beings and human cultures are very different from one another, and human beings are extremely flexible creatures. Given the unique geographic conditions, for example, and the unique history of a people, the kinds of customs and standards developed by a culture can be strikingly diverse. A universalist's solution to the problem of human nature, by contrast, points to the shared biological and psychological deep structures present in human nature, and shared rational and logical standards. The universalist ethical tradition views human beings as having a shared universal human nature. Fully solving the problem of human nature and fully answering its questions would involve providing a well-developed account of human nature that would draw on research from many fields of study, including the sciences and the humanities.

Concepts, Theories, and Traditions Introduced in Chapter 1

Concepts

Folkways – The concept that customs are developed by average people (folk) over long periods of time.

Objective universal values and principles – The concept that some values and principles obtain independently of whether human beings believe in them or not.

Relative rights – The concept that rights (whether moral, legal, or contractual) are always relative to context.

Right/wrong is relative – The concept that matters of right and wrong are always relative to a context.

Relative values – The concept that values are always relative to a context.

Tolerance – The concept that we should tolerate, accept, and not criticize others who have different values and ways of living than we do.

Universal human nature – The concept that human beings have a shared, universal, set of essential characteristics.

Universal reason/rationality – The concept that human beings have a shared, universal, capacity for thinking and reasoning.

Universal rights – The concept that there are certain rights that all human beings have, no matter what culture or society they belong to.

Theories

Cultural relativism – The theory that, as a matter of fact, different cultures have different practices, standards, and values.

Ethical relativism (relative ethics) – The theory that *all* ethical standards are relative, to the degree that there are no permanent, universal, objective values or standards.

Ethical universalism (universal ethics) – The theory that at least some ethical values, rules, and standards are universal.

Traditions

Relativism – A tradition of thought that holds that matters of knowledge, truth, value, and ethics are always relative to a context.

Universalism – A tradition of thought that holds that matters of knowledge, truth, value, and ethics admit of universal standards.

For Further Reading

Harman, Gilbert. 1975/2007. "Moral Relativism Defended," in R. Shafer-Landau and T. Cuneo (eds.) *Foundations of Ethics: An Anthology*. Oxford: Blackwell, pp. 84–92. A contemporary defense of moral relativism.

Harman, Gilbert. 1984. "Is There A Single True Morality?" In D. Copp and D. Zimmerman (eds.) *Morality, Reason and Truth: New Essays on the Foundations of Ethics*. Totowa, NJ: Rowman & Allanheld, pp. 27–48. A contemporary defense of moral relativism.

Harman, Gilbert and Judith Jarvis Thomson. 1996. *Moral Relativism and Moral Objectivity*. Oxford: Blackwell. A defense and critique of moral relativism.

Krausz, Michael (ed.). 1989. *Relativism: Interpretation and Confrontation*. Notre Dame, IN: University of Notre Dame Press. An anthology of articles for and against different kinds of relativism.

Levy, Neil. 2002. *Moral Relativism: A Short Introduction*. Oxford: Oneworld. An exploration of moral relativism.

Meiland, Jack W. and Michael Krausz (eds.). 1982. *Relativism: Cognitive and Moral*. Notre Dame, IN: University of Notre Dame Press. A collection of articles for and against ethical relativism.

Moser, Paul K. and Thomas L. Carson (eds.). 2001. *Moral Relativism: A Reader*. New York: Oxford University Press. A collection of articles for and against ethical relativism.

Wong, David B. 1991. "Relativism." In P. Singer (ed.) *A Companion to Ethics*. Oxford: Blackwell, pp. 442–50. A short overview article about ethical relativism, written by one of its contemporary defenders.

Wong, David B. 2006. *Natural Moralities: A Defense of Pluralistic Relativism*. New York: Oxford University Press. A book-length defense of a moderate version of ethical relativism.

Online Resources

William Graham Sumner's *Folkways* (1906), https://archive.org/details/folkwaysastudys01sumngoog Accessed October 1, 2016.

Ruth Benedict's *Patterns of Culture* (1934), http://203.200.22.249:8080/jspui/bitstream/2014/10368/1/Patterns_of_culture.pdf Accessed 1 October 2016.

Michael Ruse & Edward O. Wilson's "Moral Philosophy as Applied Science" (1986), http://joelvelasco.net/teaching/167win10/ruse%20and%20wilson%2086%20-%20moral%20philosophy%20as%20applied%20science.pdf Accessed 1 October 2016.

Pope John Paul II's *Splendour of Truth* (1993), http://w2.vatican.va/content/john-paul-ii/en/encyclicals/documents/hf_jp-ii_enc_06081993_veritatis-splendor.html Accessed 1 October 2016.

Review Questions

1. What is the main question that both Relative Ethics and Universal Ethics seek to answer? Explain how they answer this question.
2. What evidence supports Relative Ethics? In your view, how strong is that evidence?
3. What evidence supports Universal Ethics? In your view, how strong is that evidence?
4. What is the difference between Cultural Relativism and Ethical Relativism? Do you think this distinction helps to solve the problem of relativism? Explain.
5. How is it possible to reconcile Cultural Relativism with Ethical Universalism?
6. If I am firmly committed to tolerance and human rights, is my view more supported by Ethical Relativism or Ethical Universalism? Why?

Discussion Questions

1. What do you think cultural diversity tells us about the ultimate nature of ethics? Does it lead you to accept Ethical Relativism? Why or why not?
2. If Ethical Relativism is true, can there be genuine moral progress? For if all ethical standards are relative, then by what standard would you determine that moral progress, as opposed to mere moral change, is taking place? Explain.
3. In many countries around the world, women do not have equal rights with men. What would Cultural Relativism, Ethical Relativism, and Ethical Universalism imply about this fact? Explain.
4. Around the world, human beings engage in divergent sexual practices. When it comes to human sexuality, does it make sense to say

there are any universal ethical standards or values? In your answer, be sure to distinguish between Cultural Relativism, Ethical Relativism, and Ethical Universalism.

5. In many countries around the world, we find police brutality. What would Cultural Relativism, Ethical Relativism, and Ethical Universalism imply about this fact? Explain.

Chapter 2

Virtue Ethics

In October of 1997 a drivers' education teacher was in a car with two students. During the driving lesson they were cut off by another motorist. The instructor told the student driver to chase the car down. When they caught up to the car, which was stopped at a red light, the driving teacher leapt from the car, went to the other car, and punched the driver. This is a case of road rage: an assault brought about by an incident that occurred on a roadway. According to the US National Highway Traffic Safety Administration, one-third of all fatal car crashes could be attributable to road rage.

What would compel a person to commit acts of road rage? How could an emotion – anger – prompt a person to go to such great lengths, as in the above example? Anger, as a natural feeling, gives us a clue as to how we feel about a situation. There is a difference between a feeling and a behavior, however. An angry feeling does not have to become an angry action; it is possible to vent the emotion into a different, less violent, behavior. But by one estimate, one out of five Americans has an anger management problem. Anger mismanagement can be a major cause of conflict. And when we cling to the resentment of having been wronged, we continue to carry the anger inside, a behavior that some health care professionals say can lead to future illnesses. Virtue ethics is an ethical tradition that has much to say about how emotions are related to actions and how human beings have the ability to control their actions, and, in the process, gain happiness for themselves. Virtue ethics is an ancient ethical tradition that stretches far back in time, even before the era of Socrates.

Ethics: The Basics, Second Edition. John Mizzoni.

Socrates, the ancient Greek philosopher, is well known. The kind of philosophy that most interested Socrates was ethics (moral philosophy). Socrates was keenly interested in asking philosophical questions about ethics. The three most famous ancient Greek philosophers, Socrates, Plato, and Aristotle, all agreed that basic questions about ethics cannot be answered without also answering questions about human nature.

"Know thyself" was a saying in ancient Greek culture that Socrates took very seriously. Essentially, the saying "know thyself" pertains to the philosophical problem of human nature. Human beings, as creatures capable of asking intellectual questions, cannot avoid asking questions like: "Who am I?" and "What am I?" But in addition to pursuing solutions to the problem of human nature, Socrates also pursued solutions to the philosophical problem of the origins of ethics, the philosophical problem of relativism, and the philosophical problem of conduct.

In this chapter we will look at virtue ethics, the tradition of ethics that Socrates worked in. Socrates made it his mission in life to examine and question whether he and his fellow Athenian citizens were living good, virtuous lives. Virtue ethics is a very rich ethical tradition that spans many different cultures over many, many centuries. Virtue ethics addresses all four of the ethical problems we are considering.

The first thing we must come to grips with in virtue ethics is the basic question – tenaciously pursued by Socrates, Plato, and Aristotle – what is a virtue?

> [V]irtue appears to be present in those of us who may possess it as a gift from the gods. We shall have clear knowledge of this when, before we investigate how it comes to be present in men, we first try to find out what virtue in itself is. (Plato's *Meno*, 380 BCE: 32)

In Chapter 1, we mentioned tolerance as an example of a virtue and dealt with the question of whether genuine tolerance was more consistent with an ethical relativist framework or a universalist ethical framework. In this chapter we will seek to be a bit more precise about concepts like tolerance, generosity, integrity, honesty, kindness, etc., which, in ethics, are known as virtues.

The basic (and ancient) question, "What makes something right or wrong?" opened Chapter 1 and led to the problem of the origins of ethics and the problem of relativism. In this chapter, the basic (and ancient) question, "What is a virtue?" will also lead us to these ethical problems, as well as lead to a solution to the practical problem of conduct.

2.1 What Are Virtues?

A virtue is a trait of character of a person that is good for that person to have. Consider the ethical concepts of tolerance, generosity, integrity, honesty, and kindness. In their noun form they are traits of a person. Even though perhaps most of them can be put into the form of an adjective and applied to actions (a tolerant action; a generous action, an honest action; a kind action), the focus in virtue ethics is on traits of character of a person. Thus in this ethical tradition, the focus will be on a person who has (or lacks) tolerance, generosity, integrity, honesty, kindness, etc.

> *Character*: The concept that each person possesses a distinctive grouping of traits.

Aristotle, the ancient Greek philosopher, in addition to defining a virtue as an excellent trait of character, in 337 BCE offered another way to define a moral virtue. A moral virtue, he argued, is a mean between two extremes. This is known as his principle of the golden mean.

> *Principle of the Golden Mean*: A moral virtue is a mean between two extreme vices (the vice of excess and the vice of deficiency).

In ancient China, Confucius recommended a similar principle regarding virtues; and in ancient India, the Buddha called his philosophy of life the middle way. The central idea of the principle of the golden mean is that a moral excellence – a moral virtue – consists in a mean state. Aristotle explains:

> By virtue I mean virtue of character; for this [pursues the mean because] it is concerned with feelings and actions, and these admit of excess, deficiency and an intermediate condition. We can be afraid, e.g., or be confident, or have appetites, or get angry, or feel pity, in general have pleasure or pain, both too much and too little, and in both ways not well; but [having these feelings] at the right times, about the right things, towards the right people, for the right end, and in the right way, is the intermediate and best condition, and this is proper to virtue. Similarly, actions also admit of excess, deficiency and the intermediate condition. Now virtue is concerned with feelings and actions, in which excess and deficiency are

> in error and incur blame, while the intermediate condition is correct and wins praise, which are both proper features of virtue. Virtue, then, is a mean, in so far as it aims at what is intermediate. (Aristotle 337 BCE: 44)

In Aristotle's ethical theory, the moral virtues are concerned with both the feelings and the actions of a person. Aristotle describes that how we handle our feelings, and the rational judgment we use in developing our virtues, are important for human flourishing (i.e., important for ethics, living an ethical life). In Aristotle's view, each human being possesses a soul, a rational soul. The rational soul provides human beings with the capacity to control their feelings, either well or poorly. If feelings are controlled well, then virtues develop; if feelings are controlled poorly, then vices develop and stand in the way of flourishing. Aristotle writes:

> We have found, then, that we wish for the end, and deliberate and decide about what promotes it; hence the actions concerned with what promotes the end will express a decision and will be voluntary. Now the activities of the virtues are concerned with [what promotes the end]; hence virtue is also up to us, and so is vice. (Aristotle 337 BCE: 66)

The virtue courage, Aristotle explains, is a mean between cowardice on the one extreme and rashness or fearlessness at the other extreme. The issue is about how one handles fear. If one is overcome with fear, then one will be cowardly. On the other hand, if one ignores fear altogether, that is the other extreme: one is fearless or rash. Excellence is navigating between the two extremes. Since we are rational creatures we are in a position to control our behavior. If we allow feelings to overcome us, we are not in control. On the other hand, if we deny that we have certain feelings then we are denying our own human nature, which is not a rational thing to do, but rather a foolish and irrational thing to do (see Figure 2.1).

Besides courage, temperance is another example of a virtue. Here again, by using the principle of the golden mean we can recognize what the virtue temperance consists in. Temperance is a mean that has to do with our desires. If we let our desires control us, then we are intemperate. At the other extreme, if we deny our desires then we are denying our human nature. The excellence is controlling one's desires to the proper degree. In virtue ethics, controlling one's desires to the proper degree – developing the virtue of temperance – is something we ought to do in order to bring about our own well-being.

Figure 2.1

1. Moral virtues contribute to happiness and well-being.
2. Cowardice, a deficiency of courage, does not contribute to happiness and well-being.
3. Fearlessness, an excess of courage, does not contribute to happiness and well-being.
4. A moral virtue is a mean between two extreme vices (*Principle of the Golden Mean*).

---

5. Therefore, courage is a moral virtue.

There are two further clarifications to be made about the principle of the golden mean. First, the golden mean is not a mathematical mean. A helpful analogy is with archery. Hitting the middle of the target is not average; on the contrary, it is excellent. Developing virtues (hitting the bull's eye of a target) requires effort. A beginner might be lucky enough to hit the bull's eye once, but to do it over and over again involves practice and skill development. The Buddha once said that it is easier to conquer others than it is to conquer oneself. What he is highlighting is the difficulty of controlling one's feelings and actions appropriately in a consistent manner. Developing moral virtues is a challenge, and when one achieves success in developing a moral virtue, that is excellent. A contemporary example involving the inability to control one's feelings and actions is road rage. Should we allow anger to control us (as in road rage), or should we control anger to the point where we don't become angry at all? For Aristotle, the virtue regarding anger is to feel it and express it to the proper degree, not too much and not too little.

The second point to notice about the golden mean is that it is not a precise mean but rather a mean relative to us. Another sports analogy would be the sweet spot on a baseball bat. The best place to hit the ball on the bat is not the exact center of the bat; the mean is relative because the excellent place for the ball to meet the bat is toward the thick end of the bat. This is only an analogy. But the point is that the golden mean is not always exactly in the center; it may be off-center if that is what will allow the person to flourish. For Aristotle, ethics is not a precise science: ethics is about living a good life, and that is not something one can do with absolute precision. Human lives, even excellent ones, often take the form of a zigzag, not a straight line. A virtue, a golden mean, is not a one-size-fits-all concept; it may not look the same in different people.

2.2 Aristotle, Happiness, and the Virtues

Over the centuries there have been slightly different ways of defining a virtue, but the basic idea has been rather constant. The basic idea was given its first systematic treatment and analysis by Aristotle in ancient Greece. Although Socrates and Plato also worked in virtue ethics, it was Aristotle who composed the first book-length treatment of virtue ethics in 337 BCE.

Aristotle was interested in many subject areas, ethics being only one of them. He studied humans in the same way that he studied many other beings and organisms. In an attempt to do a systematic study he wished to understand all facets of human beings, including their biology, their psychology, their social aspects, their political aspects, their art, their logical abilities, etc. Aristotle begins his famous book on ethics, not by discussing the virtues, but by discussing human nature and human happiness. He observes that all humans seek happiness, and he uses logical argument to show that it is reasonable that all human beings seek happiness, since it is the only thing valuable for its own sake.

He then turns his attention to finding a way to properly understand happiness. What is happiness? What does the happy or good life consist in? His answer leads to a discussion of the virtues, which he understands as "excellences." A virtue is an excellent trait of character that is good to have. It is good to have because it leads to an individual's achievement of happiness, or flourishing. Happiness, Aristotle argues, consists in the full development of one's potential. (Rather than use the word "happiness," it may be more appropriate to translate the Greek term he uses with the terms "well-being" or "flourishing").

Aristotle observes that all humans are seeking to achieve well-being and seeking to flourish. He is not claiming, of course, that because humans seek after happiness, they will necessarily achieve it. Developing one's natural talents into virtues is challenging. It is deserving of praise when one does so, since developing virtues is an excellent achievement. In modern English, Aristotle's study of human behavior and his inquiry into the elements that contribute to human well-being and flourishing is known as the study of human nature. Inquiring into human nature, as we will see in all subsequent chapters of this book, is an important concern for anyone who studies ethics. For, after all, if we are to discuss how we ought to live (i.e., discuss ethics), isn't it important to get clear for ourselves about what kind of being we are, so that we can then determine what kind of life is appropriate for the kind of creature we are?

Two easy phrases sum up significant aspects of Aristotle's theory of human nature: (1) Humans are rational animals, and (2) humans are social/political animals. Both phrases characterize human beings as kinds of animals. This indicates the kind of inquiry Aristotle was conducting. He was in the habit of studying all aspects of the world around him, from stars, to physical objects, to animals, to humans. He is known for his system of classification, and in his view humans are classified as animals. But humans are very unique beings, since they have rational powers that no other creatures possess.

The second major characteristic – that humans are social/political animals – tells us that humans flourish in groups. They have social origins (mother/father/child) and they succeed in social pursuits, such as having friends and allies, and living in communities, towns, nations. Living a good, happy life, then, will involve living a life in accord with our rational and social natures, and developing all of the virtues associated with the natural abilities of rational and social creatures.

2.3 A Developmental Model

Human beings are not born with moral virtues. A moral virtue is a trait that gets developed by habit. As Aristotle describes it:

> Virtue of character results from habit ... Hence it is also clear that none of the virtues of character arises in us naturally...Thus the virtues arise in us neither by nature nor against nature, but we are by nature able to acquire them, and reach our complete perfection through habit. (Aristotle 337 BCE: 33–4)

Good habits (virtues) are the building blocks of good moral character. Humans are born with the potential, and they are also born with the power to control their own actions and to guide their own moral, physical, and mental development (see Figure 2.2). Because humans are rational creatures, they are aware of what they are doing. They

Figure 2.2

Potential ⇒ Repeated actions ⇒ Formation of habits ⇒ Character have the choice about which actions to perform. If we stopped to reflect on our own actions, we should see that repeated actions become habits, and these habits can be either good or bad for us. Although doing the right thing and doing what is good for you can often be a struggle, virtue ethics teaches that repeated actions become habits. When one has developed a habit, it makes doing particular actions much easier. Good habits (virtues) contribute to one's growth and development as a person.

In thinking about virtues, there is a kind of input/output dynamic to consider. There is a time in one's life when one is attempting to develop virtues – this is the input phase. It is during the input phase that one's character is in the process of being developed. But then, once habits are established, and one's character is well formed, particular actions and the fruits of those good actions seem to flow effortlessly from one's character. When we have developed an ingrained habit, it makes doing the task at hand much easier; we can perform difficult actions without even trying. This is the output phase, and the dimension of character we are familiar with in different common expressions like, "she is acting out of character today." When you have a developed character, people will come to expect what kind of actions you will perform.

Just as bad habits are hard to break, those who are convinced of the effectiveness of virtue ethics remember and realize that *good* habits are also hard to break. Helpful analogies to use for this input/output dynamic are learning to play a musical instrument and driving a car. At first, playing an instrument is difficult – it can be painful and one moves at a very slow pace. But when mastery of the instrument is achieved, one can then do things with little effort. Similarly, in learning to drive a car, at first it seems difficult to steer, to apply the right amount of pressure to the gas and to the brake, to see the road and cars ahead, and at the same time see the cars to one's side and in the rear. But when driving a car is mastered, one seems to be driving effortlessly. The old saying about riding a bike also applies here: once you learn how to ride a two-wheeler, you will never forget how to do it. Through repetition, certain actions become second nature to us. In the words of St. Francis of Assisi: first do what is necessary, and then do what is possible. Before you know it you'll be doing the *im*possible. St. Francis's phrase sums up the input/output dynamic of developing virtues.

In Aristotle's developmental model, the idea of a role model (*mimesis* in Greek) is also seen as very important. This is because one of the natural ways that human beings learn is by imitating others. Think of the expression "monkey see, monkey do." With the help of role models we learn which virtues are important and we also learn what kinds of actions one engages in when one has a particular virtue. In the Christian tradition, for example, we see that Jesus often reminds his followers to imitate the various perfections of God, e.g., God is loving, God is forgiving, God cares for us, and so we too must behave in like manner to the people we interact with: "Forgive us our trespasses, as we forgive those who trespass against us." Further, in St. Paul's letters – which make up the bulk of the writings in the New Testament of the Christian Bible – Paul continues this approach because he advises that the good life is to imitate the life of Jesus. St. Francis, St. Dominic, and many other saints, using the same virtue ethics model, took Paul's advice. They attempted to live lives modeled after the life of Jesus. A phrase attributed to St. Francis poetically sums up the notion of modeling: "Preach the gospel at all times, and sometimes use words."

Another way to make the point about role models in virtue ethics is to refer back to Aristotle's description of humans as social animals. This fact of our human nature again points to our being affected by others. In addition, although some virtues seem more focused on us as individuals – for example, courage is about how we handle fear, and temperance is how we handle our desires – we should notice that many of the virtues, such as honesty, generosity, tolerance, have to do with our dealings with others. Many excellent traits are social traits.

Role Model: The concept of a role model is a person who possesses and thus displays developed character traits.

One dimension of all of the virtues is the fact that not only are virtues good for the individual who possesses them, but they are also good for those who have social contact with the virtuous person. An obvious example of this that we have already mentioned is that one who has a virtue is modeling for others, and others will benefit from that. But there are a number of different ways that others benefit from our virtues. For example, if I am generous, I am generous to others; if I am honest, I am honest to others; if I am tolerant, I am tolerant of others. People who interact with a virtuous person will benefit.

The flipside of this is also true: the people who deal with the individual who lacks virtues and has many vices (i.e., vicious people) will be negatively affected. Thus, I will be harmed by dishonest people, by unkind people, by people who lack integrity, and by those who cannot control their desires.

2.4 Universalism and Relativism Again

Under Aristotle's virtue ethics theory, certain virtues are good for *anyone* to have, no matter what culture one is from. Similarly, the Egyptian text *The Instruction of Ptahhotep,* written more than 4,000 years ago, states that the following virtues should be practiced toward everyone: self-control, moderation, kindness, generosity, justice, truthfulness, and discretion. For Aristotle, because we have a shared human nature, there are human traits that are important for any rational and social animal to possess. All human beings share enough features so that some virtues are necessary and important no matter what particular cultural circumstances we could imagine. Other virtue theories, such as the Christian virtue theory, also link together virtue ethics and universalism.

But some virtue theorists maintain that the character traits a particular society chooses to regard as virtues and the character traits it chooses to regard as vices are purely relative to that society. Virtue relativists will point to the fact that each culture has its own catalogue or list of virtues it thinks is appropriate and necessary for living a good life in its society. It is quite possible, then, to have a relativistic interpretation of the virtues (see Figure 2.3). While a universalist virtue ethics will acknowledge that different cultures emphasize different virtues, it nevertheless asserts that there are at least some virtues that are universally important. A relativist virtue ethics, by contrast, notes that different

Figure 2.3

Possible combinations:

Relativist virtue ethics:
Cultural relativism & ethical relativism & virtue ethics

Universalist virtue ethics:
Cultural relativism & ethical universalism & virtue ethics

cultures emphasize different virtues and then asserts that there are no universal ethical standards or virtues – all ethics is relative.

Here we can review a point from Chapter 1. Although virtue ethics is compatible with both cultural and ethical relativism, when people interpret the different inventories of virtues as they relate to different eras and different cultures (i.e., *cultural* relativism) as proof of *ethical* relativism, then they are being too hasty with their conclusion.

As we saw in Chapter 1, universalists contend that there are *at least some* ethical values, standards, principles that are *not* relative. In the context of virtue ethics, a universalist would contend that there are *at least some virtues* that are not relative. So, even though Aristotle's list of the virtues is different from a Christian list of virtues, a universalist will point out that there are *some* virtues that appear on both lists, for example, justice, courage, and honesty. A universalist will notice that even though Greeks such as Aristotle, and Christians such as St. Paul, have different worldviews, nevertheless, there are certain common elements in both traditions. For example, not only do both traditions agree on the importance of some particular virtues, but they both conceive of ethics as having to do with the search for happiness (the Christian view of happiness involves eternal salvation, instead of earthly happiness) and they both use the concept of a role model.

As was mentioned in Chapter 1, the perception that there are universal human traits having to do with our language, our facial expressions, the way our minds work, our food preferences, etc. is very much alive in some of the sciences today. If so, then there is a natural place for a universalist virtue ethics. Evolutionists say these traits and the human potential Aristotle spoke of have been put into place by natural selection, while theologians will say these traits and this potential have been put into place by God. Nevertheless, the view that we can observe common human traits comes from many different disciplines of study and fits in with a universalist virtue ethics.

Thus, we can use virtue ethics to think about the problem of relativism. To consider the issue a bit further, we could ask ourselves: does it make sense to conclude that all human virtues are relative? Does it makes sense to say that if a culture values a certain trait as virtuous then that trait will come to be looked upon as virtuous, instead of vicious? Does it make the most sense to say that in identifying virtuous behavior, all human experience is entirely dependent on its own era, historical circumstance, and the influence of one's society?

It seems that the motives, actions, emotions, and relationships that give rise to virtues in other cultures and societies will often have a counterpart in our own lives. This seems to tell us that there are shared human values and virtues, if not apparent on the surface, then below the surface. Hence we can reach the same conclusion about the problem of relativism as we did in Chapter 1: ethical relativism seems to be an exaggeration of cultural relativism.

2.5 Virtue Ethics: A Guide to Good Behavior

Although virtue ethics can be linked with relativism or universalism, in a very important respect virtue ethics is unlike both of those theories. Ethical Relativism and Ethical Universalism primarily address the basic question: "What is ethics?" in the sense of, "Where do ethical standards come from?" As we saw in Chapter 1, Ethical Relativism and Ethical Universalism are offered as solutions to the problems of relativism and the origins of ethics. Virtue ethics, on the other hand, addresses more practical questions such as, "How should I live my life?" and, "What kind of person should I try to become?" These questions are central to the problem of conduct, which is a practical ethical problem.

When compared to relative ethics and universal ethics, then, virtue ethics offers us more help and guidance when we are trying to decide what we ought to do or what kind of person we ought to become. Even though Aristotle's basic virtue ethics framework is over 2,000 years old, we can fruitfully use it in thinking about how to live our lives today.

But Aristotle's virtue ethics is not a rigid formula for how to live the good life. In the first few pages of his book on ethics, Aristotle qualifies his ethical theory:

> Our discussion will be adequate if its degree of clarity fits the subject-matter; for we should not seek the same degree of exactness in all sorts of arguments alike … Moreover, what is fine and what is just … differ and vary so much that they seem to rest on convention only, not on nature. Goods, however, also vary in the same sort of way … Since these, then, are the sorts of things we argue from and about, it will be satisfactory if we can indicate the truth roughly and in outline; since we argue from and about what holds good usually, it will be satisfactory if we can draw

> conclusions of the same sort ... since the educated person seeks exactness in each area to the extent that the nature of the subject allows. (Aristotle 337 BCE: 3–4)

Aristotle is doubtful that ethics admits of the same degree of precision as science and mathematics; he offers an ethical theory that honors the complexity and richness of human experience.

One area of Aristotle's ethical theory that I will *under*emphasize is his view that because we are essentially rational, that is our ultimate purpose. If we only think of ourselves as rational beings, then the good life would be the life of contemplation and thinking. But this overlooks the other sides of the human person – because, even by Aristotle's own admission, we are not only rational beings, we are also emotional, social, and political beings. This more controversial aspect of Aristotle's ethical theory – where he recommends a life of contemplation over a life of action – can be safely set aside. One recent interpretation has it that Aristotle meant that the life of contemplation is the ultimate purpose only for people at the end of life, those in retirement, which is an intriguing interpretation.

A more modest aspect of Aristotle's claim that humans are rational animals is simply that human beings have cognitive abilities; they are aware of the choices they make and can control the choices they make. This is why the actions they choose to take, the habits they form, and the characters they develop, are all their responsibility. Human beings have help, of course, from their social surroundings and from their role models but, according to virtue ethics, human beings are not fully conditioned by their environment. There is an innate potential that all humans share (a universal human nature), and it is up to us individually to have a hand in developing that potential.

Another interesting way in which we can see that virtue ethics has practical applications is by noticing how it fits in with literature. There are some ethical theorists who insist that studying great literature that touches on ethical themes is a highly effective way to study ethics, especially virtue ethics. Universalists will emphasize how literature can help us to recognize universal human needs, and universal human values and virtues. Relativists will emphasize how literature can introduce us to values, ways, and customs that are totally foreign to us.

Character is a key ethical concept and a key literary concept. Think about the characters in books and movies. What virtues and vices do they possess that animate the plot? Narratives provide true-to-life illustrations of what the philosopher Bernard Williams calls "thick" ethical concepts (such as *treachery* and *promise* and *brutality* and *courage*), and so narratives can help those moral philosophers who might be preoccupied with "thin" ethical concepts like *right, good, is,* and *ought*. Virtue ethics focuses on the whole person and on the concrete experiences of living a good life. Great writers can skillfully describe characters, their choices, the lives they lead, and the virtues they either have or lack.

2.6 Pros and Cons of Virtue Ethics

Though virtue ethics is a rich and varied ethical tradition, this chapter has primarily focused on Aristotle's virtue theory. As an ethical theory generally, though, virtue theory has some good things going for it. Based on the brief description of virtue ethics in this chapter, we are now in a position to point to some of the attractive qualities of virtue ethics: it is reasonable, somewhat flexible, and it focuses on the whole person and thick concepts, all of which contribute to its being easily understandable. Furthermore, virtue ethics fits well with common sense, especially when it emphasizes that good habits lead to good results such as happiness, well-being, and flourishing.

One of the challenges in applying virtue ethics to one's own life is that one must choose which virtues to aspire toward. Who are our role models? As relativists are quick to point out, we have many lists of virtues to choose from (see Figure 2.4). Here are two contemporary examples.

Figure 2.4 Sample lists of virtues

Aristotle (350 BCE)	*Christian* (300 CE)	*Benjamin Franklin* (1771)	*Boy Scouts* (1909)	*Stephen Covey* (1989)
Courage	Faith	Temperance	Trustworthy	Be proactive
Temperance	Hope	Silence	Loyal	Begin with the end in mind
Gentleness	Charity	Order	Helpful	Put first things first
Modesty	Prudence	Resolution	Friendly	Think win/win
Righteous indignation	Justice	Frugality	Courteous	Seek first to understand, then be understood
Liberality	Courage	Industry	Kind	Synergize
Magnificence	Temperance	Sincerity	Obedient	Sharpen the saw
Proper pride		Justice	Cheerful	
Honesty		Moderation	Thrifty	
Wittiness		Cleanliness	Brave	
Friendliness		Tranquility	Clean	
		Chastity	Reverent	
		Humility		

The Boy Scouts of America require each scout to memorize and live by a list of Boy Scout virtues – they call it the Scout Law: a scout will be trustworthy, loyal, helpful, friendly, courteous, kind, obedient, cheerful, thrifty, brave, clean, and reverent. The book *The 7 Habits of Highly Effective People*, which was on the best-seller list in the late 1990s for several years, recommends seven habits for success, and its author, Stephen Covey, claims that he is interested in restoring the character ethic. Even though Covey never uses the word "virtue," it is clear that his approach fits well within a virtue ethics framework, for he emphasizes good habits, living a good (effective) life, and developing good character.

When faced with many lists of virtues, we can simplify things by remembering that within a given tradition there is often one animating virtue that sets the tone for the rest of the virtues valued by that particular tradition. In religious ethical traditions we will notice that for the Christians, even though they value many different virtues (faith, hope, charity, prudence, temperance, justice, courage, etc.), St. Paul says it is *charity* – love – that is the most important Christian virtue: "So these three things continue forever: faith, hope, and love. And the greatest of these is love" (1 Corinthians 13:13). St. Augustine furthers the point by saying that all of the other virtues are simply forms of charity. A contemporary writer recently claimed that the virtue *hospitality* sums up the Franciscan ethical tradition. The one most important virtue emphasized by Confucius in ancient China is *jen*, which is translated as goodness, benevolence, compassion, or simply, humanity. The one most important Islamic virtue is *obedience*, for human beings are called to obey the will of God. In fact, the word "islam" actually means submission, surrender.

In non-religious ethical traditions like Aristotle's virtue ethics, some have said that *moderation* sums it up, for, after all, doesn't Aristotle endorse the principle of the golden mean? That is not quite right, though, because this interpretation takes away from the notion that a virtue is an excellence, not a modest, or mellow, or average middle-of-the road position. Think of a grading system where a grade of A is excellent, B+ is very good, B is good, C is average, etc. A virtue is an excellence, it is not middle-of-the-road, moderate, C for average; it is earning an A! The word "virtuoso" means having exceptional skill; we should use that word not only in music, where we most frequently hear it, but in ethics too. So, saying we can sum up Aristotle's ethic as emphasizing the one virtue "moderation" is a bit misleading. Instead of trying to zero in on one virtue, perhaps we can focus on a few. The eighteenth-century moral philosopher David Hume, for example, emphasizes two virtues: *benevolence* and *justice.*

Another challenge to virtue ethics that contemporary philosophers raise is that while virtue ethics gives us good reason to try to develop virtues in ourselves as individuals, it does not overtly require us to have concern for human beings generally. If we are looking for an ethical theory that tells us that we must have concern for all human beings – as a moral obligation – we do not seem to find it in virtue ethics.

2.7 Conclusion

This chapter has dealt with all four philosophical problems in ethics. With regard to the philosophical problem of the origins of ethics, Aristotle's virtue ethics claims that ethical standards come from a combination of human nature and society; ethical standards do not come from God or religion. Ethical standards are not solely derived from one's society because there is a universal human nature that cannot be totally ignored. Human flourishing cannot solely be determined by what a society decides because human flourishing and well-being are tied to human nature. Societal standards that are contradictory to human nature would not lead to human happiness.

It is easy to see how Aristotle's virtue ethics also provides a solution to the problem of human nature. Not only does he argue that there is a universal human nature, but Aristotle goes some way toward filling in some details about what that human nature consists in, beginning with the observation that all human beings are striving after happiness. And, as we have seen, Aristotle describes human beings as rational animals and as social/political animals. As rational beings, humans can control their feelings and actions, and can choose what kinds of habits they will develop.

When faced with the philosophical problem of relativism and its main question – "Is ethics relative to society?" – someone might simply respond that, yes, ethics and virtues are always relative. Aristotle, though, when faced with the relativist question, might answer, "Yes" and "No." As an ethical universalist, Aristotle will say that *cultural* relativism may be true because we do observe diversity among cultures, but *ethical* relativism couldn't be true because there are some virtues that are important to have, no matter what culture one belongs to.

Finally, as a solution to the problem of conduct, virtue ethics answers questions about how to determine the right thing to do and how one should live a life, and what counts as a life lived well, and what kind of person I should become, in terms of virtues and universal human nature. A trait is virtuous if it is a product of our developed natural potential and if it contributes to our happiness, well-being, and flourishing.

Concepts, Principles, Theories, and Traditions Introduced in Chapter 2

Concepts

Character – The concept that each person possesses a distinctive grouping of traits (traits such as generosity, integrity, honesty, and kindness).

Excellence – The concept that a virtue is a perfection, a perfected trait, an excellent trait.

Good life, the – A life of happiness, well-being, and flourishing.

Habit – The concept that repeated actions eventually become second nature, because over time repeated actions will require less effort. A moral virtue is a good habit.

Happiness – For Aristotle, happiness is that which all human beings seek. It is a condition of well-being and flourishing in which one has developed one's full potential.

Lists of virtues – The concept that different individuals, societies, and cultures have assembled different lists of what they believe are the appropriate and necessary character traits (virtues) for living a good life.

Role models – One of the natural ways human beings learn is by imitating others. The concept of a role model is a person who possesses and thus displays developed character traits.

Vice – A character trait that stands in the way of one's flourishing.

Virtue – A character trait that contributes to one's flourishing. Examples include generosity, integrity, honesty, and patience.

Principles

Principle of the Golden Mean – The principle that says a moral virtue is a mean between two extreme vices, the vice of excess and the vice of deficiency.

Theories/Traditions

Virtue ethics – The ethical theory and tradition that focuses on discovering which character traits are most important for living an ethically good life.

For Further Reading

Ackrill, J. L. (ed.). 1987. *A New Aristotle Reader*. Princeton, NJ: Princeton University Press. An anthology that collects Aristotle's contributions to areas beyond ethics, such as metaphysics, logic, politics, etc.

Aristotle. [337 BCE] 1985. *Nicomachean Ethics*, trans., T. Irwin. Indianapolis, IN: Hackett Publishing. Offers a systematic analysis of virtue ethics.

Baron, Marcia W., Philip Pettit, and Michael Slote. 1997. *Three Methods of Ethics: A Debate*. Oxford: Blackwell Publishers. Contrasts virtue ethics with consequentialist ethics and deontological ethics.

Chan, Wing-Tsit. (ed.). 1963. *A Source Book in Chinese Philosophy*. Princeton, NJ: Princeton University Press. An anthology that contains more on Confucian ethics.

Comte-Sponville, André. 2001. *A Small Treatise on the Great Virtues*. New York: Henry Holt & Company. A recent exposition of eighteen different virtues.

Crisp, Roger. 1996. *How Should One Live? Essays on the Virtues*. New York: Oxford University Press. A recent collection of articles on virtue ethics.

Crisp, Roger and Michael Slote. (eds.) 1997. *Virtue Ethics*. New York: Oxford University Press. A collection of articles for and against virtue ethics.

Gardiner, Stephen M. (ed.). 2005. *Virtue Ethics: Old and New*. Ithaca, NY: Cornell University Press. A recent collection of articles on virtue ethics.

Gupta, Bina. (ed.) 2002. *Ethical Questions: East and West*. Lanham, MD: Rowman & Littlefield. An anthology that contains both Western and non-Western examples of virtue ethics.

MacIntyre, Alasdair. 1984. *After Virtue: A Study of Moral Theory*, 2nd edition. Notre Dame, IN: University of Notre Dame Press. Gives an analysis of the virtues in chapter 14, and relies heavily on Aristotle.

Pojman, Louis P. (ed.). 2004. *The Moral Life: An Introductory Reader in Ethics and Literature*, 2nd edition. New York: Oxford University Press. An anthology that emphasizes the connection between (virtue) ethics and literature.

Rosenstand, Nina. 2000. *The Moral of the Story: An Introduction to Ethics*, 3rd edition. Mountain View, CA: Mayfield Publishing Co. A text that highlights the connection between (virtue) ethics and literature.

Slote, Michael. 2001. *Morals from Motives*. New York: Oxford University Press. Attempts to move virtue ethics away from an Aristotelian model.

Online Resources

Plato's *Meno* (380 BCE), http://classics.mit.edu/Plato/meno.html Accessed October 2, 2016.

Plato's *Euthyprho* (380 BCE), http://classics.mit.edu/Plato/euthyfro.html Accessed October 2, 2016.

Plato's *Apology* (380 BCE), http://classics.mit.edu/Plato/apology.html Accessed October 2, 2016.

Aristotle's *Nichomachean Ethics* (337 BCE), http://classics.mit.edu/Aristotle/nicomachaen.1.i.html Accessed October 2, 2016.

Martha Nussbaum's "Non-Relative Virtues: An Aristotelian Approach" (1988), http://puffin.creighton.edu/phil/Stephens/History_of_Ethics/Nussbaum~Non-relative%20Virtues.pdf Accessed October 2, 2016.

Review Questions

1. List several virtues and vices that you possess.
2. Use the principle of the golden mean to help explain that honesty is a moral virtue.
3. According to Aristotle, why should we bother to develop virtues? Do you agree? Why or why not?
4. In what way does Virtue Ethics employ a developmental model?
5. Explain how Virtue Ethics can be joined with Ethical Relativism, and how it can be joined with Ethical Universalism.
6. Name a few virtues you would like to develop as part of your character. Who could you use as a role model?

Discussion Questions

1. Do you have a hero? If not, why not? If so, who is your hero? Explain why. What are the virtues and vices of your hero?
2. What virtues do you think are most important for political leaders? Use the principle of the golden mean in developing your answer.
3. Andrew Weil, the director of the integrative medicine program at the University of Arizona College of Medicine, in response to the trend of fast food restaurants being located in hospitals, says that doctors should model healthy lifestyles for their patients, and hospitals should be places of inspiration and education as well as centers for the treatment of disease, not fast food. Explain how you can develop Weil's case with concepts from Virtue Ethics.

4. Joseph DesJardins, the author of a book about business ethics, suggests that some business professions can be thought of as gatekeepers, for instance, attorneys, auditors, accountants, and financial analysts. This is because in a market-based economic system, markets should function within the law and be free from fraud and deception. Gatekeeper business professions must ensure that market transactions are performed according to legal rules in order to ensure that the market functions as it should. What virtues do you think would be important for these gatekeepers? Use the principle of the golden mean in developing your answer.
5. Scientists say that in the next few decades we will experience large scale catastrophic climate change. Which virtues and vices do you think are relevant to thinking about this situation?

Chapter 3

Natural Law Ethics

Gianna Beretta Molla was a working mom, a medical doctor with three children. While she was pregnant with her fourth child, she noticed an unusual swelling of her abdomen, and was subsequently diagnosed with uterine cancer. She agreed to have surgery to remove the tumor that was growing alongside her uterus. There were only two ways to remove the *entire* tumor, however. She could either have an abortion, which would facilitate the removal of the entire tumor, or have her whole uterus removed. An abortion would directly cause the death of her fetus. Having her uterus removed (an operation known as a hysterectomy), would also cause the death of her fetus, but indirectly. Gianna decided against both of these options, as she did not want to do anything that would harm the growing fetus.

Gianna's fourth child was born on April 21, 1962, delivered through Caesarian section. Tragically, Gianna died one week after the child's birth. Many years after her death several miracles of healing were attributed to Gianna. On May 15, 2004 she was canonized St. Gianna; she is the first working mom to become a saint.

Natural law ethics says an abortion in Gianna's situation would have been unethical, because it would have directly taken the life of an innocent fetus. But natural law ethics says removing the uterus to save Gianna's life would not have been unethical, even though such an operation would still have brought about the death of the fetus. The natural law ethics tradition has developed a principle of double effect for dealing with complicated ethical situations where the ethical thing to do is unclear. The principle of double effect is an ethical principle that applies to situations where an unintended evil happens during the course of a good action. In this case the good action would have

Ethics: The Basics, Second Edition. John Mizzoni.

been a hysterectomy that would have protected the life of Gianna, and the unintended evil would have been the death of her fetus.

The main theories looked at in the first two chapters – virtue ethics, universal ethics, and relative ethics – all surfaced in the ancient world. Natural law ethics, which was developed in the medieval period, is an ethical tradition that grew out of these ancient traditions. Aristotle's virtue ethics was very influential in the development of natural law ethics. Many of the key concepts are the same, but there is enough difference to warrant giving natural law ethics a separate chapter. In natural law ethics, we see the incorporation of Christian ethics into Aristotle's original framework.

A common way of thinking that feeds into a natural law ethics approach has to do with seeing things that are natural as good. Consider when products are advertised with "all natural ingredients," or when people try to do things that are natural, like camping. Why do people go into the woods without electricity, electronics, or running water, and "rough it," with nothing more than a backpack and a tent? Some of them, at least, seem to be aspiring to a temporary period where they can live a simpler, more "natural" life, i.e., life more closely attuned to nature. Or, think of those who simply "live off the land." In all these examples there is a premium put on "getting back to nature" and associating what is natural with what is good. Thomas Aquinas (1225–1274) is the most famous philosopher who takes this basic idea and develops it into a full-scale ethical theory.

3.1 What Is Natural Law and Where Does It Come From?

The best way to get to the meaning of the natural law is to put it in the context of other laws that we are more familiar with. We are all familiar with law as something that legislators and governments are involved with. These are what Aquinas calls human laws, because they are designed, proposed, passed, and enacted by humans. The kind of law that humans design, however, is not the only kind of law there is, because humans are not the only law givers. For Aquinas, the supreme law giver is God.

God's plan for all of reality involves laws. Since Aquinas's worldview includes a belief in God as the creator, then everything that exists anywhere in nature has its ultimate source in God. Another characteristic of God is that God is all-knowing (omniscient). God has a plan or blueprint of some kind for all of reality, thus God knows why reality is designed the way it is. A big difference between God and the natural world as we know it (creation), is that God is eternal, while the natural world – as something that God has created – is finite. While it is possible for the natural world to go out of existence, it is not possible for God to go out of existence. God was not created; God has always existed and always will exist. Thus, in addition to believing there are human laws, Aquinas also believes there is an eternal law. The eternal law is God's plan as God understands it. Humans, as finite beings, can never understand God's plan as God understands it. In the following passage, Aquinas describes the eternal law:

> Just as craftsmen must have in mind plans of what they are making – blueprints – so those who govern must have in mind plans of what those subject to their government ought to do – laws. God's wisdom, thought of as the plan by which he created everything, is a blueprint or model; thought of as the plan by which he directs everything to its goal, it is a law. The eternal law is indeed nothing else than God's wise plan for directing every movement and action in creation. (Aquinas 1270: 284)

So far, then, we have described two kinds of law – human law and eternal law. The difference between these two kinds of law is emphasized in the Bible, and St. Augustine memorably captures the difference between the two of them by using the phrases "city of God" and "city of man." While the city of man has human laws to organize it, the city of God has the eternal law as its ultimate guide.

We are finally in a position to make a first approximation of what natural law is. In the words of Thomas Aquinas, "natural law is the rational creature's participation in the eternal law." Even though *everything* in creation bears the mark of its creator, only rational creatures are able to consciously become aware of this and understand what the eternal law requires of them. Aquinas describes the natural law:

> Reasoning creatures follow God's plan in a more profound way, themselves sharing the planning, making plans both for themselves and for others; so they share in the eternal reasoning itself that is imprinting them with their natural tendencies to appropriate behaviour and goals. This distinctive sharing in the eternal law we call the natural law, the law we have in us by nature. For the light of natural reason by which we tell good from evil (the law that is in us by nature) is itself an imprint of God's light in us. (Aquinas 1270: 281)

But because the eternal law is only intimately known by God, human rational creatures must settle for a somewhat second-best understanding of the eternal law. After all, it does not seem realistic that human beings would be able to understand God's plan in the way that God understands it. So, again, the natural law is the rational creature's understanding of the eternal law: the natural law is only a partial glimpse into God's plan for human beings. But even though the natural law is only a partial glimpse of God's plan, it is nonetheless a reliable guide for determining the basic outlines of an ethical life. We can see how Aquinas is working out a solution to the problem of the origins of ethics. He is arguing that ethical standards have their ultimate origin in God's plan.

There is yet another type of law that is significant: divine law. Even though there is a natural law through which all rational beings know the difference between right and wrong, yet what human beings can figure out by their reason and reflection alone will not be sufficient for them to achieve eternal salvation. In Aquinas's religious worldview, it was necessary for God to have revealed more specific guidance about how human beings ought to live their lives, because living according to the dictates of the natural law would not be seen as sufficient guidance for people to reach eternal salvation.

> *Natural Law*: The rational creature's participation in and (limited) understanding of the eternal law. (A concept.)

Aquinas quotes St. Paul's Letter to the Romans as an example of an ancient reference to the natural law. Although poetic, Paul's phrase "the natural law is written on the human heart," is helpful in capturing some of the elements of natural law ethics. "For though the pagans do not have God's law," Paul says, "nevertheless they know the difference between right and wrong for they have the law written on their hearts." We can see how Aquinas's analysis of the different kinds of law is important, because it helps us to more clearly understand what Paul is getting at. Paul's claim seems confusing at first because he uses the same word, *law*, to refer to two different kinds of law. To clear up this ambiguity Aquinas has distinguished between divine law and natural law.

3.2 The Natural Law and Universal Ethics

Because natural law ethics emphasizes that there is one natural law that all human beings ought to follow and the ultimate source of the natural law is the one God, it is pretty obvious that natural law ethics, like Aristotle's virtue ethics, is another form of universalist ethics.

A question that we will immediately ask, though, is why, if everyone has the same natural law written on their hearts, do we see such ethical variety in the world? This is a question that Aquinas addresses. In other words, natural law theory attempts to solve the problem of relativism.

Aquinas's answer is basically that everyone does indeed have the same moral law available to them as long as they are rational beings. But when we are embroiled in the complex and complicated daily affairs of countless individuals, then things begin to get messy. As we attempt to apply right and wrong to our unique situations, our judgment can become clouded by bad habits or misguided passions. For Aquinas, there are indeed universal moral standards and we come to know these universal moral standards, not through human law, not through human feelings or emotions, not through our society's customs, but through human reason. Though we come to know these standards through reason, their ultimate source is of divine origin. Aquinas, like Aristotle, holds that ethics is rooted in human nature and that human nature is universal. When Aquinas talks about our natural inclinations to preserve life, to propagate, and to seek knowledge, he was referring to every member of *Homo sapiens*.

3.3 Natural Law Ethics and Human Nature

The method that Aquinas suggests for moving from the abstract idea of a natural law to more specific ethical duties or obligations is the following. If we observe human nature and human natural inclinations, then we will recognize that humans are naturally directed toward basic and fundamental values/goods. In saying that humans are naturally directed toward certain universal goods, Aquinas is echoing Aristotle's view of human nature. Aquinas says that the things to which human beings have natural inclinations are naturally apprehended by human reason as good, and therefore are objects to be pursued, while their opposites, as evils, are to be avoided. Centuries earlier, Aristotle advanced a similar ethical approach. For Aquinas, we need to look at human natural inclinations (human nature), to figure out what the natural law is and what the natural law requires us to do.

Aquinas identifies four categories of fundamental human goods: life, procreation, sociability, and knowledge. The first fundamental human good is our own life. If we observe human behavior we will notice that people have a natural inclination to preserve themselves. This natural inclination reveals itself in many, many ways, from the most basic to the more complex. A simple way in which this natural inclination reveals itself is in our very bodily actions. If you tried to fall flat on your face, literally, you will probably not be able to do it. You will likely put your hands out in front of you to break your fall. You have a natural inclination to preserve yourself; it is instinctual. A more complex example of how the natural inclination to preserve oneself operates in human beings is by having a job. One of the basic objectives of work is to "make a living," to preserve one's life.

The second fundamental human good Aquinas identifies is the human natural inclination toward sexual reproduction. Like the first inclination to self-preservation, this inclination toward sexual activity (and hence reproduction) can be thought of as instinctual in human beings. Here it is important to recognize that these natural inclinations are not necessarily conscious. One cannot say that he or she is inclined to sex, but is not inclined toward reproduction. Sexuality naturally leads to reproduction.

The third natural inclination is toward sociability. Here again we can hear the echoes of Aristotle. In Chapter 2, we observed that Aristotle's solution to the problem of human nature included the notion that humans are social animals. This is what Aquinas is getting at here. We have a natural inclination to sociability in that we naturally have social relationships from the day we are born – with our parents, our siblings, our friends, our own children, etc. It is inescapable that all humans come from a social environment, and humans seem to strive naturally to be in a community environment. Think of peer pressure, for instance. We naturally want to be accepted by our peers, and so we often cave in to the pressure they put on us.

The fourth natural inclination Aquinas identifies – our natural inclination toward knowledge – also has echoes of Aristotle. As Aristotle said, we are rational animals. The opening line of Aristotle's book *Metaphysics* is that "all men by their nature, desire to know." Since this is a natural inclination that all human beings have, we should think broadly about what is claimed here. A very basic example of this natural inclination is that we are curious creatures; we want to know things. Human beings ask questions. We ask questions because we want to know things. And when we ask questions we want the truth. We have a natural inclination to knowledge and the truth. And for Aquinas's religious worldview, we have a natural yearning to know the truth about God.

Our natural inclinations incline us toward certain goods. The words "incline" and "inclination" are helpful. Think of their meaning in terms of an inclined plane, a slant. On an incline, a ball will naturally go in a certain direction: down. We, too, have natural directions; our natural inclinations slant us toward certain goods. Another way to describe this is to say that human beings naturally value life, sexuality, social interaction, and knowledge. If human beings naturally value these things, then we can call them values. Thus, natural law theory asserts that there are fundamental human values. Now that we have looked at Aquinas's solution to the problem of human nature, we can consider how he provides a solution to the problem of conduct.

How should we behave toward these goods, these fundamental values? The natural law ethic says we ought to preserve and promote these values, not destroy them or contradict them. This then is the main principle of natural law ethics:

> *Principle of Natural Law*: We ought to perform those actions that promote the values specified by the natural inclinations of human beings.

What does that mean, practically speaking? Let's take the first inclination, toward self-preservation. Natural law ethics tells us that we ought to perform actions that promote our self-preservation and avoid actions that will destroy or contradict our self-preservation. At the extreme, we should not kill ourselves. To directly contradict our natural inclination to preserve ourselves is wrong, hence suicide is immoral. Less extreme examples would include that we ought to take care of our health; we should not engage in risky behavior that will harm ourselves, like drug addiction, self-mutilation, reckless driving, etc.

Given the fact that we are rational beings, we have the capacity to realize that not only do *we* have these natural inclinations, but other human beings have them too. Thus, we ought not to stand in the way of others as they pursue their own self-preservation. This is precisely what the Golden Rule asks us to do:

> *Principle of the Golden Rule*: Do unto others as you would have them do unto you.

The principle of the golden rule is not only part of the Christian heritage, but also appears in many other religious traditions such as Confucianism, Buddhism, Jainism, Zoroastrianism, Hinduism, Judaism, and Sikhism (see Figure 3.1).

Figure 3.1

The Golden Rule

Confucianism
Never do to others what you would not like them to do to you. (5th century BCE)

Buddhism
Hurt not others with that which pains thyself. (5th century BCE)

Jainism
In happiness and suffering, in joy and grief, we should regard all creatures as we regard our own self, and should therefore refrain from inflicting upon others such injury as would appear undesirable to us if inflicted upon ourselves. (5th century BCE)

Zoroastrianism
Do not do unto others all that which is not well for oneself. (5th century BCE)

Classical Paganism
May I do to others as I would that they should do unto me. (Plato, 4th century BCE)

Hinduism
Do naught to others which if done to thee would cause thee pain. (Mahabharata, 3rd century BCE)

Judaism
What is hateful to yourself, don't do to your fellow man. (Rabbi Hillel, 1st century BCE)

Christianity
So in everything, do to others what you would have them do to you. (Jesus of Nazareth, 1st century CE)

Sikhism
Treat others as thou wouldest be treated thyself. (16th century CE)

Notice how a natural law argument against murder, for instance, differs from a divine law argument against murder. A divine law argument against murder might go like this: premeditated murder is wrong because, as it says in the Bible, "Thou shall not kill" (see Figure 3.2). Natural law ethical reasoning is different; it says that each person has a natural inclination to preserve their own life, hence it is wrong to stand in the way of, or go against, another person's natural inclination to preserve their own life; hence murder is immoral. Aquinas is claiming that we can reach ethical conclusions simply through natural law ethical reasoning, without consulting divine law (see Figure 3.3).

Now take the second inclination, toward procreation. Natural law ethics tells us that we ought to perform actions that promote procreation and avoid actions that will destroy or contradict our inclination toward sexual reproduction. Thus, we ought to allow for sexual unions that yield children, and we ought to refrain from actions that stand directly opposed to procreation, like artificial contraception, sterilization, homosexual activity, and masturbation. This is the kind of reasoning that Catholic theologians have used in developing their sexual ethic.

With regard to the third inclination, toward sociability, we can think back to the social virtues that Aristotle said we are naturally predisposed to develop because of our social nature: generosity, honesty, and

Figure 3.2

1. Divine law instructs us as to what is right and wrong.
2. One of the commandments says thou shall not kill.

---

3. Therefore, murder is ethically wrong.

Figure 3.3

1. The ethical principle of natural law says we ought to perform those actions that promote the values specified by the natural inclinations of human beings.
2. A person has a natural inclination to preserve her life, she has value; in killing her you are destroying that value.

---

3. Therefore, murder is ethically wrong.

friendliness. Aquinas mentions that we ought to avoid offending the people we live and associate with. Thus natural law ethics advises us to behave socially, to get along with others, and be cooperative.

The last natural inclination, toward knowledge, may not seem to be directly about ethics, but if we have a natural inclination toward the truth and people feed us lies, then they are in violation of the natural law. Also, if we ourselves are naturally inclined toward knowledge, yet we do not allow ourselves to gain in knowledge and wisdom, then we are not living up to the obligation we have to ourselves and to others to seek the truth. For Aquinas, we must shun ignorance.

> *Natural Inclinations*: The concept that human nature directs human beings toward certain fundamental goods, which human beings then naturally value.

3.4 Natural Law Ethics and Virtue Ethics

Natural law ethics incorporates virtue ethics. In the same way that Aristotle sees a certain direction in human needs and actions (what I have called the developmental aspect of his views on human nature), Aquinas sees the same. Virtues are perfections; they are the natural outcome of following the directionality that is built into human nature. In Aquinas's view, our human nature was intentionally created and designed by God, and our lives only reach their natural end when they take us closer to God. The virtues are the fruits of performing actions toward a goal – our human good.

But the Christian list of virtues that Aquinas promotes differs from Aristotle's list of virtues. The most important difference is that Aquinas's list, in addition to having moral virtues, also includes *theological* virtues. While moral virtues are formed through repeated actions and habit, the theological virtues – faith, hope, and charity – have their origin in God's grace. This makes sense if we think of expressions like "faith is a gift." We cannot earn faith in God as we would develop a moral virtue, but rather, it is through God's grace that we are given the gifts of faith, hope, and charity. So, for Aquinas's religious version of virtue ethics, there are some virtues where we must rely heavily upon God's grace. The theological virtues have a similar place in natural law ethics as the divine law. Just as the divine law is needed for people to achieve supernatural happiness, so too, are the theological virtues necessary for supernatural happiness.

Overall then, the virtues have a place in Aquinas's natural law ethics: when one is working to develop one's moral virtues, one is living in accord with the natural law. When one is putting oneself in a position to receive God's grace, one is preparing oneself for the theological virtues.

3.5 When Following the Natural Law Is Unclear: Use the Pauline Principle

It seems rather straightforward to say that when we are working toward developing virtues then we are living in a way that is consistent with natural law ethics. Now, though, we must consider situations where it is not clear what the natural law requires of us.

In his writing, Aquinas deals with ambiguous moral situations. He recognizes that even if we are trying to follow a natural law ethic, there are still times when it is difficult to decide on the right thing to do. For Aquinas, this is a very real aspect of living a human life. Just as we saw in Aristotle's virtue ethics, living a human life can be a zigzag. As human beings, we have many ethical responsibilities and we have a great deal of potential that requires our efforts before it can manifest itself in virtues. There are times, though, when these responsibilities pull us in different directions.

There is an important New Testament principle that Aquinas incorporates into his natural law ethic. It is called the Pauline principle because we find it in Paul's Letter to the Romans. A more popular phrasing of the principle is: the end does not justify the means.

> *Pauline Principle*: It is not morally permissible to do evil so that good may follow. (The end does not justify the means.)

There may be situations where we are tempted to perform an action that we are not proud of, but we consider doing it just for the purpose of bringing about some further goal we have. Is it OK, for example, to turn the other way sometimes in order to bring about a greater good?

Take lying, for instance. Because of our natural inclination toward knowledge and toward sociability, we ought to tell the truth. So lying is not in keeping with the natural law ethic. There are situations, though, where we feel that we are justified in telling a lie because we are anticipating that there will be better results if we told the lie than if we tell the truth. On occasions like these, Aquinas advises us to remind ourselves of the Pauline principle. It is not permissible to do evil so that good may come.

Take a more extreme example: a lifeboat situation. A group of people have survived a cruise disaster. The lifeboat can only hold 20 people but right now there are 28 people in the boat. It appears that the lifeboat is sinking and will not hold this many people. There are some survivors who are severely injured and have now become comatose. One of the healthy survivors suggests throwing some of the injured overboard in order to save the majority of survivors. Is such an action morally justifiable under natural law ethics?

We know that this is a direct action of killing – throwing people overboard will certainly lead to their death. The natural law would say that directly killing is wrong. But yet, if a few sick and comatose people were sacrificed, then 20 healthy people would be saved. Isn't that worth it? Here is where the Pauline principle can remind us that we should not do evil in the hopes that good may come from it.

So would the natural law ethic really say that in this lifeboat situation we ought to do nothing? But then *everyone* will die! This is where the religious worldview of natural law ethics can help us see how we could possibly live with such a tragedy. By *not* doing an immoral action to try to bring about a good result, we are leaving it in God's hands. Perhaps God will help the *whole* group to be saved by sending a fishing boat in its vicinity just in the nick of time. Or it could turn out that the sick are not thrown overboard, and all 28 people die. But, by the ethical standard of the Pauline principle, it would still count as the morally correct thing to do, because, according to the principle, the rightness or wrongness of an action is not determined by the outcome, but by the principle of the thing. It is simply wrong, in principle, to directly kill a few comatose people in the hope that a future good may come of it.

3.6 When Following the Natural Law Is Unclear: Use the Principle of Double Effect

Let's look at another, more complicated, case. We know from above that it is in accord with natural law to protect our lives. And we also know that it is against natural law to take another's life. But how about a situation where we are being physically attacked? Is it morally permissible to kill in self-defense? Is it contrary to natural law to kill others who are attempting to preserve themselves (even if they are attacking)?

Since Aquinas is working out of a biblical tradition, there is an obvious reference here to the fifth commandment of the Hebrew Bible, "Thou shall not kill." As a Christian philosopher, Aquinas will want to make his ethical theory consistent with the Bible's commandments. But does that mean that natural law ethics prescribes that we ought not to kill, even in cases of self-defense? If we apply the Pauline principle we seem also to reach the same conclusion that killing in self-defense is morally wrong. For in killing in self-defense wouldn't we be doing evil (killing our attacker) so that good may come (our life will be preserved)?

Aquinas, though, would say that we have not yet properly analyzed the situation from the perspective of natural law ethics. If we look closely at the main principle of natural law ethics – that we ought to perform those actions that promote the values specified by the natural inclinations of human beings – we should notice that one of the key elements of natural law ethics is that we need to use our free will to perform these actions. In assessing the morality of a particular action it is important to note where we are putting the energies of our free will. What are we willing? What are we intending?

If we are intending to preserve our own life, then we are acting in accord with the natural law. If we are intending to destroy a life then we are not acting in accord with the natural law. The question about the morality of killing in self-defense should therefore center on our intentions.

In a situation when an attacker is threatening our life, if we struggle to protect ourselves and in that process our attacker gets killed, we have not committed an action inconsistent with natural law ethics. If our intention is genuinely to protect our lives, then we are acting in accord with the natural law. If an accidental by-product of this morally good action involves the destruction of a human good, this is unfortunate, but it does not render our action immoral (see Figure 3.4). Here is how Aquinas describes the situation:

Figure 3.4

	⇒ Consequence 1 (Save my own life)
Intention ⇒ Action	
	⇒ Consequence 2 (Take attacker's life)

> An act of self-defence may have two effects: it may save one's own life and cost the attacker his. Now intending to save one's own life can't make an act illegitimate, since it is in the nature of all things to want to preserve themselves in being as far as they can...Somebody who uses more force than necessary to defend himself will be doing wrong, though moderate use of force can be legitimate...However, it is not licit for a man actually to intend to kill another in self-defence. (Aquinas 1270: 390)

Thus, Aquinas has given us a principle of double effect:

> *Principle of Double Effect*: It is morally permissible to perform an action that has two effects, one good and the other bad, if certain conditions are met.

The first condition is that the act itself must be good; the second is that we must be intending the good outcome, not the bad; the third is that the action must not violate the Pauline principle (the evil effect is not pursued for the sake of a further good effect); and fourth, it must be a serious situation, for, after all, a basic human value or good is being destroyed.

Take a case that is different from life and death. Consider the second natural inclination, toward procreation. If we have a natural inclination to procreate, we ought to promote that good by performing actions that preserve that value. To perform actions that destroy that value is inconsistent with the natural law. Thus, to sterilize oneself would directly destroy that value. But what if I am ill and the only way to cure my illness is to perform an operation that will cause me to become sterile? If I am intending to undergo the operation because I am intending to protect my life (following from the natural inclination to preserve one's life), and the sterilization is only a side effect, then we have a case where one action will have two effects, one good and one evil. If I am intending the good one, though, and there is a serious reason for this operation, then, according to the principle of double effect, I am performing an action that is consistent with the natural law, and is therefore, moral.

Let's look at one example from each natural inclination. That takes us to the third one, the natural inclination to sociability. Here is an example that relates to smoking. Every year during national smoke-out week people are told about the hazards of smoking and are given tips on how to break the habit. One tip involves keeping yourself out of a situation where you will be tempted to smoke. Thus you should avoid other smokers. So let's say the action in question involves an invitation to go out with a group of friends who, unfortunately, all smoke. You can go with them or not. If you go with them, you will likely to be tempted to smoke because smokers will surround you; secondly, their second-hand smoke will surround you. You choose not to go out with them, say. That chosen action has a good effect and a bad effect. The bad effect is that you are going against your inclination to be social and be with your friends. The good effect is that you are preserving your health. If you are intending to preserve your health, then declining the social invitation from your friends is merely a negative side effect.

A fourth example involves the natural inclination to knowledge. One way to fulfill your natural inclination to acquire knowledge is by reading. When you do a lot of reading, however, it causes eye strain, and because you have eye problems your eye doctor has advised you to limit your daily reading. The action we are considering is continual reading. The good effect is that you gain more knowledge; the bad effect is that you damage your vision. When we apply the principle of double effect we must ask if you are intending to damage your vision. If not, but you are intending the good effect only (more knowledge), and the bad effect is not the means to the good effect, then your action, though it has negative side effects, is morally permissible.

3.7 Conclusion

Although the virtues, which are more about one's character than one's actions, are incorporated into the natural law framework, natural law ethics places much more emphasis on the analysis of moral actions and the application of principles to determining the morality of actions. When applying natural law ethics, the main element to focus on is one's intention – are we intending to follow the natural law? Another aspect that differentiates medieval natural law ethics from ancient virtue ethics is that natural law ethics is cast into a religious framework. Thus, according to natural law ethics, when we as individuals develop the virtues, we are following a law that ultimately stems from God's will.

Natural law as a moral law does have limitations even from the perspective of Aquinas himself, because, as he points out, the divine law and the theological virtues are aids from God that are necessary to achieve supernatural happiness. Today, natural law ethics is thought to have even more limitations. One major reason for this is that today many moral theorists are skeptical about any kind of reasoning that proceeds from observations about human natural inclinations to moral conclusions. Individuals who share the religious worldview that undergirds natural law ethics, however, will be less skeptical about this kind of reasoning.

Natural law ethics offers solutions to all four philosophical problems in ethics. Its solution to the philosophical problem of the origins of ethics is that ethical standards have their ultimate origin in God's plan for the world. Ethical standards are not solely derived from one's society. Since God has created human beings, Aquinas believes we can discern God's plan for us by examining and reflecting upon the natural inclinations of human beings. Natural law ethics therefore has a considerably developed solution to the problem of human nature. Human beings are rational and social beings that are naturally striving toward basic goods. Ethical standards are importantly rooted in human nature, though human nature is not their ultimate origin, since God is responsible for human nature being what it is.

With regard to the problem of relativism, Aquinas maintains that the apparent relativity of ethics does not detract from the ultimate universal features of ethics, which are grounded in the universal features of human beings. Like the other universalists we have looked at, Aquinas will accept the fact that there is cultural diversity and disagreement in ethical standards, and will advise us not to take the ethical disagreement and cultural relativity we observe as conclusive proof that there are no permanent and universal standards in ethics. For Aquinas, the standards exist just as surely as God exists, and human skepticism alone concerning these matters does not disprove their existence.

As a solution to the problem of conduct, natural law ethics answers questions about how to determine the right thing to do and how one should live a life, in terms of the natural law. An action is right when it is consistent with the natural law. As a highly developed solution to the problem, natural law ethics offers several ethical principles that offer guidance in making such a determination: the Principle of Natural Law, the Golden Rule, the Pauline Principle, and the Principle of Double Effect. As an ethical theory, it offers much practical guidance.

In this chapter we have sketched the basic outline of natural law ethics. Our next chapter will also use the concept "laws of nature" but in a very different way, a way that is critical of religious natural law. Our next chapter will address our first modern ethical theory: social contract ethics, a theory and tradition that for the most part attempts to avoid religious and divine references. It is a view influenced by modern science as it began to develop in the seventeenth century.

Concepts, Principles, Theories, and Traditions Introduced in Chapter 3

Concepts

Divine law – The revealed word of God that provides guidance as to how human beings can achieve eternal salvation.

Eternal law – God's plan as God understands it.

Human goods – Aquinas identifies four categories of fundamental human goods: life, procreation, sociability, and knowledge.

Human law – Laws that are designed, proposed, passed, and enacted by humans.

Natural inclinations – The concept that human nature directs human beings toward certain fundamental goods, which human beings then naturally value.

Natural law – The rational creature's participation in and (limited) understanding of the eternal law.

Supernatural happiness – Happiness in the afterlife; eternal salvation.

Principles

Principle of Natural Law – The ethical principle that says we ought to perform those actions that promote the values specified by the natural inclinations of human beings.

Principle of the Golden Rule – The ethical principle that says you ought to do unto others as you would have them do unto you.

Principle of Double Effect – The ethical principle that says it is morally permissible to perform an action that has two effects, one good and the other bad, if certain conditions are met.

Pauline Principle – The ethical principle that says it is not morally permissible to do evil so that good may follow. (The end does not justify the means.)

Theories/Traditions

Natural Law ethics – The theory and tradition that says there are universal ethical standards discoverable through human reflection on human natural inclinations.

For Further Reading

Arnhart, Larry. 2001. "Thomistic Natural Law as Darwinian Natural Right," in E. F. Paul, F. D. Miller, and J. Paul (eds.), *Natural Law and Modern Moral Philosophy*. Cambridge: Cambridge University Press, pp. 1–33. Defends the view that a Darwinian view of human nature can support the natural law reasoning of Aquinas.

Barcalow, Emmett. [1994] 2006. "Problems for Natural Law Theory," in Mark Timmons (ed.), *Conduct and Character: Readings in Moral Theory*, 5th edition. Belmont, CA: Thompson, pp. 84–7. A view critical of natural law ethics.

Boyd, Craig A. 2007. *Shared Morality: A Narrative Defense of Natural Law Ethics*. Ada, MI: Brazos Press. A recent defense of natural law ethics.

Boyle, Joseph M. Jr. 1980. "Toward understanding the Principle of Double Effect," *Ethics* 90: 527–38. A defense of the principle of double effect.

Boyle, Joseph M. Jr. 1984. "The Principle of Double Effect: Good actions entangled in evil," in *Moral Theology Today: Certitudes and Doubts*. St. Louis, MO: The Pope John Center, pp. 243–60. A defense of the principle of double effect.

Cicero. 52 BCE. *Treatise on the Laws*. The notion of natural law was also discussed in ancient Rome. Cicero, for example, as a statesman, writes about natural law and how it is foundational to his general understanding of what laws are.

Foot, Philippa. [1967] 2007. "The problem of abortion and the Doctrine of the Double Effect," in Russ Shafer-Landau (ed.), *Ethical Theory: An Anthology*. Oxford: Blackwell Publishers, pp. 582–9. An article critical of the principle of double effect.

Gomez-Lobo, Alfonso. 2001. *Morality and the Human Goods: An Introduction to Natural Law Ethics*. Washington, DC: Georgetown University Press. A recent defense of natural law ethics.

Laing, Jacqueline A. and Russell Wilcox. 2014. *The Natural Law Reader*. Oxford: Wiley-Blackwell. An extensive collection of articles on natural law.

McInerny, Ralph. 1982. *Ethica Thomistica: The Moral Philosophy of Thomas Aquinas*. Washington, DC: The Catholic University of America Press. A short introduction to Aquinas's natural law ethics.

O'Connor, D. J. 1967. *Aquinas and Natural Law*. London: Macmillan. A short introduction to Aquinas's natural law ethics.

Sigmund. P. E. (ed.). 1988. *St. Thomas Aquinas on Politics and Ethics*. New York: W. W. Norton & Company. Contains excerpts of Aquinas on ethics.

Woodward, P. A. (ed.). 2001. *The Doctrine of Double Effect: Philosophers Debate a Controversial Moral Principle*. Notre Dame, IN: University of Notre Dame Press. A collection of articles on the principle of double effect.

Online Resources

St. Paul's "Letter to the Romans" (56 CE), http://biblescripture.net/Romans.html Accessed October 3, 2016.

Cicero's *Treatise on the Laws* (52 BCE), http://oll.libertyfund.org/titles/545 Accessed October 3, 2016.

Thomas Aquinas's *Summa Theologiae* (1270), http://www.sacred-texts.com/chr/aquinas/summa/Accessed October 3, 2016.

Germain Grisez's "First Principle of Practical Reason: A Commentary on the *Summa Theologiae*, 1-2, Question 94, Article 2" (1965), http://scholarship.law.nd.edu/cgi/viewcontent.cgi?article=1106&context=nd_naturallaw_forum Accessed October 3, 2016.

Pope Paul VI's *Humane Vitae* (1968), http://w2.vatican.va/content/paul-vi/en/encyclicals/documents/hf_p-vi_enc_25071968_humanae-vitae.html Accessed October 3, 2016.]

Review Questions

1. Name a few aspects of Aristotle's Virtue Ethics that Aquinas incorporates into his Natural Law Ethics.
2. What differentiates natural law from civil law, eternal law, and divine law?
3. Explain how Natural Law Ethics depends on a certain view of human nature.
4. Is it always obvious what natural law requires of us? Why not? What should we do when it is not obvious to us?
5. Can you think of a situation in which the principle of double effect is applicable? Explain how the principle applies.
6. What are the fundamental human goods that are promoted by the natural law? Can you think of others?

Discussion Questions

1. Why is stealing wrong? Illustrate how divine law ethical reasoning and natural law ethical reasoning differ in how they answer this question. Be sure to mention the principle of natural law, natural inclinations, and distinguish between human law, divine law, and natural law.

2. In Martin Luther King, Jr.'s "Letter from the Birmingham City Jail," he asks the question, "How does one determine when a law is just or unjust?" He answers his question with the following: "A just law is a man-made code that squares with the moral law or the law of God. An unjust law is a code that is out of harmony with the moral law." Develop King's point by distinguishing between human law, divine law, natural law, and eternal law.
3. According to Aquinas's Natural Law Ethics, which of the following actions is morally permissible? Artificial contraception, killing in self-defense, masturbation, gay sex. Be sure to mention natural inclinations, the principle of natural law, and the principle of double effect.
4. Suppose that some prisoners have information that will save a large number of lives. The only way to obtain the information is to threaten to kill the prisoners, but you know they will not reveal what they know unless your threat is serious. To show them how serious you are, you have one prisoner shot before their eyes. Because of your action, the information is revealed and many lives are saved. Is killing the one prisoner morally justified? Explain by using the principle of double effect and the Pauline principle.
5. The Ebola virus causes a serious disease in humans. When a person affected by the Ebola virus is brought to a hospital the patient is quarantined. To have contact with the patient, a health care worker needs to put on a full body suit, for protection against the virus. Normally, if a patient goes into cardiac arrest, health care workers rush into resuscitate the patient. But if no one is suited up and the infected patient goes into cardiac arrest, health care workers are instructed not to go in and perform the resuscitation because of the possible spread of the virus. With natural law ethics, analyze the ethics of such a decision.

Chapter 4
Social Contract Ethics

Jerry Bowles was driving along on a rainy night. On the road up ahead he saw an accident scene, so he pulled over to offer some help. As he was opening the trunk of his car to get out a flashlight, he was hit by another car swerving to avoid the accident scene. Jerry woke up in the hospital with part of one leg missing and the other needing to be amputated. He had gone through 55 pints of blood.

One unit of whole blood can help five people. The red cells can help people who need surgery, have anemia, or who have lost a lot of blood in accidents. The white cells can help patients with white cell disorders, such as leukemia. Blood platelets can help patients who are undergoing chemotherapy treatments. The blood's plasma can help burn victims. By donating a pint of blood every 56 days, an individual could save up to 18 lives every year. It is pretty clear that the simple act of donating blood can do a lot of good for a lot of people.

Some people are regular blood donors. Jerry Bowles, for instance, prior to his accident, had been a regular blood donor for nearly 50 years. Yet, even though human beings are the only source of this blood supply, only five percent of the eligible population donates blood. Is this because human beings are naturally selfish? That's what social contract theorist Thomas Hobbes thought. Even so, it would seem that we ought to agree to donate blood because the chances are fairly high that we, or our loved ones, will need some pints of blood one day. In that case, perhaps donating blood is not only a generous thing to do, but it may also be a rational thing to do. People like Jerry Bowles are convinced that donating blood yields good karma.

According to social contract ethics, ethics is about participating in a social contract. An action, for instance, is a right action when it is consistent with the contract you have agreed to. An action is wrong when

Ethics: The Basics, Second Edition. John Mizzoni.

Figure 4.1

The Social Contract Tradition

Seventeenth century	Thomas Hobbes, England (1588–1679)
Eighteenth century	John Locke, England (1632–1704) Jean-Jacques Rousseau, Switzerland (1712–1778)
Twentieth century	John Rawls, USA (1921–2002) Jan Narveson, USA (1936–)

it goes against the agreement you made. Beginning with Thomas Hobbes in the early 1600s, modern philosophers gave serious consideration to this way of thinking about ethics (see Figure 4.1). The early 1600s was an era that saw the development of a new tradition for thinking about ethics, a view of ethics heavily influenced by modern science. The methods of scientists like Galileo, Kepler, and Bacon color Hobbes's understanding of the laws of nature. It was Hobbes who developed the first full-scale defense of social contract ethics, a modern ethical theory deeply influenced by the new scientific approach to understanding reality. In this chapter we will focus on many aspects of Hobbes's contributions to the social contract ethics tradition.

4.1 Continuities and Discontinuities with Natural Law Ethics

Hobbes and most other social contract theorists avoid basing their ethical theory on a religious worldview. Unlike natural law theorists, Hobbes does not assume that God is the creator who has created the universe with universal laws that can be discerned by human reason. Clearly, there are aspects of natural law ethics with which Hobbes disagrees; nevertheless, there are parts of natural law ethics that Hobbes agrees with and even incorporates into his theory. Most notable of the aspects of natural law ethics that Hobbes incorporates into his ethical theory is concern with human inclinations. Like Aquinas and other philosophers, Hobbes was a keen observer of human behavior.

In addition to the discontinuity in worldview from natural law ethics to social contract ethics, there is also a discontinuity in their characterizations of human nature. The solution to the problem of human nature Hobbes develops is rather unique in comparison to the views of human nature we have considered so far in this book. Hobbes offers a rather unflattering view of human nature. But this should be understood in the context of science. For, after all, isn't science supposed to tell us how things *are* and how things work, and avoid our personal prejudices and hopes about how we *wish* things to be and how we *wish* things worked? Hobbes's theory of human nature, in keeping with a hard-nosed scientific account, claims to explain what humans are *really* like, not what we would hope them to be like.

Part of the new modern scientific approach involves a new method, one that emphasizes observation and experiment. When one adopts this method, a rejection of classical philosophy will quickly follow, since the way that classical philosophy was taught in medieval universities meant studying the authoritative works of past writers and thinkers. Thus, moderns were quick to reject any trace of Aristotle, because they believed Aristotle's authority had become too great, and certain claims of his were open to serious criticism and were out of keeping with a modern scientific outlook.

So even though Hobbes will agree with Aquinas's basic approach of looking at human inclinations as a starting point for solving philosophical problems in ethics, Hobbes will want to avoid any elements of Aristotle that are found in Aquinas's account of human nature. For instance, the two human natural inclinations for sociability and knowledge that Aquinas had emphasized (like Aristotle before him) Hobbes now sees as idealized thinking about human nature. Hobbes believes it is rather naïve and self-deceiving to think that humans are naturally social creatures who have a natural inclination toward knowledge and the truth.

> *Psychological Egoism*: The theory and tradition that says all human behavior is, as a matter of fact, motivated by self-interest.

As far as having a natural inclination to self-preservation, though, Hobbes thinks that Aquinas is right on target. In fact, he believes that our natural inclination to preserve ourselves swamps all the rest of our natural inclinations. Contemporary thinkers have called this solution to the problem of human nature that characterizes all human behavior as motivated by self-interest, *psychological egoism*. The term captures the notion that self-interested behavior is part of our very psychology, that is, part of our human nature. Although this view of human nature has been given a contemporary name, it is actually a view that is quite old. Hobbes, as a modern philosopher, though, uses it as the cornerstone of his social contract ethics. Thus, in some ways, social contract ethics is similar to natural law ethics, but in other ways, it is very different. It is a distinctly modern ethical theory and tradition. As we will see, the social contract tradition offers a new way to conceive of ethics and human freedom.

4.2 The Principle of Self-Interest (Ethical Egoism)

In the social contract ethical tradition, the human natural inclination to preserve ourselves is regarded as so important that it even gets elevated to the status of a moral principle. This seems to be true even in natural law ethics, because in following the basic natural law argument, not only do we naturally and instinctually seek to preserve ourselves, but it is *right* that we do so. For both natural law ethics and social contract ethics, we are ethically required to protect ourselves and promote our own safety and well-being. But in social contract ethics, the principle of self-interest (that says one ought always to perform those actions that benefit oneself) is the very centerpiece of ethics. This principle is called *ethical egoism*, because it is emphasizing how people *should* behave, the *right* way to behave, the way they *ought* to behave. And for Hobbes, it is the key to solving the problem of conduct.

> *Principle of Self-Interest*, i.e., Ethical Egoism: One ought always to do whatever is in one's best interest.

This principle should not be confused with a narrowly selfish and shortsighted principle. For if one is genuinely attempting to do what is in one's best interest, one may find benefit in refraining from an immediate selfish gain, if over the long term this tactic will be in one's best interest. For instance, a stock investment strategy that yields immediate cash benefits may not be the strategy that will be in one's ultimate best interest.

4.3 The State of Nature

Just as scientists focus on studying the natural world, so Hobbes, too, in following the modern scientific approach, also focuses on the natural world. A scientific understanding of the natural world will differ from a theological understanding of the natural world. While theological worldviews usually emphasize how human beings are unique and distinct from nature, a scientific worldview, on the other hand, emphasizes how human beings are part of the natural world. Hobbes focused all of his philosophical efforts on human affairs. The main issue for him – one that is central in the social contract ethical tradition – is: how should we understand human social institutions if we take a scientific worldview seriously?

What is life like in a state of nature, in a condition where there is no human law, no human government, no police, no infrastructure, no civilization, and no society? A theological perspective of the state of nature – like the one incorporated into natural law ethics – tells us that since all human beings have the natural law written on their hearts, and every single human being of the age of reason intuitively knows the difference between right and wrong, the state of nature may not be that terrible a condition to live in.

But Hobbes's worldview is very different. In Hobbes's view, human beings in nature have nothing to stop them from following their main inclination to preserve themselves. Since there are no laws, people are totally free to do whatever they need to do to help and protect themselves. In the state of nature each person is free

> to use his own power, as he will himself, for the preservation of his own nature; that is to say, of his own life; and consequently, of doing any thing, which in his judgment, and reason, he shall conceive to be the aptest means thereunto…in such a condition, every man has a right to every thing; even to one another's body. (Hobbes 1651: 103)

Given the psychological fact of psychological egoism, every human being has the same tendency. We are all in the same boat; that is, we are equal in this regard. In the state of nature, we are free to do whatever we choose, for there are no natural moral laws. The only laws are those laws we agree to follow.

Are people naturally directed by their natural inclinations to develop virtues? Not according to Hobbes's social contract way of thinking. To think that there are natural inclinations to develop virtues is, according to contractarians like Hobbes, another example of the idealistic virtue ethics that natural law theorists borrowed from ancient virtue ethics.

What is life like in the state of nature, though, when everyone is pursuing their own interests with no regard for others? In Hobbes's view, the state of nature is really a state of war, because conflict would be the norm for selfish creatures like these. Here is how Hobbes describes it:

> [T]hey are in that condition which is called war; and such a war, as is of every man, against every man…In such condition, there is no place for industry; because the fruit thereof is uncertain: and consequently no culture of the earth; no navigation, nor use of the commodities that may be imported by sea; no commodious building; no instruments of moving, and removing, such things as require much force; no knowledge of the face of the earth; no account of time; no arts; no letters; no society; and which is worst of all, continual fear, and danger of violent death; and the life of man, solitary, poor, nasty, brutish, and short. (Hobbes 1651: 100)

In the state of nature there is no such thing as right or wrong, so we really cannot legitimately object to others' behavior. Hobbes explains:

> To this war of every man, against every man, this also is consequent; that nothing can be unjust. The notions of right and wrong, justice and injustice have there no place…They are qualities, that relate to men in society, not in solitude. (Hobbes 1651: 101)

State of Nature: The state of nature is a condition, hypothetical or actual, in which there is no human law, no government, no police, no infrastructure, no civilization, and no society. For Hobbes, since in this condition human beings will experience continual conflict and strife, it is appropriate to think of it as a state of war. (A concept.)

In the state of nature, there is nothing wrong with psychological egoism or ethical egoism.

4.4 A Contract Involves Cooperation

But social contract ethics tells us that in a state of nature and state of war, people do not really get what they want. In a state of nature with constant conflict and strife caused by unlimited freedom, people do not get the security, stability, and creature comforts they want. Hobbes observes that human beings are rational creatures; they are clever problem solvers who know how to figure things out in order to get what they want. As clever creatures, then, human beings will devise a way to escape from the state of nature: they will enter into mutually beneficial contracts with others. Sometimes people contract with rulers and give them absolute power, or sometimes people informally contract with the people they live with.

For Hobbes, humans don't enter into cooperative ventures like contracts because they are naturally cooperative creatures with natural inclinations toward sociability. They enter into cooperative ventures because they realize they have a better chance of getting what they want when they form contracts with others.

Recall from Chapter 3 that Aquinas discusses eternal law, divine law, natural law, and human law. For Hobbes, there are basically only two kinds of law: scientific laws of nature and human-made laws. These are the only laws that really exist. What Hobbes is doing is developing a view of ethics from the perspective of someone who believes in scientific laws of nature but does *not* believe in eternal law, divine law, or natural law from God.

Our focus in this chapter and in this tradition, then, is on ethical standards that are derivable from human laws and human-made contracts. Thinking in this way is not very difficult to do; we can easily think of contracts from the perspective of the legal and business world. An obvious example is trade and commerce. For every commercial transaction, there is some kind of trade agreement: I'll give you this, you give me that. Whether in the Stone Age or the information age, the dynamic is the same: I'll trade my axe for your stingray spear, my dollar bills for your cup of coffee, or an increased balance on my credit card for your computer program. Reciprocity is part of a contractual arrangement: you do this, and I'll do that. The commonly used Latin phrase *quid pro quo* captures the idea. The Latin literally means: "this for that." Other common phrases that capture the basic idea are "you scratch my back and I'll scratch yours," and "tit for tat." Because Hobbes was writing in England in the 1640s, the language he uses to make this point about social contract ethics is much more formal:

> Whensoever a man transferreth his right, or renounceth it; it is either in consideration of some right reciprocally transferred to himself; or for some other good he hopeth for thereby. For it is a voluntary act: and of the voluntary acts of every man, the object is some *good to himself.* And therefore there be some rights, which no man can be understood by any words, or other signs, to have abandoned, or transferred. As first a man cannot lay down the right of resisting them, that assault him by force, to take away his life; because he cannot be understood to aim thereby, at any good to himself. (Hobbes 1651: 105)

When one agrees to enter into a contract, one is giving up a degree of freedom: one agrees to behave in certain ways, and agrees *not* to behave in other ways. Thus, the nature of a contract has to do with the amount of freedom possessed by each individual in the state of nature. In a contract, then, there are boundaries on what individuals are allowed to do and what they should do. When individuals are totally free, there are no boundaries. But that ends up being a state of war where everyone is worse off. Hobbes envisions a strategy of cooperation as a better bet for satisfying one's desires for peace, stability, security, and creature comforts.

The social contract tradition wants us to see that in addition to the many individual explicit and signed contracts, there are also many implicit and unsigned contracts; there is a social contract for *all* social contexts. This is the only sense that Hobbes concedes that we are social creatures – we will seek to benefit ourselves by participating in cooperative ventures. The main principle of social contract ethics is:

> *Principle of the Social Contract*: One ought to agree to participate in social contracts.

Hobbes shows how a straightforward ethical egoism will not work. For if we all straightforwardly followed an ethical egoism then we would put ourselves in a state of nature, a condition that any rationally self-interested being would want to avoid. Therefore, we need to follow an enlightened egoism, or "rule-egoism," i.e., social contract, in order to escape from the unhappy and unprofitable state of nature. With the thought experiment of a state of nature and state of war, Hobbes shows that human beings, as rationally self-interested, will agree to enter into a social contract precisely because they are naturally self-interested. They will agree to follow a set of rules (a contract) only if they believe they stand a good chance of benefiting themselves through receiving security and other benefits.

4.5 A Contract Involves Rationality

Rationality is a prerequisite for entering into a contract. Can you make contracts with non-rational creatures like lions, tigers, wolves, birds, or mollusks? There is a story of how St. Francis of Assisi (from the thirteenth century) made an arrangement with a wolf that was terrorizing the little Italian village of Gubbio. St. Francis negotiated an agreement between the wolf and the villagers: if the wolf would stop attacking the villagers, then the villagers would provide food for the wolf.

Someone like Hobbes, who only takes a scientific worldview seriously, would likely say that such a story is simply legend, for people cannot make agreements with wild animals. Hobbes would more likely point to incidents such as the man in Taipei, Taiwan who in 2003 leapt into a lion's den at the Taipei Zoo and tried to convert a lion to Christianity. Luckily, because the lion was already fed that day, the man was only bitten in the leg. Hobbes would also point to the example of Roy Horn of Siegfried and Roy, who was unexpectedly attacked by one of his tigers during a performance. Wild animals are unpredictable and we cannot rely on the contracts we make with them. We cannot talk to them and make agreements that "we'll do this, and they'll do that." In Hobbes's words:

> To make covenants with brute beasts, is impossible; because not understanding our speech, they understand not, nor accept of any translation of right; nor can translate any right to another; and without mutual acceptation, there is no covenant. (1651: 109)

Hobbes, like many moral theorists, maintains that for a being to engage in morality and perform moral actions, the being has to possess rationality and have the ability to reason (see Figure 4.2).

Another ground for asserting that rationality is a prerequisite for morality is that beings must be able to understand that there are rewards

Figure 4.2

1. We cannot make contracts with non-rational creatures.

---

2. Therefore, rationality is a prerequisite for entering into a contract.
3. Following morality is following a contract.

---

4. Therefore, only rational beings can be considered to be moral beings.

and punishments attached to their actions. Even when animals are trained with methods using rewards and punishments, there is still a rather high degree of probability that the animals will not live up to "agreements" made with their trainers. Although there may be extended periods of training, and the animals may have long relationships their trainers, wild animals can turn on their trainers.

Rational beings are also known to break their contracts. But with rational beings – as compared with non-rational beings – the chances are much higher that the contract will be observed; this is because the being is rational and conscious of the benefits and the punishments. In Hobbes's view, "a covenant needs a sword"; words alone will not ensure that people follow the rules of the contract: "[C]ovenants, without the sword, are but words, and of not strength to secure a man at all" (Hobbes 1651: 129). This is how ethics and laws must necessarily overlap. Punishment must be looming or else whenever human beings get the chance, their selfish nature will prompt them to break the rules and the agreements they have made with others.

As proof that rules must have teeth if they are to do the job we want them to do, Hobbes reminds us of what happens when the structure of a society temporarily breaks down. Consider how people behave when there is a catastrophe or disaster of some sort, cases where there are no authorities to enforce the law. People behave lawlessly when laws are temporarily suspended. They loot and riot. This is the kind of activity that also happens during war. The common expression "raping and pillaging" captures the kind of activity that goes on during war.

What this means for Hobbes is that when the structure of society breaks down and people fall back into the state of nature, they simultaneously fall back into a state of war. And according to traditional wisdom, all is fair in love and war, i.e., anything goes. In sum, then, in order for a contract to work effectively, the contract must: (1) be between individuals who are rational beings who have the capacity to agree to the contract and who will understand the terms of the contract, and (2) have some mechanism in place to penalize those individuals who violate the contract.

4.6 Common-sense Morality (Properly Understood)

Even though social contract theorists build egoism into their background assumptions, they nevertheless still endorse common-sense morality. From the perspective of social contract ethics, it is in our rational self-interest to follow basic rules: we should tell the truth, keep our promises, not deceive, not steal, not kill, etc. Social contract ethics is a practical ethic; it gives us a reason to act and a reason to follow these basic rules. The clearest evidence that social contract ethics endorses common-sense morality is that, according to Hobbes, the golden rule sums up social contract ethics. Hobbes realizes that ethical theory can be subtle at times and not thoroughly understood by everyone; but it is inexcusable for someone to claim that he or she does not understand social contract ethics, he says, because it has been summed up in a principle that anyone can understand: "Do not that to another, which thou wouldest not have done to thyself" (1651: 122).

But social contract theorists will interpret the golden rule with an egoistic slant. Think of it this way: why should I not lie to you? A social contract theorist will say that the reason is: I don't want *you* to lie to *me*. Thus, treat others as *you* wish to be treated (the golden rule). From this perspective, the golden rule has egoism built right into it. Hobbes finds no trouble with incorporating into his non-religious ethic a principle traditionally thought to have religious roots. Similarly, he makes use of the concept of "contract." (He often uses the word "covenant" too, which has obvious roots in the Judeo-Christian tradition in which he was immersed, a tradition that believes there is a covenant between God and his people).

The concept of karma, which has had an important role to play in Indian ethics since ancient times, would also be seen by contractarians as an ethical principle having an egoistic element built right into it. The notion of karma is that every single action an individual performs contributes to what will happen to that individual in his or her next life. Doing bad actions stores up bad karma and then in the next life one would be demoted in some way from one's current position in society. Doing good actions, on the other hand, stores up good karma and then in the next life one would improve one's future position over one's current position in society. What an egoist notices about the law of karma is that playing by the rules and doing good actions helps oneself in the long run, while breaking the rules and performing bad actions only serves to harm oneself in the long run. In fact, in this tradition, since everyone is responsible for their current position in society (because of their own past actions), others don't *deserve* your help at all. Contractarians offer similar reasoning in that they claim that in following the rules of society (abiding by the contract) one will benefit, and that the reason for helping others is not born of altruism but of enlightened egoism.

We need not venture into such metaphysical speculations about a future life after death in order to use this reasoning. The social contract tradition puts its emphasis on living in today's society. The questions to ask are: "Will I prosper in today's society if I participate in the social contract?"; "Will I prosper if I break the social contract?"; and "Will I be better off if there were no social contract at all?"

Let's look at a few easy examples of how social contract ethics claims to support common-sense morality and claims to offer us the best understanding of what common-sense morality actually is. If I need money right now, where should I get it? Will my needs best be served if I steal it from the nearest convenience store? No, because shortly after I demand the money from the salesperson at the convenience store, I will likely get caught by the police. Getting arrested will set me back in a *worse* situation than I am in right now in needing money. Would I want to live in a society where people do not get caught for stealing?

No, because I then run more of a risk that people will steal from *me* when *they* need money. Social contract ethics, then, provides a good explanation of why we need to have a rule prohibiting stealing and a good explanation of why I ought to follow that rule.

If someone asks me a question, should I tell that person the truth? Or, will my interests best be served if I lie to that person? When people say that honesty is the best policy, they are referring to the idea that if I adopt a policy of lying to people, then my lies will eventually catch up with me and I will be in a worse-off position than if I had made honesty my policy. From a social contract egoistic perspective, honesty is the best policy *for me*; I will be better off in the long run if I do not get involved in lying to people, trying to cover my tracks, starting to believe my own lies, etc. For example, if I want to do well in a job interview, should I deceive my interviewer? Will my interests best be served if I deceive the interviewer, or will my dishonesty likely become exposed when I am hired and asked to do something that I am not capable or qualified to accomplish? Social contract ethics claims to put commonsense morality on a solid footing and claims to give the best understanding of why we follow the ethical rules that we do. And why we *should* follow ethical rules.

4.7 Social Contract Ethics Applied

Before we consider more applications of social contract ethics, let us consider social contract ethics and the problem of relativism. Social contract theorists assert that all ethical standards everywhere are aspects of social contracts. There are many individual contracts, but the nature of morality is a contract, and a prerequisite for morality is rationality. Social contract ethics is rationally based and has an egoistic aspect. Because social contract ethics says that ethical standards depend upon the standards enacted by societies, social contract ethics may seem similar to cultural or ethical relativism. But in the face of the wide variety of even contradictory ethical standards in different societies, social contract ethics will respond that even though the terms of the various contracts are different (there is wide variety), nevertheless, the framework of the ethical standards developed by various societies is still a contract. Thus, social contract ethics is a form of ethical universalism, not a form of ethical relativism. As such, it can accept that there is cultural relativism, but it will disagree with ethical relativism's claim that ethics is a purely relative enterprise without any kind of universal dimensions.

To see more clearly how social contract ethics solves the problem of relativism, consider what ethical relativism implies about following the rules and laws of one's society. Cultural and ethical relativism, when taken together, would imply that people ought to be obedient to the folkways and standards of their society; whatever is right is in the folkways, because right and wrong are determined by the folkways. A robust ethical relativism says that ethics is always relative to a society; there are no ethical standards outside a society's standards. If the rules and laws that are in the folkways are always right, then people ought to always follow the rules and laws.

But social contract theorists do not argue that people should have blind obedience to the rules and laws of one's society. In fact, the social contract tradition provides a strong argument justifying civil disobedience in cases where the rules and laws of a society are unjust. In an ethical relativist view, it would not make much sense to *dis*obey the rules or laws of one's society. But social contract theorists have famously endorsed civil disobedience in situations where the terms of the contract are unjust, or where all parties are not equally observing the terms of the contract.

In the social contract ethics tradition, a main issue is whether the contract is a good contract or a bad contract. We have to check to see if the conditions of the contract are fair and whether people are doing what they are supposed to be doing. Is the social contract indeed giving everyone who agreed to participate in it the payoff they deserve, in return for giving up some of their unlimited freedom? The likely situation is that the contract is beneficial in some way to some parties, for how else would the contract be created in the first place?

But given the selfish nature of human beings, it is also a likely bet that *some* people in the contract are benefiting more than others, because the ones in the position to take advantage of others and get away with it are tempted to do so. The result? Some individuals or groups are being taken advantage of either because the contract itself is rigged against them, or because the terms of the contract are not truly being honored by all parties. An ethical concept that sums up whether the contract is a good contract or a bad contract is *justice*. Is the social contract just or unjust? As a practical ethic, social contract theory can help us justify particular moral rules (like "don't lie," "don't steal," "don't kill"), and it can help us show how some moral rules that a particular group may endorse are not truly just (see Figure 4.3).

Figure 4.3

1. A just social contract is a contract in which those who give up a freedom get a benefit in return.
2. Persons are not obligated to follow unjust social contracts.

---

3. Therefore, civil disobedience is sometimes justified.

For instance, in the United States there used to be so-called Jim Crow Laws, which were segregation laws to separate the races in public spaces. Blacks were forced to use separate facilities, whether in hotels, restaurants, railway cars, restrooms, or water fountains; and there were also laws banning interracial marriages. These Jim Crow laws were supported and upheld by many rulings of the United States Supreme Court. Can social contract ethics help us show that Jim Crow laws, although endorsed by white Americans and the US Supreme Court, were not really just?

According to social contract ethics, people – as rational beings – will agree to follow a set of rules (a contract) only if they believe they stand a good chance of benefiting themselves. Were adult black Americans rational beings with the capacity to agree to a contract and understand the terms of the contract? Yes. As rational beings in a state of nature, would they agree to give up some of their freedom and follow Jim Crow laws because they believe that they will receive security and benefits in this arrangement? No, not at all. As rational beings, why should they accept different standards from what everybody else must follow? Jim Crow laws do not recognize blacks as individuals with equal standing in the wider community; these laws were designed to limit where blacks could carry out their normal tasks of everyday living. Jim Crow laws are indications that an unjust social contract was functioning in the United States.

Here is another example. From the time that the United States declared its independence from the British government in 1776, it took the 15th Amendment to the Constitution of the United States in 1870 for blacks to gain the right to vote, and the 19th Amendment in 1920 for women to be granted the right to vote. Social contract ethics helps to show that laws prohibiting blacks and women from voting, although endorsed by white men, are really unjust. For again, the individuals we are talking about are rational egoists who are capable of agreeing or disagreeing with a contract. In using a social contract ethic, adult blacks and women would not accept this kind of arrangement: why would they give up the unlimited freedom that they enjoy in the state of nature for the terms of this unjust contract?

Thus, it is clear that with social contract ethics we are not talking about following rules and laws simply for the sake of following rules, or being obedient to the status quo for the sake of being obedient. No, we are talking about following the rules *if they are reasonable rules for rational and selfish beings to follow*. What makes them reasonable, according to this tradition, is determined in the light of rational egoism: a rule is reasonable to me when I am benefiting from it, and not only benefiting in the short run. We are talking about the rules that are necessary to have a reasonably organized and stable society where people can exercise the most amount of freedom without that freedom bringing down the whole framework. Managing the terms of the social contract will always be a balancing act. According to social contract ethics, eternal vigilance is necessary, for we are all selfish, and there must be watchdogs and gatekeepers who ensure that people are following the rules and not taking advantage of their positions of power in society.

4.8 Conclusion

Even though the social contract tradition observes and endorses egoism, it realizes that the state of nature is undesirable and the only way out of the state of nature is through cooperation. It realizes there is no "I" in "team." We even see examples of cooperation in nature, as when Canada geese fly in a V-formation because it makes the flying easier for each individual goose. For humans, a social contract is necessary for conditions of social cooperation.

Nevertheless, critics of social contract ethics will point out that there is something about common-sense morality that does not sit right with social contract ethics. A commonsensical expression about ethics, for instance, is that ethics and being ethical are about doing the right thing even when no one is watching. Even though social contract ethics sounds convincing when it says that a social contract is necessary for conditions of social cooperation, if that is what we truly believed that ethics amounted to, would we have good reason to act ethically when no one is looking? If Hobbes is correct about human nature – that all people are self-interested – then wouldn't they be motivated to cheat and take advantage when they knew they were not going to get caught? True, social contract ethics will say we need a general rule against cheating if we are to effectively and productively cooperate, but when it comes to a particular situation, if no one knows I'm cheating, as an egoist I will want to cheat *and* agree to the general rule that cheating is wrong. As an egoist, won't I try to have my cake and eat it too? Discussions about social contract ethics call this kind of person a *free rider*: one who wishes to benefit from the rules but who will violate the rules if he or she can get away with it. Because of issues like this, some social contract theorists attempt to de-emphasize the egoistic dimensions of social contract ethics.

Social contract ethics does provide solutions to all four problems in ethics, though. With regard to philosophical questions about human nature, Hobbes argues that all human beings are ultimately self-interested: psychological egoism is his solution to the problem of human nature. This view is also known as rational egoism, because in addition to being selfish creatures (like any animal), humans are rational. So human beings have created rules for themselves in order to escape the state of nature. The solution to the problem of the origins of ethics, then, is that ethical standards come from human beings who have created these standards by creating contracts. Although social contract ethics says that ethical standards depend upon the standards enacted by societies, and it grants that the terms of the various contracts are different, it responds to the problem of relativism by saying that all ethical standards are still contracts and all human beings are rational and self-interested. So it accepts cultural relativism and universalism, but denies ethical relativism.

As a solution to the problem of conduct, social contract ethics holds that you should do what will benefit you. Social contract ethics realizes, though, that a near-sighted understanding of ethical egoism leads to a state of war. So when asking the question about what you should do, the focus should be on the rules, laws, and contracts of one's society (aka, rule-egoism). Individuals must ask themselves if the ethical rules their society is asking them to follow yield benefits for them. A society's particular contract will often provide answers about right and wrong, but the rational participants in the society must critically evaluate the contract to make sure it is a just contract, one where people give up some of their freedoms, but only in order to get the benefits of a stable and secure society.

In the next chapter we will look at another tradition of modern ethics, utilitarian ethics. In some ways utilitarian ethics continues Hobbes's project, in that it tries to ground ethics in a scientific rather than a religious worldview. Utilitarianism also follows contractarianism in thinking of ethics in a *consequentialist* way, so-called because rules and laws are regarded as right or wrong depending on the consequences they will bring to people.

In other ways, though, utilitarianism is a departure from social contract ethics. Hobbes was thought of as radical because he straight-facedly endorsed egoism, but Hobbes was still traditional because he rested ethics on rationality. Utilitarians, as we will see, are regarded as radical not because of their views on egoism, but because they broke with the longstanding rationalist tradition that sees ethics as resting on rational foundations. The utilitarians regard ethics as not grounded in human rationality, but rather in human feelings.

Concepts, Principles, Theories, and Traditions Introduced in Chapter 4

Concepts

Equality – In social contract ethics, each person entering the contract has the same status, due to his or her rational ability to enter the contract in the first place.

Justice – The ethical concept that sums up whether a social contract is a good contract (a just one) or a bad contract (an unjust one).

Law – A law is a standard enacted by human beings through a social contract.

Liberty, freedom – In the state of nature, human beings possess unlimited freedom; there are no legitimate laws that can constrain their behavior.

Reciprocity – The concept that in a contractual arrangement a person gives something up in order to get something in return.

Social contract – An agreement between people, whether implicit or explicit, to follow a set of mutual beneficial rules.

State of nature – The state of nature is a condition, hypothetical or actual, in which there is no human law, no government, no police, no infrastructure, no civilization, and no society.

State of war – Since in the state of nature human beings will experience continual conflict and strife, it is appropriate to think of it as a state of war.

Principles

Principle of Self-Interest – The ethical principle that says one ought always to do whatever is in one's best interest.

Principle of the Social Contract – The ethical principle that says one ought to agree to participate in social contracts.

Theories/Traditions

Consequentialism – The theory that an action (or rule or law) is determined to be ethically right or wrong depending on the consequences it brings to people.

Ethical egoism – The theory and tradition that says individuals ought always to do whatever is in their best interest.

Psychological egoism – The theory and tradition that says all human behavior is, as a matter of fact, motivated by self-interest.

Rational egoism – The theory that humans are rational and selfish beings.

Rule-egoism – The theory that says people should follow a set of rules (a contract) that will yield for them the best consequences.

Social contract ethics – The theory and tradition that says ethical standards are, and should be, the products of a social contract.

For Further Reading

Darwall, Stephen. 1998. *Philosophical Ethics*. Boulder, CO: Westview. Discusses the pros and cons of social contract ethics, see chapters 10 and 11.

Gauthier, David. 1986. *Morals by Agreement*. New York: Oxford University Press. Offers a contemporary version of social contract ethics.

Hobbes, Thomas. [1651] 1962. *Leviathan*, ed. M. Oakeshott. Introduction by R. S. Peters. New York: Collier Books. For more on Hobbes and the modern scientific tradition, see R. S. Peters' Introduction.

Kagan, Shelly. 1998. *Normative Ethics*. Boulder, CO: Westview Press. Discusses the pros and cons of social contract ethics, see chapter 7.1.

Kahane, Howard. 1995. *Contract Ethics*. Lanham, MD: Rowman & Littlefield. A contemporary version of social contract ethics that connects social contract ethics to evolutionary biology.

Locke, John. [1689] 1980. *Second Treatise of Government*. Indianapolis, IN: Hackett Publishing. A characterization of the state of nature and state of war that differs from Hobbes's. See chapters 2 and 3.

Rawls, John. 1971. *A Theory of Justice*. Cambridge, MA: Harvard University Press. A contemporary version of social contract theory.

Scanlon, T. M. 1998. *What We Owe to Each Other*. Cambridge, MA: Harvard University Press. Offers a contemporary version of social contract ethics, a version that *de*-emphasizes the egoistic dimension.

Online Resources

St. Francis and the Wolf of Gubbio (1390), http://tamingthewolf.com/saint-francis-and-the-wolf/ Accessed October 4, 2016.

Thomas Hobbes's *Leviathan* (1651), http://socserv2.socsci.mcmaster.ca/econ/ugcm/3ll3/hobbes/Leviathan.pdf Accessed October 4, 2016.

John Locke's *Second Treatise on Government* (1690), http://www.earlymoderntexts.com/assets/pdfs/locke1689a.pdf Accessed October 4, 2016.

Jean-Jacques Rousseau's *The Social Contract* (1762), http://www.earlymoderntexts.com/assets/pdfs/rousseau1762.pdf Accessed October 4, 2016.

Review Questions

1. In what ways does Social Contract Ethics differ from Natural Law Ethics? In what ways are they similar?
2. Based on how Hobbes defines the concept of "the state of nature," are we currently living in the state of nature? Explain.
3. Given what the chapter says in Sections 4.6 and 4.8, do you think Social Contract Ethics captures common-sense morality? Why or why not?
4. What is the difference between psychological egoism and ethical egoism?
5. Explain how justice is a key concept in Social Contract Ethics.
6. Explain why Social Contract Ethics is considered a consequentialist ethical approach.

Discussion Questions

1. Do you think, as Hobbes does, that rules are ethical because they are part of a social contract? Or, do you think that rules are part of the social contract because they are ethical? Explain.
2. Natural Law Ethics seems to require a strict sexual ethic. How would a sexual ethic based on Social Contract Ethics differ from a sexual ethic based on Natural Law Ethics? (If you write out your answer, underline each natural law concept and principle and social contract concept and principle you mention.)
3. In 1919 the freedom to manufacture, sell, or distribute intoxicating liquors was taken away from Americans with the 18th Amendment to the United States Constitution. (It was subsequently repealed by the 21st Amendment in 1933.) The period between 1920 and 1933 is known as "Prohibition," because alcohol was prohibited. By using as many concepts and principles from Social Contract Ethics as you can, make a case for or against prohibition. (In your answer, underline each social contract concept and principle you mention.)
4. The United States has experienced many school shootings in recent years. Should there be stricter handgun laws? Develop a response by using Social Contract Ethics. (In your answer, underline each social contract concept and principle you mention.)
5. What would Social Contract Ethics say about legalizing marijuana for recreational use? In developing your answer, use at least three concepts/principles from Social Contract Ethics.

Chapter 5

Utilitarian Ethics

In 2002 the chef Charlie Trotter stated that he would no longer serve foie gras at his five-star restaurant. Foie gras is a special kind of duck liver. In French *foie gras* means "greasy/fatty liver" (*foie* = liver; *gras* = greasy). Foie gras is produced by the forced feeding of ducks and geese so that the birds develop overly enlarged livers. A tube is inserted into the bird's throat and it is fed against its will. It is an ancient practice. Regular-sized duck or goose liver does not have the same taste and texture as oversized duck or goose liver, which is the reason for the overfeeding.

Having witnessed ducks being fed by tubes, chef Trotter, a prominent chef, became affected by what he saw as cruelty to the animals. The production of foie gras is banned in some countries, and some US states have introduced bills that would ban the production or sale of foie gras. In 2005, the state of Illinois sold 46,000 pounds of foie gras. A restaurant owner in Chicago, where a ban on foie gras was recently instituted (and later overturned), complained that, "This ban is embarrassing Chicago ... What's next? Some other city outlaws Brussels sprouts? Another outlaws chicken? Another, green beans?"

In response, an advocate of utilitarian ethics would point out that neither Brussels sprouts nor green beans can suffer. It doesn't make sense to say that farmers are being cruel to Brussels sprouts or green beans. Since vegetables don't have nervous systems, they cannot experience pain. But ducks and geese *can* experience pain. Isn't that fact morally significant?

In this chapter we look at another modern ethical tradition. It has its origins in the eighteenth-century writings of David Hume and Jeremy Bentham (see Figure 5.1). Like social contract ethics, utilitarian ethics

Ethics: The Basics, Second Edition. John Mizzoni.

Figure 5.1

The Utilitarian Tradition

Eighteenth century	David Hume, Scotland (1711–1776)
	Jeremy Bentham, England (1748–1832)
Nineteenth century	John Stuart Mill, England (1806–73)
Twentieth century	Peter Singer, Australia (1946–)

Figure 5.2

Two kinds of consequentialist ethics
Social Contract Ethics asks: What will be the consequences for me?
Utilitarian Ethics asks: What will be the consequences for all concerned?

focuses on outcomes, or consequences; so both of these ethical theories are called *consequentialist* ethical theories.

The big difference between social contract ethics and utilitarian ethics is that social contract ethics has an egoistic base, while utilitarianism has an altruistic base. In other words, social contract ethics assumes that the reason that people are willing to get involved with a social contract is that they as individuals will benefit. But utilitarian ethics accepts that people can be genuinely motivated for the sake of others, not only self-benefit. Whereas with social contract ethics I judge a rule or law to be right or wrong depending on the consequences it will have for me if I participate in the contract, with utilitarian ethics I judge a rule or law to be right or wrong depending on the consequences (or utility) that it will have on all who will be affected (see Figure 5.2).

5.1 Ethics Is Based on Feelings

Upon first learning about social contract ethics one might think it to be an odd ethical theory because it endorses egoism, a view that many people find unethical on its face. In a different way, one might think utilitarian ethics to be an odd ethical theory too, because its solution to the problem of the origins of ethics rejects the traditional view that characterizes ethics as having a rational foundation.

David Hume (1711–1776) is the grandfather of utilitarian ethics. His famous book, *A Treatise of Human Nature* (1739), is, as one can tell from its title, as much a work on human nature as it is on ethics. In the book, Hume puts forward a powerful argument about the nature of ethics. We will look at the argument, one step at a time. But first, here it is in Hume's words:

> Since morals, therefore, have an influence on the actions and affections, it follows, that they cannot be deriv'd from reason; and that because reason alone, as we have already prov'd, can never have any such influence. Morals excite passions, and produce or prevent actions. Reason of itself is utterly impotent in this particular. The rules of morality, therefore, are not conclusions of our reason. (Hume 1739: 457)

The first step, or premise, in Hume's argument is simply the commonsense observation that ethics concerns how we ought to live and what we should do. His next point has to do with human nature and is more controversial. He observes that human reasoning is not the kind of thing, or kind of capacity, that can motivate human beings into action. Reason, he says, is powerless for producing or preventing actions. As simply a statement about what human beings are like, Hume observes that people are moved to act by desires, feelings, and emotions, not by reasoning alone. For example, just *knowing* that I have an exam tomorrow is not enough to *motivate* me to study. Or just *knowing* that I need to lose weight is not enough to *motivate* me to loss weight. There are plenty of times where, through my reason, rationality, and capacity for understanding, I *know* what I need to do, but I nevertheless cannot get motivated to act. For Hume, it is an emotional state of some kind, like a feeling, passion, or desire, that spurs us into action; rational thinking alone does not get us off the couch. Thinking about it simply won't do the trick. Hume sums up his solution to the problem of human nature with his memorable phrase: "Reason is, and ought only to be the slave of the passions, and can never pretend to any other office than to serve and obey them" (Hume 1739: 415).

Hume then takes his solution to the problem of human nature, couples it with his first premise (that ethics is commonly thought to be about how we should live and act), and he reaches the striking conclusion that ethics cannot be based on human reason and rationality. If ethics has to do with actions and guiding our actions, he argues, then ethics must have to do with feelings and emotions, because those are the only things that can really motivate us into action (see Figure 5.3).

Figure 5.3

1. Morals have an influence on our actions.
2. Reason alone cannot influence our actions.

---

3. Therefore, morals are not based on human reason.

With this brief but incisive argument, Hume offers a critique of the centuries-long tradition in ethics that characterizes ethics as based on human rationality. Let us consider the upshot of Hume's argument. If he is correct, it would mean that whenever anyone acts, he or she is motivated by some feelings, not just reasons and thinking. So, for example, if I plan to attend college and I then do a lot of research on ten colleges, comparing them and trying to narrow the list down to my top choice, when I make that final choice I am not choosing by pure logic and reason alone and only looking at the evidence. There is always some feeling, most likely unstated, that guides my choice.

Or, when I make a moral judgment that so-and-so is a good or bad person, or that my neighbor's action is a bad action, not only is my human reason and logic involved in making such judgments, but feelings and emotions are prompting me, even if subtly, to make the judgments that I make.

The same holds true for any ethical statement I make. When I say that suicide is morally wrong, I am expressing my feelings about suicide; when I say that racism is wrong, I am expressing my feelings about racism; when I say that killing in self-defense is morally permissible, I am expressing my feelings about it, etc.

Hume put forward his view about ethics and human psychology in the early 1700s, but this way of thinking about the human mind gained more momentum in the late nineteenth and early twentieth century through the psychological theories of Sigmund Freud. Like Hume, Freud claimed that when we make decisions in our lives and take action, we may be deluded into thinking that we are in total control of our own choices. Freud developed theories about unseen and unknown forces that operate deep in the (unconscious) human mind. These questions about human nature and the human mind have wide-ranging implications, but for our purposes we are simply noting that Hume has contributed this way of thinking as the foundation for the utilitarian ethical tradition. According to the utilitarian tradition, humans are not simply rational or clever creatures; humans are feeling creatures and everything about them – including their ethics – has to do with feelings and emotions. For Hume, ethics has its ultimate origins in the feelings of human beings.

In addition to using the words "feeling," "emotion," "passion," and "desire," Hume often uses the word "sentiment" and his theory is sometimes called a *theory of moral sentiments*. As we will see later in this chapter, the word "sentiment" and variations of it will prove to be highly significant for the utilitarian ethical tradition. It comes from the Latin word *sentire*, which means *to feel*. So, it is not incorrect for us to use the word "sentiment" interchangeably with the word "feeling." An important concept for utilitarians (especially after Hume) is the concept of *sentience*, which comes from the same Latin root. There is a Spanish expression, "Lo siento mucho," which translates into English as, "I'm very sorry," but the literal translation is "I feel it much." The Spanish word *siento* comes from the same Latin root, *sentire*. *Sentience* is the ability to feel, and *sentient* creatures are creatures that have an ability to feel; it is not surprising that this will be a key concept for utilitarians who are following in the Humean tradition.

5.2 Is $\nrightarrow$ Ought: Shorthand for Hume's Theory of Moral Sentiments

Hume's theory of moral sentiments centers on the idea that whenever anyone acts or makes a moral judgment, he or she is motivated by some feelings, not just reasons and thinking. Hume has famously summed up his view by using the words *is* and *ought*.

First, consider the concept *ought*. If we go back to the original argument by which Hume seeks to establish his theory about the nature of ethics, we will recall that his first premise was the uncontroversial view that ethics is about how we ought to act and how we should live our lives. What is the key word in that premise? The concept of *ought*. For Hume, as with virtually all moral philosophers, the word *ought* sums up when something is ethical. Ethics is about how we should live our lives; ethics is about what we ought to do; ethics is about doing the right thing. The premise is uncontroversial, and *ought* as a summary way of talking about the realm of ethics is also an uncontroversial idea.

The concept *is* comes up in the second premise of Hume's argument. In that premise he makes a claim about human nature and brings in the concept of human reason, which has to do with rationality, logic, and understanding; or simply, the capacity humans have for knowing (not necessarily doing). What is the ideal that human reason, rationality, and logic try to live up to? Human reason strives to understand things, distinguish truth from falsity, separate fact from fiction, and gain facts. Human reason seeks to analytically and impartially gather and logically process information without bias, without prejudice, and with detachment. The word that sums up what reason and rationality is concerned with is *is*. Reason wants to know about what *is*; it wants the facts, not our hopes, not what we *want* to be true, but the actual truth. And even if the truth hurts, reason still strives after the facts.

Hume observed that human beings pride themselves on their ability to think and their ability to consciously know the world around them – they have even given themselves the name *Homo sapiens*, "the species of hominoid that knows." Hume claimed, however, that while this ability makes us unique among all creatures that exist, nevertheless, we are still animals, and as such, we are driven by our desires, feelings, and emotions. He claims that reason is the slave of the passions, and he means that emotional forces are most often out of our conscious control. Even though we think our heads and minds are doing the driving, it is really our feelings, emotions, and desires that are driving *us*. Recall what this view of human nature implies about ethics: reasoning itself is not sufficient to make a moral judgment or to perform an action; more is needed. Feelings, desires, and emotions are needed. Hume sums up his theory of moral sentiments with the concise phrase: one cannot derive an *ought* from an *is*; which simply means that ethics is not grounded in human reason, and ethics cannot be determined by reason, or derived from human reason (see Figure 5.4). Hume's position is that from reasoning, thinking, and logic alone (*is*), we cannot derive any ethical (*ought*) conclusions. If we wish to draw ethical conclusions we need to feel something.

The statement that *one cannot derive an ought from an is*, in addition to being a shorthand way that Hume recaps his theory of moral

Figure 5.4

Is ↛ Ought

sentiments, has also become a handy way to distinguish the ethical realm from the non-ethical realm. Even theorists who disagree with Hume's theory of moral sentiments still believe that the is/ought distinction is important. In the previous chapter, on social contract ethics, for example, the is/ought distinction was implicitly used in distinguishing between psychological egoism and ethical egoism. Psychological egoism, a theory about human nature, is put forward as a factual theory, a statement of *is*. Ethical egoism, on the other hand, is put forward as a practical ethical theory; it advises us what we ought to do – thus it makes an *ought* claim. We can acknowledge that psychological egoism and ethical egoism are importantly different, while being neutral on whether Hume is correct about ethics being grounded in our feelings rather than our reason. Some theorists have referred to the rule that *one cannot derive an ought from an is* as "Hume's law."

5.3 Feelings, Utility, and Consequences

How do we go from saying that ethics is based on feelings to talking about a "utilitarian" ethics? The word *utility* just means "usefulness," so the question is, "useful for what?" What is a "useful" ethics? The answer is uncomplicated: a useful ethic is one that is beneficial, it brings benefits; it brings about things that we desire and that will benefit us.

> *Utility*: Usefulness. In utilitarian ethics, an action, for example, has utility if it is useful in bringing about happiness. (A concept.)

The philosopher Jeremy Bentham (1748–1832) provides an easy way for us to make the connection between a theory that says ethics is based on feelings, and a "utilitarian" ethic. The first thing to do is consider the feelings that human beings experience. What is the most basic way to categorize our feelings? The most basic way is to categorize them as good feelings or bad feelings. So what makes all the good feelings, good? According to Bentham, the issue is straightforward. Good feelings are pleasurable, and it is the experience of pleasure that makes good feelings good. Similarly, it is the experience of pain that makes bad feelings bad.

In the following passage Bentham somewhat poetically describes how ethics is based on feelings – the feelings of pain and pleasure – and how utilitarian ethics incorporates these facts:

> Nature has placed mankind under the governance of two sovereign masters, *pain* and *pleasure*. It is for them alone to point out what we ought to do, as well as to determine what we shall do. On the one hand the standard of right and wrong, on the other the chain of causes and effects, are fastened to their throne. They govern us in all we do, in all we say, in all we think: every effort we can make to throw off our subjection, will serve but to demonstrate and confirm it. In words a man may pretend to abjure their empire: but in reality he will remain subject to it all the while. The *principle of utility* recognizes this subjection, and assumes it for the foundation of that system, the object of which is to rear the fabric of felicity by the hands of reason and of law. (Bentham 1789: 1–2)

The view that says "good" should be understood in terms of pleasure is known as *hedonism*, which comes from the Greek word *hedon*, a term that simply means pleasure. Bentham, like other early utilitarians, identified a utilitarian ethic as an ethic that says humans ought to increase human pleasure and decrease human pain and suffering. As mentioned at the beginning of the chapter, utilitarianism is an ethic that focuses on consequences. In evaluating whether an action, policy, rule, or law is good, we need to check to see whether the action, policy, rule or law is bringing about good consequences, i.e., more pleasure than pain. Utilitarian ethics thus provides a straightforward solution to the problem of conduct.

> *Hedonism*: The theory and tradition that says "good" should be understood in terms of pleasure.

Beginning with theorists like Hume, utilitarians also recognized that the feelings we have, whether good pleasurable ones or bad painful ones, are affected by our interactions with others. As we have seen with Hume, the true source of our moral judgments is not our rationality but our feelings. We are moved to judge or act by what we feel. When you make the judgment that serial killers are immoral, for instance, you are expressing your feelings about serial killers. When you make the judgment that parents who abuse their small children to death are immoral, you are expressing your feelings about them. You feel negatively toward these wrongdoers and you feel badly about their victims. An expression that we would use today is that you "feel for the victims," you "feel their pain and suffering."

But why do we feel others' pain and suffering when it is not happening to us? If psychological egoism were true and we were selfish through and through, it wouldn't matter to us what happens to other people, especially other people we don't even know and have never even met. The utilitarians reject psychological egoism; they claim that we have natural feelings of sympathy (*sym* "together" + *pathy* "feeling") for other human beings. This is a view about human nature. Unlike Hobbes's theory of human nature (psychological egoism), the utilitarian tradition asserts that human beings are not solely self-interested, but rather they have genuine feelings for the well-being of others. Instead of saying that humans are natural-born egoists, utilitarians hold that humans are natural-born altruists. The prefix *alt*-simply means *other*. The utilitarian view of human nature is that human beings have genuine feelings for others (in addition to feelings for themselves).

In utilitarian thinking, as soon as we care about what is happening to others we then begin to analyze events and actions in terms of how they contribute to the pleasure or suffering of others. We care about the consequences of our actions on others. We consider whether our action will contribute to their good feelings; we consider whether our action will contribute to their suffering. In other words, we think about the usefulness, or utility, of a particular action on our feelings and on others' feelings. Even though Hume claims that ethics is ultimately based on feelings, he does admit that reasoning and thinking has a supporting role to play in ethics. In the following passage from Hume, note how he claims that assessing utility and consequences will require the use of reason:

> One principal foundation of moral praise being supposed to lie in the usefulness of any quality or action; it is evident, that *reason* must enter for a considerable share in all decisions of this kind; since nothing but that faculty can instruct us in the tendency of qualities and actions, and point out their beneficial consequences to society and to their possessor. (Hume 1751: 82)

Now, what is the argument that goes from saying that we *do* care about how our actions will affect others – that's what human are like – to the *moral* claim that we *should* care about how our actions will affect others? Here it is: We genuinely feel for others, we feel their joys and their pains. We feel our own joys and pains too. Is there a difference

Figure 5.5

1. We genuinely feel for others, we feel their joys and pains.
2. We feel our own joys and pains too.
3. There is no genuine difference between our joys and pains and their joys and pains.

---

4. Therefore, we should regard others' joys and pains as just as important as ours.

between our joys and pains and their joys and pains? If there is no difference, then we *should*, purely as a matter of consistency, regard their suffering as just as important as ours (see Figure 5.5). Thus, the main utilitarian principle is the

> *Principle of Utility*: One ought always to do whatever will have the most utility for all concerned.

As a solution to the problem of conduct, the principle of utility says you should do what will increase utility, and you should not do actions that decrease utility.

The ancient Chinese philosopher Mo Tzu advocated an ethical theory that is similar to utilitarianism in many respects. Moism and Confucianism were the two dominant philosophical schools of thought in China from the fifth to the third century BCE. According to the teachings of Mo Tzu, moral life is desirable for the benefits it brings. Mo Tzu advocated that if people benefited each other, they would be living moral lives. If people cared not only for their own parents, families, and country, but in addition cared for other people's parents, families, and countries, then there would be good consequences for all concerned. Mo Tzu's ethical theory is known as a doctrine of universal love. In his writings, he gives examples of specific Chinese rulers who have practiced this ethic and who have met with success.

5.4 Utility and Happiness

In Chapter 1, we saw how Aristotle claimed that all human beings are seeking after happiness. And we saw how Aristotle defines happiness in terms of human flourishing and developing one's potential.

The early utilitarians, by contrast, defined happiness differently: they defined it along hedonistic lines, that is, in terms of pleasure. The utilitarians are attempting to offer a straightforward, easily understood and easily applicable ethics, and since they make happiness one of their key elements, they also provide a straightforward and easily understood definition of happiness. They endorse a commonsensical claim that a happy life is simply a life filled with pleasures, while an unhappy life is a life filled with pain and suffering.

Utilitarianism is regarded as a consequentialist ethic because the view recommends that in deciding whether an act, rule, policy, or motive is morally good, we should look to see if it has good consequences for all who will be affected. Instead of asking whether an action has good consequences for someone, we can simply ask if the action contributes to someone's happiness. Thus, utilitarianism is often characterized as an ethical approach that focuses on happiness, not only on the individual's happiness, but everyone's happiness. The Principle of Utility, then, is also known as the Greatest Happiness Principle:

> *Principle of Utility*, i.e., the Greatest Happiness Principle: One ought always to do whatever will have the most utility for bringing about happiness for all concerned.

5.5 Utilitarianism: Relativist or Universalist?

Some theorists claim that because of utilitarianism's emphasis on outcomes, utilitarians must hold that the problem of relativism is solved with the theory of ethical relativism. This interpretation usually comes from the critics of utilitarian ethics. Critics of utilitarian ethics argue that since utilitarians say the morality of an action depends on what the outcome of the action will bring to all who are affected, then just about any action can be regarded as moral. In other words, because it is a consequentialist ethic, we cannot say if an action is wrong until we see its bad consequences. Because utilitarian ethics in some sense holds the morality of an action hostage to and dependent on the outcome, the morality of the action seems *relative*.

Those who *defend* utilitarian ethics, on the other hand, deny ethical relativism, and see utilitarian ethics as a form of universalism, given its basis in a belief in universal human nature. Utilitarians say that all human beings have egoistic and altruistic elements, and all human beings are interested in avoiding pain and increasing pleasure. Instead of ethical relativism, then, utilitarians support an objective ethic that recognizes there are universal values and principles.

The utilitarian view that ethics has more to do with our feelings than with our rationality might seem to provide evidence that utilitarianism is a form of relativism. For don't people have different feelings about different issues? Hume does not describe ethics in that way, though. Imagine a vicious act like premeditated murder. What makes such an act wrong? Is it because society's laws say so? Is it because of divine law, or natural law? Hume says that a person will never be able to make the moral judgment that premeditated murder is wrong until he or she feels negatively toward such an act. If there are people who do not get negative feelings from pondering the notion of premeditated murder or other heinous acts, it must be because those people have something wrong with them – they are not feeling others' pain.

"Desensitization" is a contemporary psychological term that captures why some individuals may lack feeling for the pain of others. Some individuals become desensitized; they are unable to feel others' pain. This psychological concept fits perfectly with the utilitarian concept of sentience. Hume is making claims about a universal human nature and a universal ethic, even though that ethic rests upon nothing more than human feelings and sentiments. Hume is a universalist who asserts that we can generalize our social sentiments to the rest of the human race.

5.6 Utility and Equality

At the heart of the main utilitarian argument that moves from the concern we naturally have for our own feelings of pleasure and pain, to others' feelings of pleasure and pain, is the belief that that is simply what human beings are like. When we hear about tragedies befalling others we may find ourselves cringing or grimacing.

But to go from a claim about our human nature (an *is* claim) to a *moral* claim (*ought* claim) that we *should* do this, and it is *right* that we do this, and *wrong* when we do not do this, involves an additional step in the argument. The crucial step is to ask ourselves whether there is really a difference between our joys and pains and others' joys and pains. This, for example, is a challenge to any racist. If different races feel the same pleasures and pains, then why should one race see itself as superior to another race? If there really is no difference between our pleasures and pains and others' pleasures and pains, then we *should*, just because of consistency, regard their suffering as just as important as ours. This is the core of the justification of the principle of utility – we ought to do whatever will have the best consequences for all concerned, not just for ourselves, because there really is no important difference between our welfare and others' welfare.

It is clear that equality is a key concept implied in this reasoning. Another way to describe what we have been talking about and capture the central utilitarian idea is simply to say that humans are equal: your suffering or happiness is equal to my suffering or happiness. My happiness, suffering, well-being, pleasure, and pain, are not more important than yours. Seeing ethics along utilitarian lines brings us from egoism to altruism, to equality. Another way to say it is that utilitarianism involves *egalitarianism*, the view that everyone has equal ethical standing.

In his book *Utilitarianism* (1861), John Stuart Mill says the golden rule sums up the spirit of utilitarian ethics:

> [T]he happiness which forms the utilitarian standard of what is right in conduct, is not the agent's own happiness, but that of all concerned. As between his own happiness and that of others, utilitarianism requires him to be as strictly impartial as a disinterested and benevolent spectator. In the golden rule of Jesus of Nazareth, we read the complete spirit of the ethics of utility. To do as you would be done by, and to love your neighbour as yourself, constitute the ideal perfection of utilitarian morality. (Mill 1861: 16–17)

Mill interprets the golden rule as a principle of altruism, which says that we should be impartial with regard to our well-being and others' well-being. Impartiality works hand in hand with equality. The utilitarian theory and tradition thus makes use of a principle of equality:

> *Principle of Equality*: The interests of every being affected by an action are to be taken into account and given the same weight as the like interests of any other being.

One of the unique aspects of utilitarian ethics, as compared with other ethical theories and traditions, is that utilitarians have pointed out that if we are committed to an egalitarianism based on a happiness principle, and happiness is simply defined in terms of pleasure and pain, then some *non*-humans (those who experience pleasure and pain) should be regarded as equals to humans. Although most traditional ethical theories and traditions are *anthropocentric* – that is, they view only human beings as having ethical importance – utilitarian ethics can be used to support a *non-anthropocentric* ethic, that is, one that takes the focus off the human species and puts the emphasis on pleasures and pains, whether human or non-human. It is hard to deny that there are some non-human animals that experience pleasure and pain. Utilitarian ethics requires that we extend the moral community to include all sentient beings.

Let us take a moment to compare and contrast what utilitarian ethics says about equality and what earlier ethical theories and traditions have said about equality. If we start with Aristotle's ethics, in ancient Greece, we'll notice that he did not believe in human equality. Although today it is easy for us to make virtue ethics theory accommodate the notion of equality by saying that each of us is born with the same potential and we are responsible for whether we develop that potential, Aristotle himself was not egalitarian. While Aristotle believes women are equal in status to men, he still believes that, based on their natural endowments, some people are cut out to be slaves.

Although we might think natural law ethics might be egalitarian in its base, Aquinas does not say that women are equal to men. But, as with Aristotle's virtue ethics, we could easily accommodate equality into Aquinas's natural law ethics. Hobbes does talk about equality, but he says people are equal in the sense that each human being has the ability to kill another; it is not what we would call a moral equality, in terms of moral standing. Again, though, just as with virtue ethics and natural law ethics, the social contract tradition can easily build moral equality into the basic structure of social contract theory.

We can now see what is unique about the utilitarian tradition's forceful defense of equality – it is built right into the initial formulation. The early utilitarian Jeremy Bentham is well known for his position that "each is to count for one, and none for more than one," a phrase about ethics that easily translates into a statement about democracy.

5.7 Utilitarian Applications

Utilitarians hold that their ethic provides a stable and straightforward way of putting ethics into action. To complete our look at utilitarian ethics, let us consider two applications of the principle of utility and then two applications of the principle of equality. We will start with the oldest application first. In ancient China, the philosopher Mo Tzu used a utilitarian ethical approach to condemn war and elaborate funerals. In wars, people are injured and oppressed. Mo Tzu reasoned that if we calculate the costs of war, it does not benefit the people. With regard to elaborate funerals and the practice of mourning for three years – both of which were customary in ancient China – Mo Tzu concluded that these activities were not beneficial to the people. He reasoned that the resources used with these activities could be better spent in helping to alleviate the misery of masses of people. The principle of utility says one should always do whatever will have the most utility for bringing about happiness for all concerned. Since war and elaborate funerals do not contribute to the happiness of all concerned, these practices are not ethically justified.

In early modern Great Britain, Jeremy Bentham published the book *An Introduction to the Principles of Morals and Legislation* (1789). In it, Bentham argues that the principle of utility is the sole principle to be used in evaluating ethical and legal issues. A good example of Bentham's utilitarian approach is his elaborate analysis of the act of robbery from a utilitarian perspective.

With utilitarian ethics, the way to evaluate an action is to consider all the consequences of the action on all who are affected by the action. If you are robbed, you suffer a pain because you lost your money, and suffer pain at the thought of the personal ill treatment you received. Further, if perhaps the money stolen from you was to be used to pay a debt, then your creditor is affected. If you had meant to give the money to your son, then your son has been affected. If your being robbed makes it into the newspapers, then others who read about the robbery and think about the danger they and their friends may be exposed to because they travel that road, will also feel a degree of pain. Also, this robbery may produce another robbery, because people who are tempted to rob may be encouraged. Overall, then, the action of robbery is ethically wrong because of its many negative effects (see Figure 5.6).

In John Stuart Mill's book *The Subjection of Women* (1869), we can find a good example of a utilitarian application of the principle of equality. In Mill's day, women did not have equal status with men. For Mill, though, who was committed to defending utilitarian ethics and applying utilitarian ethics to social issues, the principle of equality straightforwardly entailed that the interests of women

Figure 5.6

1. We ought always do whatever will have the most utility for bringing about happiness for all concerned. (*Principle of Utility*)
2. Robbery has many negative effects on many people.

---

3. Therefore, robbery is ethically wrong.

should be given the same weight as the interests of men. Here are the opening lines of that book:

> The object of this essay is to explain as clearly as I am able grounds of an opinion which I have held from the very earliest period when I had formed any opinions at all on social political matters … That the principle which regulates the existing social relations between the two sexes – the legal subordination of one sex to the other – is wrong itself, and now one of the chief hindrances to human improvement, and that it ought to be replaced by a principle of perfect equality, admitting no power or privilege on the one side, nor disability on the other. (Mill 1869: 1)

According to Mill's analysis, there is no good reason that the interests of women should not be taken into account. And there is no good reason that the interests of women should not be given the same weight as the interests of men; hence women ought to be treated as equals.

In Peter Singer's book *Animal Liberation* (1975), we find a more recent application of the principle of equality. Singer fully develops the utilitarian notion that sentient beings deserve our moral consideration. To take that view seriously and maintain a consistent position would require us to regard all sentient beings as equal, regardless of what species they belong to. According to Singer's analysis, there is no good reason that the interests of non-human animals should not be taken into account. And there is no good reason that the interests of non-human animals should not be given the same weight as the interests of humans; hence non-human animals ought to be treated as equals. Since we do not condone eating human animals, we should not eat non-human animals. We are therefore required to become vegetarians. Similarly, since we do not condone doing medical experimentation with human animals without their consent, we are therefore required to refrain from doing medical experimentation on non-human animals. Anything less would violate the principle of equality.

5.8 Conclusion

Utilitarian ethics offers solutions to all four problems in ethics. It serves up a solution to the problem of human nature by developing the view that one of the most essential characteristics of a human being is not rationality, as many earlier theorists had claimed, but feelings and emotions. This leads utilitarians to the view that human beings are naturally altruistic beings who have genuine concern for others. As a solution to the problem of the origins of ethics, utilitarian ethics points to the fact that ethics first and foremost has to do with emotions, and so ethical standards have their ultimate grounding and basis in human feelings. Utilitarians look no deeper than human emotion and human happiness in explaining their solution to the problem of the origins of ethics.

With regard to the problem of relativism, it may seem that by grounding ethics in human feelings, utilitarians solve the problem of relativism by endorsing ethical relativism, since different people feel differently about many ethical issues. But as with most of the ethical theories we have looked at so far, utilitarian ethics denies ethical relativism but accepts cultural relativism. Surely there are some differences in how cultures view certain human practices (cultural relativism seems uncontroversial), but because of a relatively stable and universal human nature, there are large areas of agreement in how people view certain basic practices. As a solution to the problem of relativism, then, utilitarians combine cultural relativism with ethical universalism. The principle of utility, after all, does have universal application.

As we have seen above, the principle of utility says you should do what will increase utility. Though utilitarian ethics has a theoretical base and deals with three theoretical problems in ethics, it also provides a straightforward and easily applicable solution to the practical problem of conduct. In evaluating whether we should perform an action, or follow a policy, rule, or law, we simply need to check to see whether the action, policy, rule, or law is bringing about good consequences, i.e., more pleasure than pain. Utilitarian ethics thus provides a clear-cut solution to the problem of conduct.

Utilitarian ethics has some appealing features. First of all, Hume's theory about human motivation seems persuasive. Think, for example, of parents who, when their child dies in an accident of some kind, or from some kind of disease, become dedicated to teaching others how to keep their children safe. The bereaved parents are motivated to act and take the lead in these endeavors because of the strong feelings they have. Further, utilitarian ethics tries to take the mystery out of ethics by evaluating actions, rules, policies, or law simply by looking to see whether they have good or bad consequences for all concerned. Also, utilitarian ethics is easily applicable.

Whereas social contract ethics is a consequentialist ethic grounded in egoism, utilitarianism is a consequentialist ethic grounded in altruism. It sees happiness as the main goal of human actions, policies, rules, and laws; and it asserts that everyone must be treated equally. What could be wrong with it? Well, in some ways, it is too good to be true. If we are required to make everyone's happiness the goal of all our actions, isn't that very demanding upon us? And when we extend equality beyond the human race – move from an anthropocentric ethics to a non-anthropocentric ethics – again, won't this be too demanding?

There are some highly controversial aspects to utilitarian ethics. Some of these controversial aspects will become clear in the next two chapters. One issue is that consequentialist ethical theories such as social contract ethics and utilitarian ethics deny the Pauline principle, because as consequentialist theories they endorse the consequentialist principle that the end justifies the means. Even though the Pauline principle says not to do evil in the anticipation that a greater good will come out of it (the end does not justify the means), a consequentialist ethics would seem to *justify* some actions that have traditionally been seen as evil, in the anticipation that good consequences for all concerned will come as a result. Thus, discussions of consequentialist ethics inevitably lead to grappling with hard cases involving intentionally lying, killing, or torturing one person in the anticipation that many others will be saved. In these cases, a future greater good seems to outweigh the happiness of one individual. Critics of consequentialist ethics find this to be a very disturbing implication.

Concepts, Principles, Theories, and Traditions Introduced in Chapter 5

Concepts

Altruism – The view that people can be genuinely motivated for the sake of others.

Consequences – Outcomes; effects; results.

Equality – In utilitarian ethics, my happiness, suffering, well-being, pleasure, and pain, are not more important than yours.

Happiness – In classical utilitarian ethics, happiness is pleasure.

Is vs. Ought – The statement that *one cannot derive an ought from an is*, in addition to being a shorthand way that Hume recaps his theory of moral sentiments, has also become a handy way to distinguish the ethical realm from the non-ethical realm.

Non-anthropocentrism – An anthropocentric value system centers on human beings as having ethical importance. A non-anthropocentric value system takes the focus off the human species and views non-humans (such as animals and other species) as having ethical importance.

Pleasure – The experience of good feelings.

Sentience – The ability to feel; a sentient creature has the capacity to experience pleasure and pain.

Sentiment – A feeling; an emotion.

Utility – Usefulness. In utilitarian ethics, an action, for example, has utility if it is useful in bringing about happiness.

Principles

Principle of Utility – The ethical principle that says one ought always to do whatever will have the most utility for bringing about happiness for all concerned.

Principle of Equality – The ethical principle that says the interests of every being affected by an action are to be taken into account and given the same weight as the like interests of any other being.

Theories/Traditions

Egalitarianism – The tradition that views everyone as having equal ethical standing.

Hedonism – The theory and tradition that says "good" should be understood in terms of pleasure.

Utilitarian ethics – The theory and tradition that says actions (or rules or laws or standards) ought to be judged to be ethically right or wrong depending on the consequences they will have on all who will be affected.

For Further Reading

Baron, Marcia W., Philip Pettit, and Michael Slote. 1997. *Three Methods of Ethics: A Debate*. Oxford: Blackwell Publishers. Consequentialist (utilitarian) ethics is contrasted with virtue ethics and deontological ethics.

Chan, Wing-Tsit (ed.). 1963. *A Source Book in Chinese Philosophy*. Princeton, NJ: Princeton University Press. Contains Mo Tzu's ethics of universal love (chapter 9).

Dancy, Jonathan. 1993. *Moral Reasons*. Oxford: Blackwell Publishers. A contemporary philosopher who acknowledges the influence of Hume's argument that ethics rests on sentiment not rationality, but who carefully tries to develop an alternative position.

Shaw, William H. 1999. *Contemporary Ethics: Taking Account of Utilitarianism*. Oxford: Blackwell Publishers. Provides a thorough presentation of utilitarian ethics, including a critical discussion of it.

Williams, Bernard, and J. J. C. Smart. 1973. *Utilitarianism: For & Against*. Cambridge: Cambridge University Press. For a view critical of utilitarian ethics, see part 2.

Online Resources

David Hume's *A Treatise of Human Nature* (1739), https://people.rit.edu/wlrgsh/HumeTreatise.pdf Accessed October 10, 2016.

Jeremy Bentham's *An Introduction to the Principles of Morals and Legislation* (1789), http://www.earlymoderntexts.com/assets/pdfs/bentham1780.pdf Accessed October 10, 2016.

John Stuart Mill's *Utilitarianism* (1861), http://www.earlymoderntexts.com/assets/pdfs/mill1863.pdf Accessed October 10, 2016.

John Stuart Mill's *The Subjection of Women* (1869), http://www.earlymoderntexts.com/assets/pdfs/mill1869.pdf Accessed October 10, 2016.

Peter Singer's *Animal Liberation* (1975), http://www.uvm.edu/rsenr/wfb175/singer.pdf Accessed October 10, 2016.

Review Questions

1. What argument does Hume use to prove that ethics is based on feelings? Do you think ethics is based on feelings? Why or why not?
2. What do utilitarians suggest as the way to determine if an action is right or wrong? Explain.
3. Explain how utilitarianism and egalitarianism naturally go together.
4. Why does Mill think that the golden rule is in the spirit of utilitarianism?
5. Explain how Utilitarian Ethics can shift from being a solely anthropocentric ethic to being a non-anthropocentric ethic.
6. Can you think of a context in which to apply the Principle of Utility? The Principle of Equality? Explain.

Discussion Questions

1. How would Utilitarian Ethics say you should think about voting in political elections? How does it differ from what ethical egoism says?
2. The golden rule is an ancient ethical principle, yet the modern Social Contract and Utilitarian ethical theorists have managed to incorporate the principle into their theories. Explain how Social Contract and Utilitarian theorists do this. Which of these two modern interpretations most closely captures the traditional understanding of the golden rule? Explain.
3. In Italy in November 2007 a 77-year-old man shot and killed his 82-year-old wife as she lay in bed in a hospital. His wife had been diagnosed with Alzheimer's disease eight years earlier. He told police he did it because he could not stand to see her suffer. What would Utilitarian Ethics say about mercy killing? (In your answer, underline each utilitarian ethical concept and principle you mention.)
4. Imagine that a vicious general, Pedro, is about to execute 20 innocent Indians to deter others from rebelling. Pedro offers a chance visitor, Jim, the opportunity to kill one of these Indians himself. If Jim takes up the offer, the general will spare the other 19; otherwise, all 20 will die. Would Utilitarian Ethics recommend that Jim take the offer? Explain. (In your answer, underline each utilitarian ethical concept and principle you mention.)
5. The Patient Protection and Affordable Care Act (PPACA) was signed into law in 2010, and was designed to increase the number of US citizens covered by health insurance. What would Utilitarian Ethics say about health care laws? In developing your answer, use at least three concepts/principles from Utilitarian Ethics.

Chapter 6

Deontological Ethics

In the last few years I have received many interesting emails from people I don't know. A woman by the name of Mirian Williams wrote to me that her father deposited $8.5 million for her at a private firm in Abidjan in Western Africa. Unfortunately her father was killed. She wants to invest this money outside of Africa, and she offers me 20 percent of the money if I will agree to have $8.5 million transferred into my bank account.

In a different email, Tom Arnold tells me that he works at a bank and that a multi-millionaire who deposited millions of dollars into the bank has died without a will and no next of kin. Since no one has come forward to claim the money, the transfer officers will allow me to stand in as next of kin and act as a foreign partner. For my efforts I will be allowed to keep 40 percent of the money. But the utmost confidentiality is required for this deal.

An email from BukiDiara, a woman living as a refugee in West Africa, tells me that both of her parents are dead. When her father was alive, though, he deposited $5.5 million dollars in a security company in Senegal. She would like to transfer the money to me, and then I can send some of the money to her, so she can travel to the United States.

From Sierra Leone in West Africa, Jenifer Kone sent me an email saying she lost her husband during a rebel attack. Before his death, though, he made a bank deposit of $10.5 million. Unfortunately, she has been denied access to the money. She claims that the money can only be released by the bank if it is transferred to a foreign account. She asks if I will act as her late husband's foreign business partner and have the funds transferred into my account.

Finally, an attorney writes to me that his client died as a result of a heart-related condition, and none of his client's family is alive to inherit

Ethics: The Basics, Second Edition. John Mizzoni.

their fortune. Since I have the same name as his client, the attorney says I am entitled to inherit the fund worth $3.3 million dollars.

What do all of these proposals have in common? I think they are all examples of fraud. As soon as I agree to the deal and give over my bank account number, these individuals will attempt to steal money from my bank account. In ethics, these are viewed as classic cases of deceiving someone for the purposes of using that person to acquire personal gain. Most likely, the people who sent me the above emails have fabricated those elaborate stories as a way of manipulating me so they can steal from me. A central ethical principle in deontological ethics is that we should not treat people as means, but respect them as persons.

Although "deontological" is probably not a term most people are familiar with, the ethic that the term refers to is surely one that most people are familiar with. The deontological ethical tradition is a very old tradition and you will find that you are already acquainted with the main outlines of it. A deontological ethics is simply an ethic that focuses on duty; it is a duty-centered ethics. *Deont-* merely means "duty." If you think ethics has most to do with fulfilling one's obligations, doing one's duty, and performing actions because of "the principle of the matter," then you are conceiving of ethics in a deontological ethical framework.

Recall the Pauline principle from the natural law ethics tradition, the principle that says the end does not justify the means. Consequentialist ethics denies the Pauline principle; consequentialist ethics directly contradicts the Pauline principle by saying that the end *does* justify the means. Consequences are ends and outcomes. As we saw in the last two chapters, social contract ethics is consequentialist in that one is interested in the good consequences one will reap for oneself if one participates in a social contract; it is an egoistic consequentialism. Utilitarianism is consequentialist in that one is interested in bringing about good consequences for all concerned; it is an altruistic consequentialism.

Deontological ethics, the focus of the current chapter, has more in common with natural law ethics, which was the focus of Chapter 3. Like natural law ethics, when trying to decide if an action is morally right or wrong, deontological ethics focuses more on the intention rather than the consequences (see Figure 6.1). Both deontological ethics and natural law ethics agree that the end does not justify the means. We can call them *non-consequentialist* ethical theories. Historically, most non-consequentialist ethics have been part of a religious worldview (as we saw with traditional natural law ethics). In a religious ethical view,

Figure 6.1

Intention ⇒ Action ⇒ Consequence

duty is often a key ethical concept; those who have a religious ethical view would claim that the ultimate source of our duties is God's commands. And human beings are understood not only to have ethical duties to others, but a religious duty to God.

But, beginning with the modern German philosopher Immanuel Kant (1724–1804), deontological theorists have attempted to support a duty-centered ethic without relying on a religious framework. In this chapter we will focus on a Kantian-style deontological ethic, but we will remain open to other versions of deontological ethics.

6.1 Duty-centered Ethics

A duty is something one is required to do. Here are some examples of duties: to tell the truth, to not torture people, to protect something or someone entrusted to you, to follow through on your agreements, to not break your promises, etc.

We should not get hung up on the word *duty*. There are other words that convey the same concept, terms such as *responsibility*, or *obligation*. We can talk of one's duties, or one's responsibilities, or one's obligations. The easiest examples of duties are those duties we have because of our particular role. Each of us has different roles we play. We are workers, thus we have duties that come with our particular jobs. Depending on our job, we may have duties to our employers, to our profession, to the public. If I am an accountant, for instance, I have a duty not to engage in fraudulent accounting practices; if I am a doctor I have duty to do what's best for my patients; if I am a lawyer I have a duty to do what is best for my clients. Besides being workers, we are members of families; parents have a duty to take care of their children. We are citizens too; thus we have a duty to abide by the laws of our country.

Bearing in mind these examples of different duties, think about the problem of the origins of ethics. To solve the problem of the origins of ethics with a deontological solution, we need to explain where duties ultimately come from. *Why* do I have duties to tell the truth, to not torture people, to protect something or someone entrusted to me, to follow through on my agreements, to not break my promises, etc.? One easy explanation is provided by a religious worldview: our ethical duties are the result of God's commands. This is called divine command ethics, and it provides a traditional solution to the problem of the origins of ethics. Because God commanded us to behave in certain ways, we thus have duties to behave in certain ways. In the Islamic faith tradition, for example, one's main duty is to obey the will of God. In the Jewish tradition, which also emphasizes duties, there are a total of 613 commands one must follow. In a religious worldview, the collection of God's commands can be thought of as God's law. The idea of a moral law fits well within deontological ethics, and this is one of the reasons we stated above that deontological ethics is similar to natural law ethics in many ways. Natural law ethics, as we have seen, incorporates the notion that ethics has to do with a law that has been given by God.

6.2 Ethics of Freedom and Rationality

Kant offered a different deontological solution to the problem of the origins of ethics. For Kant, we have ethical duties, but not because we have been commanded by God. Kant attempted to provide a deontological ethical theory that does not make references to God or religion. A religious worldview that accepts God as the creator will have to claim that there is some kind of relationship between God's will and human nature. We saw that in the natural law tradition, it is believed that human beings are the kind of creature they are due to God's will and God's plan, and this belief plays an important role in the formulation of natural law ethical theory.

But Kant attempts to develop an ethics that does not depend on belief in God. Many other modern ethical theorists attempt to do this as well. Rather than focus on a human being's connection to divine origins as a way to figure out what grounds our duties, Kant recommends that we solve the problem of human nature by looking at the most important and unique quality that human beings have that makes them moral beings. In Kant's view, the solution to the problem of human nature is not that human beings are made in the image of God, but that human beings have rationality, and through that rationality they have freedom. For Kant, freedom is the cornerstone to morality.

In a deontological ethic, duties, obligations, and responsibilities are center-stage. Can we legitimately hold people responsible for something they were not free to avoid? Or, instead of thinking about people (human animals), consider non-human animals. Can we hold *them* responsible for their actions? For Kant, we cannot: non-human animals are not free to choose their actions, as they are creatures of instinct. In Kant's view, human beings are unique because they are free beings; they have free will. And once a being has free will and is conscious of its actions, then it can be justly accountable for its actions. If a being is consciously aware of what it is doing, and it is free to act or not to act, this is a recipe for responsibility, obligation, and duty. Human beings *are* aware of what they do, and they *are* free to act or not to act; thus they have duties.

Kant disagreed with Hume's theory of moral sentiments and utilitarian ethics. According to Hume, one cannot make a moral judgment unless one feels something, because ethics at bottom has to do with human feelings and emotions. With his theory of moral sentiments, Hume bases ethics on feelings and desires. Kant, though, disagrees with Hume's solution to the problem of the origins of ethics. Kant thinks we can make moral judgments simply because we are rational, conscious, and free beings. He denies that ethics rests upon a foundation of human sentiments. In order to make a moral judgment, Kant believes one need *not* feel an emotion of some kind. The only thing that is required is that one can think rationally. As soon as a being is rationally conscious and can make choices, then that being is capable of duty, and capable of taking commands. But if we leave God out of the picture, who is it that is doing the commanding? Kant believes that reason and rationality command people. People have been commanded by reason – not others' reason, but their own; therefore, people have duties.

6.3 The Main Deontological Principle: The Categorical Imperative

In his emphasis on reasoning and rationality, and his attempt to leave out any reference to God or religion, one might suppose that Kant is offering a social contract ethics. But there are important differences between Hobbes's social contract ethics and Kant's deontological ethics. The most important difference is that social contract ethics, like utilitarian ethics, is consequentialist. Kant believes that any form of ethical consequentialism, whether of the social contract or the utilitarian variety, is seriously misguided.

Kant distances his view of ethics from consequentialist ethics by making a distinction between different kinds of commands. Commands can range from very basic ones, like "Beware of the dog," "Shut the window," to divine ones like "Thou shalt not bear false witness." The main feature of a command is that it is directing us to perform an action. In other words, it is *prescriptive*: it prescribes what we *ought* to do. Kant recognizes that there are different kinds of commands, and he thinks distinguishing between two main kinds is very important for ethics. Another word for command is *imperative*; accordingly, Kant tells us about a categorical imperative and a hypothetical imperative. He contrasts the two imperatives in the following passage:

> Now all imperatives command either hypothetically or categorically. The former represent the practical necessity of a possible action as a means for attaining something else that one wants (or may possibly want). The categorical imperative would be one which represented an action as objectively necessary in itself, without reference to another end. (Kant 1785: 25)

To see the difference between the two imperatives, take an example from divine command ethics. When God commands his prophets, they have a duty to obey. When God speaks directly to you, you are not supposed to ask questions. God's commands are absolute. When God gives a command, you do it, period. There are no ifs, ands, or buts. Even though Kant wants to leave out reference to God, he does believe that ethical duties have this kind of feature – they are absolute, there are some things that one needs to do, period. There are no ifs, ands, or buts. This kind of strong command, or imperative, is what Kant calls a *categorical* imperative. A deontological ethic focuses on doing one's duty for the sheer principle of the thing, simply because it is the right thing to do, period. In calling his principle a *categorical* imperative, Kant is tapping into the ethical *to-be-doneness* experience that most of us have had. Morality, as Kant understands it, has an absolute bindingness to it. And any ethical theory that does not capture that categorical nature of moral experience is deficient, and must be misguided, he thinks.

For Kant, consequentialist ethical theories are examples of misguided ethical theories that do not recognize the categorical nature of moral experience. In Kant's view, instead of recognizing a categorical imperative, a consequentialist ethics recognizes a *hypothetical* imperative. Kant's stand against consequentialist ethics is quite harsh, because, in his terms, a hypothetical imperative is not a moral imperative! So he is in effect saying that consequentialist ethics are not even ethical theories – that is how misguided they are.

Here is the big difference between a categorical imperative and a hypothetical imperative. Whereas a categorical imperative has the absolutely binding – *do it*, no ifs, ands, or buts – force behind it, a hypothetical imperative has only one's desire behind it. Think of the word "hypothetical" as describing the realm of "if," as in the word *hypothesis*. Hypothetically, I could move to Alaska. Hypothetically, I could hitchhike across the United States, or I could learn how to fly a helicopter. All of these ideas are in the realm of possibility. In what ways could they be made into imperatives? They could be made into imperatives if I *want* to move to Alaska, hitchhike across the United States, or learn to fly a helicopter. If I want to do these things, then maybe I should do these things. The "should," the "ought," the "prescriptive" nature of these imperatives are totally dependent on whether I have these desires. If I have the desires, then these imperatives are meaningful; if I don't have the desires, then these imperatives are irrelevant to me.

Here is how hypothetical imperatives are apparent in consequentialist ethical theories like social contract ethics and utilitarian ethics. With social contract ethics, the hypothetical imperative would be: if I want to protect my life and my property, then I ought to participate with the social contract. Notice how it is possible for me to say in response to that suggestion: I don't have that desire; I don't care about my life and property. With utilitarian ethics, the hypothetical imperative would be: if I want to be happy and bring about happiness for others, then I should be an ethical person. Again, see how it is possible for me to say in response: I don't care about my happiness or anyone else's happiness.

> *Hypothetical Imperative*: A command that is not absolute, but conditional, and premised on one's desires. (A concept.)

The categorical imperative, in contrast, is not dependent on one's desires. It is a command that one is to follow, period. Saying that one lacks the desire is irrelevant, because for Kant ethics is not about desires, emotions, or getting good consequences for yourself or others; it is about doing what's right, doing one's duty.

In Asian philosophy there are two examples of this point about ethics. The first is in the ethical thought of Confucius of ancient China, who, like Kant, thinks being motivated by benefits is misguided. For Confucius, one should be motivated by righteousness. The second example is in the ancient Indian book *The Bhagavad Gita*, a sacred text of Hinduism. When Arjuna, the main character of the book, is faced with the moral dilemma of whether to fight in battle or not, and is considering the different consequences of two paths of action he is caught between, he is given advice by the god Krishna. Krishna counsels that Arjuna should not concern himself with the outcome of his actions: he should not trouble himself in attempting to calculate what will be the best course of action by gauging the good versus bad consequences that will follow from his choice. Krishna tells Arjuna:

> Look to your own duty; do not tremble before it; nothing is better for a warrior than a battle of sacred duty ... Be intent on action, not on the fruits of action ... Without faith in sacred duty, men fail to reach me, Arjuna ... Better to do one's own duty imperfectly than to do another man's well. (*Bhagavad Gita*, trans. Miller, c.100 CE: 34, 36, 83, 149)

Arjuna should simply do his duty. Arjuna is a member of the warrior caste, and his responsibility is to fight in wartime.

6.4 One Form of the Categorical Imperative: The Principle of Autonomy

Kantian deontological ethics is known as a formal morality. This is because it characterizes morality as essentially having to do with rational rules, rather than, say, a set of dispositions from our human social nature. But as with all ethical theories, there is a conception of human nature that is lurking in the background.

Although Kant claims that there is one formal rule of morality, the categorical imperative, he offers different versions of the categorical imperative, which are meant as different ways of expressing the main ethical principle.

We will begin with the form that is easiest to understand.

> *Categorical Imperative*: Act in regard to all persons in ways that treat them as ends in themselves and never simply as means to accomplish the ends of others. (Principle of Respect for Autonomy)

First, notice the *form* of the principle. It is a command, an imperative, but a special kind of imperative: one that points to duties we must abide by and we absolutely ought not to neglect. The principle is categorical in another sense, too. It covers the whole category of persons (applies to all people); it is concerned not only with how you treat *others*, but with how you treat *yourself*, since you, too, are a person.

This version of the categorical imperative is sometimes called the principle of respect for autonomy. It refers to the root of Kant's ethics, the very source of our duties: the rationality and freedom of people, which is basically what autonomy is. The principle says to act so that you treat persons (where person is defined as a rational, autonomous being), always as ends in themselves and never as means only.

We may not be familiar with the language of "end in themselves" and "means," but the kernel of the idea is familiar to us to all – it is the principle that says we should not *use* people and manipulate them, because such treatment is disrespectful. We need to respect them as persons; they have moral status, they have dignity; in Kant's terms they are ends in themselves. The twentieth-century Jewish philosopher Martin Buber (1923) captures the idea in his description of different relationships: there is an I–Thou relationship in which a person, an "I," looks upon another being as a person to be respected, a "Thou." But there is also an I–It relationship in which a person, an "I," looks upon another being as an "It," a thing, a mere object that does not deserve our respect. In Buber's terms, then, we violate the principle of respect for autonomy when we wrongly treat another person as an "It" by neglecting to accord the other person the respect he or she deserves.

Another way to understand the concept of autonomy is "independence" (as opposed to dependence). As free rational beings, persons are directly responsible for the decisions they make: being free from others' interferences makes them independent. To take away a person's responsibility is to take away the person's dignity: it is to deny their personal autonomy, and to deny their independence. For Kant, "autonomy is the ground of the dignity of human nature" (Kant 1785: 41).

A contemporary way of capturing what Kant has in mind is the phrase "voluntary informed consent." To respect free rational beings is to ask them to act voluntarily, not involuntarily, and to provide them with the relevant information so they can freely choose their actions. By the principle of respect for autonomy, to attempt to direct a person's actions by withholding pivotal pieces of information from them is unethical. And to force people to do things against their will is unethical; in the area of sexual ethics, an extreme example of this is rape.

Because of the emphasis on autonomy and independence in Kant's deontological ethics, we can see how it diverges from Confucian ethics. Both Confucius and Kant agree that benefits should not be the motivation for good deeds, and we should be motivated simply because the action is right. But Confucius maintains that good role models are extremely important, a view we have seen associated with virtue ethics in Chapter 2. In Confucius' view, the very fate of the whole society depends on whether the leader has good character and provides a good role model for the citizens. If the leader is not a good role model, the people will not strive after virtue; and thus the stability of the society is threatened. As Confucius puts it, "If the ruler himself is upright, all will go well even though he does not give orders. But if he himself is not upright, even though he gives orders, they will not be obeyed" (Confucius 450 BCE: 173).

In this approach Confucius is emphasizing how humans are dependent beings: they depend on their leaders, and on their ancestors. Confucius is well known as endorsing a virtue known as filial piety, which is pious, reverent behavior toward our parents and ancestors. Kant, by contrast, does not emphasize role models. In fact, for Kant, to follow a role model is somewhat slavish and mindless, because one is not being autonomous, free, and independent. Just as we must respect others' autonomy, we must respect our own autonomy, thinks Kant.

6.5 Another Form of the Categorical Imperative: The Principle of Universality

Besides the principle of autonomy, Kant offers other versions of the categorical imperative. But he says that the different "ways of representing the principle of morality are at bottom only so many formulas of the very same law" (Kant 1785: 41).

The next version of the categorical imperative we will look at is a bit more abstract.

> *Categorical Imperative*: Act only from those personal rules that you can at the same time will to be universal moral laws. (Principle of Universality)

This ethical principle uses the concept known as universalizability, which is basically the test that says: what if everyone did that? But Kant wants to make sure that we interpret universalizability in a non-consequentialist manner. When we ask the question, "What if everyone did that?" we might interpret it in a consequentialist framework by saying that we should think about the consequences of everyone doing the action in question. Usually when the average person raises that kind of question he or she would be implying that the action would likely have negative consequences if everyone did that, and therefore, one ought not to do it.

But we can give the universalizability test a non-consequentialist interpretation, and this is the approach that Kant thinks is correct. For, if we put the universalizability test in a consequentialist framework we are really working with a hypothetical imperative, which is not a *moral* imperative. To characterize the universalizability test as a *categorical* imperative, we need to emphasize what goes into the action (the intention), not the outcome or consequences of the action. In applying the categorical imperative we are concerned with what our will is intending. In Kant's terms, we should take note of what personal rule we are following, for this is the key to what are we intending to do.

The universalizability test asks us to consider whether we could consistently *will* an action. The stress is on consistency and free will, and this should make sense since, as we saw above, deontology is an ethics of freedom and rationality. In Kant's view, consistency is a basic ground rule of rationality. If we continue contradicting ourselves and making inconsistent statements, are we rational beings? No, we would be regarded as *ir*rational. Since human rationality is the source of the categorical imperative, it is unsurprising that the principle of universality is about consistency of willing.

> *Universalizability*: A personal rule possesses universalizability – is universalizable – if it could consistently be willed to become a universal rule or law that everyone, everywhere, for all times, ought to follow.

But what does it mean to say that I am consistent (or inconsistent) when I am willing an action? Consider a broad and extreme situation like the following. Let us say that I have decided that logic and rationality are too cold and calculating, and I will henceforth live my life in total disregard of rationality and logical consistency. Can I consistently will that? No, I am being inconsistent. In the very process of deciding to be irrational I am using the rationality that I say I want to avoid! I am entertaining a self-contradictory position about how to live my life.

Figure 6.2

1. If I will it to be a universal law that people tell the truth to their family members and lie to everyone else, then I am willing that strangers lie to me.
2. As a rational being, I cannot consistently and consciously will that strangers lie to me.

---

3. Therefore, I cannot consistently will it to be a universal law that people tell the truth to their family members and lie to everyone else.

---

4. Therefore, I ought not to tell the truth to some people and lie to others, but I have a duty to tell the truth.

Here is a more standard ethical example. Let us consider a duty to tell the truth. Do I have a duty to tell the truth? In a situation where I am tempted to lie about something, can I will my personal rule to become a universal moral law? Let's say I accept that I have a duty to tell the truth to my family members but I deny that I have a duty to tell the truth to total strangers. That is my personal rule. What happens when I try to will that rule to become a universal moral law? If I am willing it to be a universal moral law that people tell the truth to their family members and lie to everyone else, I am thus willing that strangers lie to me. As a rational being, can I consistently and consciously will that strangers lie to me? No; being fed false information goes against what a rational being strives for. Therefore, I cannot consistently will my personal rule to be a universal moral law, i.e., it does not pass the universalizability test; hence I ought not to do this action. I ought not to lie to some people and tell the truth to others. I ought to tell the truth to all; this duty has an absolute bindingness to it (see Figure 6.2).

6.6 Duties Correlate with Rights (Usually)

At the outset of the chapter I mentioned how both natural law and deontological ethics have a shared commitment to the Pauline principle that says the end does not justify the means. We can use this point to remind ourselves that both natural law and deontological ethics are non-consequentialist ethical theories that place a stress on what goes into an action (the intention), rather than what results from an actions (the ends, the consequences). With non-consequentialist ethics, the way to decide if an action, rule, policy, or motive is good is not to look at the consequences that come as a result of them, but to look at the intentions – the act of willing – that goes *into* them. Think of the application of the categorical imperative as a somewhat elaborate test to check to see if our intentions are morally good: are we intending to respect the persons we are interacting with? (the principle of autonomy). Can our willing be universally consistent? (the principle of universality). Consequentialist ethical theories such as social contract ethics and utilitarian ethics, by contrast, are committed to a denial of the Pauline principle, because those theories endorse the consequentialist principle that the end justifies the means.

In this context we can introduce the concept of moral rights, because rights fit in very easily with the Pauline principle and the categorical imperative (especially the principle of autonomy version). Instead of calling it the "principle of autonomy," some theorists give it a longer label: the "principle of respect for autonomy." In this form, the categorical imperative tells us that we must treat people respectfully, as persons, and not merely as things, or means, to achieve our goals. Kant's terminology is that we ought to treat people as "ends," never as "means" only. To treat someone as an "end" is to respect that person. An easier way to capture this notion – a way that has become extremely popular in the last 200 years – is to say that people have "rights" that ought to be respected. So although Kant uses the terminology, "treat people as ends," modern and contemporary society has preferred to use a different expression, the concept of "respecting people's rights."

Thus, when we say we ought to respect the rights of persons, we are not saying anything much different from the categorical imperative. After all, if a person has rights and we are not to treat that person as a thing to be used and then discarded when no longer useful to us, that essentially means that we have duties to respect people's rights. A quick way of summing this up is to say that moral rights correlate with duties. That is, if a person has a right, then other persons have duties to respect those rights. For example, if people have the right not to be tortured then others have a duty not to torture them. If people have the right to property then others have a duty not to steal their property. Moral rights, then, have a natural home in a deontological ethical framework.

However, does the correlation between duties and rights work as well in the opposite direction? That is, if I say that you have a duty, let's say to contribute to charitable causes or to give back to the community, does that mean that others have rights? No, we may have duties that do not have a direct and precise object to which they correlate. Even though I generally ought to aid others when I am in the position to do so, which we can establish with the principle of universality, is it that specific person's right to receive aid that forms the basis of my duty? No, a legitimate right is a claim that can limit others' freedom: my right to life limits your freedom of killing, my right to property limits your freedom to take my possessions, and my right not to be tortured limits your freedom to practice your torture methods on me. But do I have a right to receive aid that limits what you can do with your wealth? No.

Another example of duties we have that do not correlate with the rights that others have is with the duties we have because of the special role we are playing, as workers, parents, or citizens. If I say I have a duty to vote, does that correlate with others' rights? No. If I have a duty to take care of my children does that correlate with rights they have? If I have a duty to do a good job at my workplace does that correlate with others' rights? No. Again, to sum up: some of the duties we have may not be direct correlates with rights. But there are plenty of circumstances in which I *do* have a duty specifically because it correlates with others' rights.

As one would expect from an ethical theory that focuses on duties, deontological theorists distinguish between different kinds of duties: positive duties, negative duties, duties to self, duties to others, direct duties, and indirect duties. The difference between positive duties and negative duties is easily understood by considering the ten commandments of the Hebrew Bible. "Thou shall not kill" commands what *should not* be done; thus it specifies a negative duty. "Honor thy father and mother" commands what *should* be done; thus, it specifies a positive duty. The difference between duties to self and duties to others is straightforward. In Kant's development of deontological theory I have a duty to myself not to commit suicide, and a duty to develop my talents, among other duties to myself. In addition, I have a duty not to lie to others, and a duty to aid others when I am in a position to do so, among others. Kant argues that each of these duties can be established by applying the categorical imperative. Those who endorse a deontological ethic within a religious worldview would say that among the duties to others are included duties to God: for example, a duty to not take the Lord's name in vain. We will consider the distinction between direct and indirect duties in a later section on deontological applications.

As we have seen, deontological ethical theory provides a natural framework for rights. An important aspect of modern rights is equality. Just as utilitarianism, a modern ethical tradition, incorporates equality into its essential formulation of the principle of utility, modern deontology also incorporates equality into its essential formulation of the categorical imperative. Like utilitarian ethics, Kant's deontological ethics has egalitarianism built right into it. The principle of universality implies universal equality, and the principle of autonomy implies equality for all autonomous beings, regardless of their sex, race, or ethnicity. This is a dimension of Kantian deontological ethics that distinguishes it from the Hindu deontological ethic that was exhibited in the Arjuna example. For as Arjuna was a member of the warrior caste, it was his duty to fight; others who are born into other castes have a different status in Hindu society. From this example, we can see that it is possible for a deontological ethic to incorporate an inegalitarian orientation.

6.7 Deontology: Relativist or Universalist?

It is obvious that Kantian deontological ethics is a kind of universalism that rejects ethical relativism, since one of Kant's formulations of the categorical imperative – the principle of universality – has the word "universal" built right into it. Kant describes that the categorical imperative is binding on *all* rational beings, regardless of their time, place, or culture. Kant solves the problem of relativism just as a universalist who endorses virtue ethics might solve it. One who endorses a universalist virtue ethics can acknowledge that cultural relativism is true – that there is cultural diversity when it comes to how different cultures view the qualities of a good person, a person with virtues. But a universalist virtue ethics also claims that there are some virtues that are important for *all* people to have no matter what the specifics of their culture, job, situation, etc. The same is true of deontological ethics. In addition to accepting cultural relativism as true – accepting that some duties are culture-specific or role-specific, deontologists have tried to show that we all have duties just because of the kind of being that we are. There are some duties that are important for *all* people to have no matter what the specifics of their job, situation, etc.

6.8 Deontological Applications

In this section we will consider applications using both versions of the categorical imperative: the principle of autonomy and the principle of universality. The first case we will consider is the ethical treatment of non-human animals. How does the categorical imperative (principle of autonomy) apply? The principle of autonomy says we ought to act in regard to all persons in ways that treat them as ends in themselves and never simply as means to accomplish the ends of others. We should respect others' freedom and rationality; we should not use people nor treat them as things; we should respect others' dignity. We must treat them as independent beings who are responsible for their own behavior.

The key question here is whether non-human animals are persons. Do they have freedom, rationality, and autonomy? Are they independent beings who are responsible for their behavior? Kant himself addresses this issue and reasons that non-human animals simply do not have these abilities. According to Kant, "Animals are not self-conscious and are there merely as a means to an end. That end is man" (Kant 1780: 239).

The ethical conclusion reached, then, is that we do not have duties to respect the autonomy of non-human animals; this is simply because they do not *have* autonomy. The very same point is true about "animal rights"; we do not have duties to respect non-human animal rights because, from a Kantian deontological perspective, they do not have rights. Again, this is simply because they do not have autonomy, freedom, or rationality (see Figure 6.3).

This ethical stance toward non-human animals fits well with what social contract ethics says about non-human animals. As we have seen in Chapter 4, a prerequisite for entering into a contract with others is that one has to be a rational being. Thus, Hobbes excludes non-human animals from social contract ethics, for they lack the capacity to enter into contracts. Like social contract ethics, Kant's deontological ethic also emphasizes rationality as a prerequisite for ethics, so Kant reaches

Figure 6.3

1. We ought to act in regard to all persons in ways that treat them as ends in themselves and never simply as means. (*Principle of Autonomy*)
2. Non-human animals are not persons – they don't have freedom, rationality, or autonomy.

---

3. Therefore, ethically, we may treat non-human animals as means.

a similar conclusion about the ethical status of non-human animals. On the other hand, we can make a contrast with utilitarian ethics here. For Kant, the fact that non-human animals can experience pain is not sufficient for conferring ethical status on them. But a utilitarian, who denies that ethics is based on rationality and asserts that ethics is based on feelings, will maintain that precisely because a non-human animal is capable of suffering (has sentience), it deserves moral standing. A utilitarian will conclude, then, that we ought to concern ourselves with how the non-human animal is affected by our actions.

We must consider one more aspect of how the principle of autonomy applies to non-human animals. We already know that in Kantian deontological ethics non-human animals are not persons that ought to be respected, but does the conclusion then follow that we can treat them simply as things to be used without *any* regard to their feelings or suffering? Is a deontological ethic so unfeeling and coldly rational?

To answer that question we must distinguish between direct and indirect duties. In an earlier section of this chapter I mentioned how a deontological ethic distinguishes between different kinds of duties: duties to self, to others, positive duties, negative duties, and direct and indirect duties. We are now in a situation to describe the difference between a direct and indirect duty. A direct duty is a duty we have toward a person. An indirect duty is a duty we have toward a pseudo-person (like a non-human animal). In Kant's thinking, we do have duties to non-human animals: we ought to be kind to them, but not because of what we owe to the non-human animal, but rather out of respect for humanity. Let's say my neighbor has a dog that persistently barks and leaves a mess on my lawn. From a Kantian deontological perspective, because this dog lacks freedom and rationality it is not a person but only a thing, an object. Since the dog is an annoyance to me maybe I should kill my neighbor's dog. But, it *is* my neighbor's dog and I should respect the dog. I thus have an indirect duty to the dog – a duty that is ultimately traceable to the fact that the dog's owner is a person. As Kant puts it: "Our duties towards animals are merely indirect duties towards humanity" (Kant 1780: 239).

While Kant, in traditional fashion, denies that non-human animals have rights, the contemporary deontologist Tom Regan has developed a version of deontology that accords rights to non-human as well as human animals (1983). As we have seen, Kant defines autonomy in terms of rationality. Regan argues that there is a different kind of autonomy other than the one Kant had in mind. For Regan, a being can be said to be autonomous if it has preferences and the ability to initiate action to satisfy those preferences. Since some non-human animals have this kind of autonomy, Regan concludes that some non-human animals have rights.

The ethical status of non-human animals concerns our duties to others; let us now turn our attention to a deontological application that concerns a duty to self, the duty to not commit suicide. Kant discusses this example in several of his ethical works. How does the categorical imperative (principle of universality) apply? Recall that the principle of universality says we ought to act only from those personal rules that we can at the same time will to be universal moral laws. So to ethically analyze an action with this principle, we need to check to see whether the personal rule we are considering following passes the universalizability test. The way to do this is to identify what we are intending, and ask whether we can consistently will that personal rule to become a universal rule.

Normally, if our life is going well, we may not have occasion to seriously consider this duty to self. But if we find that our life has taken a turn for the worse, and there doesn't seem to be any prospect of things getting better for us, what would be wrong with opting out of a miserable condition and taking our own life? There are many different lines of reasoning one could pursue in thinking about the ethics of suicide. What we are interested in, though, is how the principle of universality version of the categorical imperative would apply.

First, we must identify what it is that we are intending, that is, what is the personal rule that we are considering? Let's say my personal rule is that I am interested in living a happy life. If my life shows no signs of happiness but only misery into the foreseeable future, then my personal rule is to end my life. To ask if such an action is consistent with the categorical imperative, we must ask ourselves if we could consistently will this personal rule to become a universal law. As a free, rational being, could I will that when a person encounters prolonged misery and adversity then the will to live must turn on itself and end its own existence? For Kant, this would involve a strange kind of inconsistency, for the very act of thinking about committing suicide presupposes an actively engaged person who is willfully forging ahead with his or her life. To think that that very same will could consistently terminate itself is contradictory. In Kant's words:

> One sees at once a contradiction in a system of nature whose law would destroy life by means of the very same feeling that acts so as to stimulate the furtherance of life, and hence could be no existence as a system of

> nature. Therefore, such a maxim cannot possibly hold as a universal law of nature and is, consequently, wholly opposed to the supreme principle of all duty. (Kant 1785: 31)

Under Kant's deontological ethics, if my personal rule (what he calls in the above quotation a *maxim*) does not pass the universalizability test, then my personal rule does not pass the morality test. Thus, taking one's own life is immoral. In other words, one has a negative duty to oneself not to commit suicide.

6.9 Conclusion

For Kant, one's duties are not to be taken lightly. Take the suicide case. Even if I am suffering excruciating pain, I ought not to take my own life. Doing one's duty does not involve gaining pleasure and happiness for oneself; it involves simply doing one's duty, and sometimes that is quite difficult. Absolute duties as described by Kant might be called "heavy-duty" duties, for with ethical duties there are no ifs, ands, or buts. Doing your duty could require the loss of your life, property, or happiness, but it ought to be done nonetheless. One who is committed to "heavy-duty" duties has very high ethical standards.

In our brief introduction to deontological ethics, we can see how the theory deals with four problems in ethics. Its solution to the problem of human nature is that what is most essential about human beings is that they are rational beings who are aware of what they are doing and in control of what they are doing. Humans are free and autonomous creatures, and therefore can be meaningfully said to have obligations, responsibilities, and duties. By locating the source of the ethical standards that we should follow in human reason itself, Kantian deontological ethics solves the problem of the origins of ethics. The categorical imperative, ultimately, is a command of reason: ethical standards are derived from human reason. Just as there are universal standards of logic and reasoning, Kantian deontology holds that there are universal standards of ethics. Kantian deontology solves the problem of relativism by distinguishing between cultural relativism and ethical relativism. While some duties are culturally relative, there are some duties we are all obligated to fulfill simply because of the kind of beings we are – rational beings who ought not to perform actions that cannot be willed to become universal. There are some duties, therefore, that are important for *all* people to carry out, no matter what culture they are from.

Though deontological ethics at times uses a unique vocabulary and an abstract way of moral reasoning, it does offer an explicit solution to the practical problem of conduct. Deontological ethics is a non-consequentialist ethic, so it claims we should not solve the problem of conduct by solely looking at consequences and outcomes. Like natural law ethics, it says we need to take intentions and motives into account. Something is right if we are intending to act out of duty. The more precise way to determine if our intentions are morally acceptable and our action is right is to use the categorical imperative. We act rightly when we treat people as ends in themselves and not simply as means. We act rightly when we respect others' freedom, rationality, and dignity. We act wrongly when we use people and treat them as things. We act rightly when we follow personal rules we can will to be universal moral laws.

At first glance, what could be wrong with an ethical theory that advocates doing one's duty? Some critics, though, regard Kant's articulation and defense of deontological ethics as an over-intellectualized ethic. They point out that Kant's concept of "person" as a "rational being" is too narrow, since a real-life person is much more than a rational being. "Does the moral life *simply* consist in doing one's duty?" critics ask. Also, categorizing every entity as either a person or a thing seems too sharp a divide; aren't there grey areas in between, for example, non-human animals, the environment, the mentally disabled, and fetuses?

Different critics – consequentialists and those who take ethics to be more about feeling than thinking – make the same point in a slightly different way. They take issue with the fact that Kant counsels that we must not give in to our emotions, feelings, passions, desires, or temptations, but rather stand firm against them. In his choice of examples, Kant gives the impression that ethical actions are those done deliberately after a victory over opposing desires. In doing so, say his critics, Kant has narrowly confined ethics. However, such a position is perfectly appropriate for a non-consequentialist ethical theory.

As we have seen in this chapter, there are similarities between deontological and natural law ethics; first and foremost is that they are both non-consequentialist ethical theories. But Kant tries to develop a non-consequentialist ethic that does not rely on religious belief; he emphasizes freedom as *the* cornerstone of morality, not God. He unwaveringly emphasizes that morality is grounded in rationality (free thought, free action, and free will). But can we really have such heavy-duty absolute duties, without tracing them to God's will? His critics will say no, and that the only way his deontology will work is if the existence of God is assumed. (But this is not too strange because, after all, the name "Immanuel" means "God is with us.") Feminist critics of Kant point out that he provides an overly masculine description of ethics. In the next chapter we will consider ethics from a distinctly feminine perspective.

Concepts, Principles, Theories, and Traditions Introduced in Chapter 6

Concepts

Autonomy – The freedom and independence that rational beings possess.

Categorical Imperative – An absolute and unconditional moral command.

Command – An order that directs us to perform an action; a prescription that prescribes what we ought to do.

Dignity – The value that a person has by simply being a person; a person's value, which ought to be respected by others.

Duty – Something one is required to do; a responsibility; an obligation.

Equality – In deontological ethics, all autonomous beings deserve the same respect.

Freedom – Independence; autonomy.

Hypothetical Imperative – A command that is not absolute, but conditional, and premised on one's desires.

Imperative – A command.

Law – The collection of moral imperatives can be thought of as the moral law. As (scientific) laws of nature apply universally, so does the moral law.

Obligation – Something one is required to do; a responsibility; a duty.

Person – In traditional deontological ethics, a rational, autonomous being.

Responsibility – Something one is required to do; a duty; an obligation.

Rights – Rights are legitimate claims that limit others' freedom. Rights correlate with duties: if I have a legitimate right, then you have a duty to respect that right.

Universalizability – A personal rule possesses universalizability – is universalizable – if it could consistently be willed to become a universal rule or law that everyone, everywhere, for all times, ought to follow.

Principles

Categorical Imperative (Principle of Autonomy) – The ethical principle that says we ought to act in regard to all persons in ways that treat them as ends in themselves and never simply as means to accomplish the ends of others.

Categorical Imperative (Principle of Universality) – The ethical principle that says we ought to act only from those personal rules that we can at the same time will to be universal moral laws.

Theories/Traditions

Deontological ethics – The theory and tradition that focuses on ethical duties and says that actions are ethically right or wrong depending on whether they are in accord with one's ethical duties.

Divine command ethics – The tradition that views ethical duties as ultimately derived from God's commands.

Non-consequentialism – The theory that an action is determined to be ethically right or wrong not because of its consequences, but because of other factors, such as the person's intention.

For Further Reading

Anscombe, G. E. M. 1958. "Modern Moral Philosophy," *Philosophy* 33: 1–19. Offers a critique of Kantian deontological ethics.

Baron, Marcia W., Philip Pettit, and Michael Slote. 1997. *Three Methods of Ethics: A Debate*. Oxford: Blackwell Publishers. Deontological ethics is contrasted with virtue ethics and consequentialist ethics.

Helm, Paul (ed.). 1981. *Divine Commands and Morality*. New York: Oxford University Press. A collection of articles on divine command ethics.

Kagan, Shelly. 1998. *Normative Ethics*. Boulder, CO: Westview Press. Explains that although Kantian-styled deontology may be overly rational and seem to exclude feelings of love, compassion, and happiness, it is possible to build a deontological theory out of non-rational building blocks in order to form a moderate deontology (chapter 3.2).

MacIntyre, Alasdair. 1998. *A Short History of Ethics: A History of Moral Philosophy from the Homeric Age to the Twentieth Century*, 2nd edition. Notre Dame, IN: University of Notre Dame Press. Sketches a short introduction to Kantian deontological ethics, and includes a critical discussion (chapter 14).

Online Resources

Bhagavad Gita (100 CE), http://www.pdf-archive.com/2014/10/18/barbara-stoler-miller-the-bhagavad-gita/barbara-stoler-miller-the-bhagavad-gita.pdf Accessed October 12, 2016.

Immanuel Kant's *Groundwork for the Metaphysic of Morals* (1785), http://www.earlymoderntexts.com/assets/pdfs/kant1785.pdf Accessed October 12, 2016.

Immanuel Kant's *The Science of Right* (1790), http://intersci.ss.uci.edu/wiki/eBooks/BOOKS/Kant/The%20Science%20of%20Right%20Kant.pdf Accessed October 12, 2016.

Tom Regan, "The Case for Animal Rights" (1985), http://www.animal-rights-library.com/texts-m/regan03.htm Accessed October 12, 2016.

Review Questions

1. How does the Pauline principle fit in with Deontological Ethics?
2. What does it mean to say that Deontological Ethics is a non-consequentialist ethic? Use an example to illustrate your point.
3. Where does Kant say our moral duties ultimately come from? Where do *you* think they come from?
4. Kant argues that the categorical imperative is a moral imperative, and hypothetical imperatives are not moral imperatives. What makes the difference?
5. What do rights have to do with the concept of autonomy?
6. Give an example for each of the following: a positive duty, a negative duty, a duty to self, a duty to others, a direct duty, an indirect duty.

Discussion Questions

1. The philosopher David Rodin offers the following moral definition of terrorism: "terrorism is the deliberate, negligent, or reckless use of force against noncombatants, by state or nonstate actors for ideological ends and in the absence of a substantively just legal process" (2004: 755). Using this definition of terrorism, provide a deontological ethical analysis of terrorism.
2. Adolf Eichmann, one of Nazi Germany's most notorious war criminals, was executed in 1962. During his trial, Eichmann claimed that he was familiar with Kant's theory of ethics and went so far as to

say that he had lived his whole life according to Kant's moral precepts and the Kantian definition of duty (Arendt 1963: 135–6). Do you think that Eichmann, in his participation in the Nazis' Final Solution – their plan to annihilate the Jewish people – lived his life according to the categorical imperative? In your answer consider both formulations of the principle.

3. If developments and discoveries in the fields of cognitive science and artificial intelligence continue, human beings may eventually create androids that can think, reason, feel, and "live" in ways that are indistinguishable from humans. After creating these beings we will then have to decide if they have moral status. Describe how Utilitarian and Deontological Ethics would respond.
4. In his book *The Science of Right* (1790) Kant discusses law. He says

   > juridical punishment can never be administered merely as a means for promoting another good either with regard to the criminal himself or to civil society, but must in all cases be imposed only because the individual on whom it is inflicted has committed a crime ...The penal law is a categorical imperative; and woe to him who creeps through the serpent-windings of utilitarianism to discover some advantage that may discharge him from the justice of punishment ... For if justice and righteousness perish, human life would no longer have any value in the world ...Whoever has committed murder, must die" (1790: 257–8).

   Explain how a deontological view of punishment differs from a utilitarian view of punishment.
5. In 2014 it was discovered that the drinking water in Flint, Michigan was contaminated with lead and has caused public health problems. Some have claimed that racism is to blame for this situation, since it is largely racial minorities who have been affected by the crisis. Describe how Utilitarian and Deontological Ethics would respond. (In your answer, underline each utilitarian and deontological concept and principle you mention.)

Chapter 7
Care Ethics

God called out to his prophet Abraham: "Take your only son, Isaac, and go to the land of Moriah. There on a mountain that I will show you, offer him as a sacrifice to me." Early the next morning Abraham, with his son Isaac and two servants, set out on a journey to the place God had directed him. After three days of travel they arrived at Moriah. As Abraham and Isaac walked along, Isaac asked his father, "Father, where is the lamb for the sacrifice?" Abraham replied to his son: "God himself will provide one."

When they arrived at the place God told Abraham about, Abraham built an altar, tied up his son, and placed him on the altar. Abraham then picked up the knife to kill his son. But the angel of the Lord called to Abraham, "Abraham, Abraham, don't hurt the boy. Now I know you have obedient reverence for God, because you have not kept back your only son from me. I will richly bless you because you obeyed my command."

There are many ways to interpret this passage from the book of Genesis. Let's look at it literally.

Abraham is commanded to do something that normally is ethically forbidden, namely, to kill one's child. And out of duty to God, Abraham intends to kill Isaac, a child whose eyes are on Abraham in trust, love, and fear. As a father, Abraham has a duty to care for his children. But Abraham also has a duty to obey God's commands. Although there is a conflict between these two duties – a situation we would regard as a moral dilemma – Abraham does not waver in fulfilling his duty to God.

How would a woman in this situation feel? Nel Noddings, a proponent of care ethics, believes this situation would be horrendous for a mother. Would a woman agree to sacrifice her child for God? Would a woman agree to sacrifice her child for *any* reason, such as to save ten

Ethics: The Basics, Second Edition. John Mizzoni.

others, or to benefit the greatest good? Or instead, would a mother in Abraham's position respond to the fear and trust of her child? When Abraham acts out of principle, out of a duty to God, his love for his son takes a backseat to his love and respect for God. Is it easier for a man to do this and harder for a woman?

In this chapter, we look at our first uniquely contemporary ethical tradition. Of all the ethical traditions discussed in this book, care ethics is the only ethical tradition first articulated and defended in the twentieth century (see Figure 7.1). Care ethics began as a critique of the prevailing ethical traditions – which are regarded as masculine – and is a development of a distinctly feminine ethic.

So far, we have looked at a variety of ethical theories that attempt to solve the practical problem of conduct. A philosophical problem, as defined in the introduction of this book, is a cluster of closely related philosophical questions. Central to the problem of conduct is the philosophical (and ethical) question: What is it to live an ethical life? Proceeding backwards from our last chapter, we might wonder whether living an ethical life is about doing one's duty (deontological ethics). Or is living an ethical life about bringing about as much utility and happiness as possible for all concerned (utilitarian ethics)? Or is it about following the natural law (natural law ethics)? Or is living an ethical life about living up to the social contract that we have signed on to (social contract ethics)? Or is living an ethical life about flourishing; that is, maintaining and achieving well-being by developing excellent traits and characteristics (virtue ethics)?

Advocates of care ethics see *caring* as the key ethical ideal. Working from a particular view of human nature, advocates of care ethics recommend that we focus our attention on the concrete relationships we are

Figure 7.1

Ethical traditions

Ancient (580 BCE–200 CE)	Relative Ethics Universal Ethics Virtue Ethics
Medieval (200–1500)	Natural Law Ethics
Modern (1500–1900)	Social Contract Ethics Utilitarian Ethics Deontological Ethics
Contemporary (1900–present)	Care Ethics

in, and recommend that we attend to the concrete needs of those who are close to us. With care ethics, to live an ethical life is to care for those with whom we are in close relationship.

Feminist philosophers who write about care ethics describe it as a feminine ethic. The feminist theorists we will consider in this chapter declare that focusing one's attention on those we are close to is an ethical ideal that traditionally has more in common with how females understand ethics, rather than how males understand ethics. Males, they claim, tend to see ethics as being about principles whereas females typically do not. Thus, as we shall see, care ethics is an example of an ethics that does not have a core ethical principle.

7.1 Ethics Is Based on Feelings

As we saw with the utilitarian ethical tradition beginning with David Hume, there are some ethical traditions that solve the problem of the origins of ethics by developing the view that ethics is ultimately based on feelings. In care ethics, we again find this view. There is a limited agreement, then, between the utilitarians and care ethicists: they both agree that ethical theorists who claim that ethics has most to do with rationality and freedom are misguided.

It is indeed true to say that both care ethics and utilitarian ethics emphasize feelings; however, whereas the classical utilitarians simplified feelings into good feelings and bad feelings – describing the good ones as pleasurable and the bad ones as painful – care ethics emphasizes the feelings of love. And rather than describing feelings of pleasure, care ethicists describe feelings of joy. Joy, as they describe it, is a feeling we experience through our interactions with others.

Those who espouse a religious ethics might describe the difference between feelings of pleasure and feelings of joy as the difference between physical pleasures and spiritual pleasures. All physical pleasures, they would say, involve our physical body coming into contact with other physical bodies, for example, with food, drink, or sex. A feeling of joy, by contrast, is a spiritual pleasure that does not depend on a point of contact with a physical object. Proponents of care ethics, by and large, though, attempt to account for the nature of ethics without resorting to religious or spiritual concepts or traditions. While a religious ethic might say that a feeling of joy can come through a personal relationship with God, a non-religious care ethic will say that a feeling of joy is experienced only through our personal relationships with others.

As we saw in the chapter on utilitarian ethics, utilitarian theorists use feelings as a jumping-off point to ultimately reach a conclusion about altruism rather than egoism as their ethical ideal. In keeping with an ethic that emphasizes feelings – especially feelings for others – care ethicists use similar reasoning to reach the same conclusion. Care ethicists acknowledge that humans are feeling creatures, but would it be accurate to say that humans have feeling for themselves only, that they are only concerned with their own pleasures and pains, or feelings of self-love? Or do they experience genuine feelings of pleasure, pain, and love, for others? Utilitarian and care ethicists conclude that humans have genuine feelings for others, and then both traditions move to the conclusion that humans ought to act altruistically. Care, love, and altruism are natural tendencies of human beings, so just as utilitarian ethics in grappling with the problem of human nature emphasizes a particular aspect of human beings, namely, that humans are feeling creatures; so too does care ethics. Thus, a particular view of human nature grounds care ethics. But there is another aspect of human beings we must refer to in solving the problem of human nature, an aspect of human beings very important for the development of care ethics, a feature that makes care ethics a novel and distinctive approach. Care ethicists want to draw our attention to the fact that human beings, by their very nature, are relational beings.

7.2 Humans Are Relational Beings

In their solution to the problem of human nature, care ethicists stress that human beings are relational beings. This is an important insight about human nature, and care ethicists claim that this feature of human beings is often overlooked. Being attentive to this feature of human beings – and being consciously aware of it – moves our ethical thinking in a different direction, they say. According to Carol Gilligan, one of the earliest theorists to introduce the notion of a feminist ethics of care,

> a progressively more adequate understanding of the psychology of human relationships … informs the development of an ethic of care. This ethic, which reflects a cumulative knowledge of human relationships, evolves around a central insight, that self and other are interdependent. (Gilligan 1982: 74)

Attentiveness to the relational aspect of human nature makes care ethics unique among all previous ethical theories and traditions.

The claim that humans are relational beings is a claim about the nature of human beings. Each human being is in personal relationship with other human beings. This is an inescapable fact of 99.99 percent of all human lives. Without care, infants and small children would not survive into adulthood. At birth, a human infant has a brain that is only one-fourth the size of an adult brain. Human beings are born into a state of helplessness and need intensive caretaking. We are all born into families; our relationships to family members are our first relationships. As we get older, we form relationships with persons outside our families. At any moment in time, a human being is involved in countless relationships with others. The range of personal relationship is broad: the parent–child relationship, sibling relationships, and relationships with cousins, with neighbors, with extended family, with friends, with other children at school, with teachers, with doctors, perhaps with shopkeepers. As adults, humans have even more relationships: with co-workers, with bosses, with spouses, with spouses' families, with business associates, etc.

Note that the kinds of relationships care ethicists are highlighting are concrete personal relationships. As a way to be specific about a *caring* relationship, Nel Noddings (1984) has formulated the terms "the one-caring" and "the cared-for." The formative relationship between mother and child gives the easiest example, and it is an example feminists commonly use as a sort of ideal model.

The one-caring is the care giver; the mother, for example. The cared-for is the person being cared for; the child, for example. It is a concrete personal relationship in that the one-caring doesn't merely think fondly about the cared-for, but the one-caring actually attends to the needs of the cared-for. Moreover, in order for there to be a genuine relationship, and not merely an abstract formal relationship, the person designated as the cared-for responds in some way to the caring with some kind of acknowledgment. This is an important aspect because it is what would be expected in a *concrete* relationship, not an abstract relationship in which a person *imagines* that he or she is caring for another, when all the while the cared-for is not aware in the slightest of the one-caring's efforts or intentions. The caring relationship can indeed be a subtle relationship; there are obviously circumstances in which parents and children are estranged from each other, or siblings from each other, or neighbors; the list could go on and on. There can be good caring relationships between people, or bad relationships between them, for example, an exploitive relationship. The focus with care ethics is with those concrete relationships about which there is no doubt.

Care ethicists recommend that we take note of the fact that we are relational beings who exist in relationship with many people, and accept it as an inescapable fact about human nature that human beings exist in personal relationships with others.

> *One-caring*: The care giver; the care provider. (A concept.)
> *Cared-for*: The person being cared for. (A concept.)

Earlier I mentioned that one could make a religious interpretation of the feeling of joy that comes as a product of the relationships we have with others. The notion of personal relationship is important for *theistic* religions, that is, religious traditions that hold that humans can have personal relationships with God. Theism is a religious tradition that is distinguished from *deism*, the view that human beings *cannot* enter into personal relationships with God, even though God does exist. Since theism involves belief about a relationship with a personal God, the caring relationship of the one-caring and the cared-for can apply to the relationship between God and humans. Theists will say that when human beings enter into this relationship they will experience spiritual joy. Just as care ethics emphasizes a relationship of love, there are many theistic religious traditions that conceive of the relationship between God and humans as a caring and loving relationship.

A critic, however, might ask how it is possible for one God to have personal relationships with seven billion humans (and countless billions of other creatures). In response, a theist might point out that God has the unique characteristics of being omniscient (all knowing) and omnipotent (all powerful); therefore, simultaneously having seven billion personal relationships is possible for such a uniquely capable being. In addition, theists assert that God is good and loving; thus, God cares for us, God loves us, God knows what we need, and God attends to our needs.

However, even if care ethicists concede that God could have a personal relationship with humans, they would ask if *humans* could have a personal relationship with God. Does God really have needs that we could attend to, and further, can God acknowledge when we are caring for Him? Some people believe they can receive signs from God acknowledging their caring actions toward God. Care ethicists who wish to leave references to God and religion out of their ethical theory would consider interpretations of such signs to be wishful thinking on the part of the imaginative and interpretive human mind.

In addition, they would say that God does not have concrete needs that humans could attend to; while on the other hand, we are surrounded and immersed in concrete relationships with others who most definitely are in dire need of our help. Breast cancer, for example, affects one out of every eight women; 13 percent of the world's population lives in extreme poverty; and 17 percent of the adult population in the world is illiterate.

Theists will, of course, respond to this charge. They will likely say they attend to God's needs *by* attending to the needs of others, thus by caring for those who are close to us we are, at the same time, attending to God's needs. This is not a fully satisfactory response, though, as it really sidesteps the original question about whether humans can have a personal relationship with God. If the response is that we ought to care for those humans who are in relationship with us, then what role does *God* have in the relationship? Care ethicists will observe that if the theists wish to emphasize that we are to attend primarily to the concrete needs of others, then, in effect, God features in the picture only as an abstract idea.

7.3 Ethics of Principles

Advocates of care ethics emphasize the concrete relationships we are in, and emphasize that we ought to attend to the concrete needs of those who are close to us. Therefore, they recommend that we should simply provide care to our loved ones rather than pay allegiance to abstract principles (or abstract beings like God). Nel Noddings points out that there has been too much killing and violence done in the name of principle. When we have our attention focused on obedience to principles, we can become blind to the concrete needs of others.

Think of all the ethical principles we have considered in this book, from the Pauline principle, to the principle of natural law, the principle of self-interest, the principle of the social contract, the principle of utility, the principle of autonomy, and the principle of universality. According to some feminist theorists, such principles are the product of masculine thinking about ethics. The primary thinkers who have had the most influence in the development of ethical theories over the centuries have been men. The theories and principles they developed are born out of a male experience of life. The ethical concepts they focus on in their theories reveal a masculine orientation.

For example, in the last chapter we saw how deontological ethics recommends that we act for the principle of the thing, just for the sake of doing our duty, and not determine the morality of our actions by looking at their consequences. Consider the ethical perspective of two civil war generals. "Duty," General Robert E. Lee (1807–1870) once said, "is the most sublime word in our language. Do your duty in all things. You cannot do more. You should never wish to do less." General Thomas Jonathan "Stonewall" Jackson (1824–1863) held that, "Duty is ours; the consequences are God's." An ethic that advises us *not* to consider the concrete effects our actions have on those who are close to us does not fit with a feminine ideal. Deontological ethics is an example of an ethic that prioritizes an abstract principle over a tangible need. A non-consequentialist ethic of principle like deontological ethics would at times seem to justify indifference and unconcern, for, after all, one needs to keep a steady focus on one's duty and not be distracted by others' personal needs.

We might think that a deontological ethic, which focuses on duties, might fit with what care ethicists have in mind if we think that we have a duty to care for those who are in need. This would be like saying we have the duties we have because of our role. For example, if I am a woman with children then, because of my role, I have a duty to care for my children. But the care ethicist Nel Noddings has pointed out that, "Mothering is not a role, but a relationship" (Noddings 1984: 128). Caring for someone simply because it is your duty has an impersonal dimension to it; being motivated to act out of duty is very different from being motivated to act out of love and care. These considerations drive care ethicists to reject the deontologist's claim that the principle of universality is the heart of morality. Making universality a prominent part of one's ethics (rather than concrete relationship), is considered to be the height of abstraction.

Having seen that a deontological (non-consequentialist) ethic is at odds with care ethics, let us look to see whether consequentialist ethical theories are in keeping with care ethics. We have already said above that there are some similarities and some differences between the utilitarian consequentialist ethic and care ethics. In the utilitarian ethics chapter, we mentioned that Mo Tzu of ancient China advocated an ethical theory of universal love that resembled utilitarian ethics. And Christian ethics also takes a universal love approach. But care ethicists distance their theory from the universal love approach. Although care ethicists make care and love center-stage in their ethical theory, they disagree with tying a principle of universality to care and love. It is impossible to be in a concrete, loving, personal, and caring relationship with *all* human beings. To presume that such a thing is possible is nothing but an abstraction, the very thing care ethicists wish to avoid.

A further problem with utilitarian ethics, according to proponents of care ethics, is that determining the morality of an action by calculating the best overall consequences for all concerned seems like an attempt to make ethics mathematical, and mathematics is abstract. Although utilitarian ethics incorporates sentiment and altruism – aspects that care ethicists agree with – the principle of utility when used to determine the morality of actions can sometimes conflict with care ethics. Care ethicists wish to emphasize that ethics is not mostly about being rational or calculating. Also, the principle of utility, as we have seen in the chapter on utilitarian ethics, connects closely to the principle of equality, and equality generates impartiality. But care ethics recommends that we be *partial* to those who are close to us, not impartial for all concerned. The ideal of impartiality is an example of an abstract ethic.

> *Partiality*: Impartiality is a position of neutral detachment that shows an equal regard for all concerned. Partiality is giving special regard to those who are close to us. (A concept.)

The other modern consequentialist ethic we have looked at in this book – social contract ethics – also contains elements that conflict with care ethics. The first troublesome element is its rational egoism. Social contract ethics characterizes people as rational and selfish beings. According to care ethics, both of these assumptions are incorrect. Another incongruity is the social contract notion that ethics is about a contract. Since care ethicists characterize humans as relational beings who naturally find themselves in relation, to claim that the relations between people are contractual gives a distorted view of human relationships. Care ethicists would only concede that an exceedingly small subset of all our relationships are contractual, not *all* of our social relationships, as contractarians seem to assert.

7.4 Virtue Ethics and Partiality

Of all the ethical theories we have looked at in this book, virtue ethics is the most similar to care ethics, although care ethics is still a distinct ethical theory. In both care ethics and virtue ethics there is a de-emphasis on principle and actions, and a stress put on the person in relationship.

But virtue ethics *could* degrade into an ethic that would be just as masculine as Kantian deontology. It is possible to imagine a virtue ethics that might suggest that the good life consists in developing virtues for oneself so that one may achieve well-being. And this potentially could lead to treating the people one interacts with as faceless and nameless individuals. A "virtuous" person such as this may indeed develop virtues and achieve a degree of well-being, but the personal dimension would be missing. Care ethicists disagree with a virtue ethic that would consider a hermit virtuous, for instance, because he or she developed a few core virtues.

In terms of virtue ethics, care ethics emphasizes the social virtues, the other-regarding virtues like generosity, patience, and sensitivity, as opposed to the self-regarding virtues involved in attempting to master one's fears or desires, like courage or temperance. But not only does care ethics spotlight the social virtues, it also redefines the social virtues so they have a personal dimension. For example, we might think of generosity as a social virtue, in that we develop it by being generous with others. But care ethicists, in emphasizing concrete personal relationships, would stress that we ought to be generous to those with whom we are in personal relationship. In sum, we *could* consider care ethics a form of virtue ethics, one that prioritizes a certain set of virtues: those social virtues appropriate for concrete, personal, and caring relationships.

There is an interesting similarity between care ethics and Confucian virtue ethics, which we would expect if care ethics is a kind of virtue ethics. In contrast to Mo Tzu's teaching of universal love, Confucius endorsed a doctrine of love with distinctions. According to Confucius, one should not love everyone equally; there is a gradation in human relations. For Confucius, a good person is occupied with loving and honoring their parents. To have this character trait is a kind of piety, filial piety, which is a notion we mentioned in the deontological ethics chapter when contrasting Kantian deontological ethics and Confucian virtue ethics.

7.5 Feminine Ethics

As noted above, care ethics does not emphasize ethical principles, because it views ethical principles as part of a masculine-oriented approach to ethics. In other words, principles are "the language of the father," while care ethics is an attempt to spell out ethics in "the language of the mother." Thus, care ethics aspires to be a feminine ethics. However, although it is accurate to say that care ethics is an example of a feminine ethic, we should not take that to mean that *all* feminists would endorse care ethics. There is a difference between a feminine ethic and a feminist ethic. In general, feminism involves various efforts and initiatives to advance the interests of women in society. A feminine ethic, on the other hand, is simply an ethic that is "rooted in receptivity, relatedness, and responsiveness," as Nel Noddings puts it in her book *Caring: A Feminine Approach to Ethics & Moral Education* (1984). A feminine ethic involves committing oneself to caring, and defining oneself in terms of the capacity to care. Although more women than men have tended to understand ethics in these terms, according to Noddings, "all of humanity can participate in the feminine as I am describing it" (Noddings 1984: 172).

To repeat, feminism is a broad spectrum and care ethics is only part of that spectrum. We are certainly aware of feminists who have endorsed a deontological ethics and emphasized equal rights for women. But for care ethicists, a deontological feminist ethic is not a true *feminine* ethic; it is not "rooted in receptivity, relatedness, and responsiveness"; rather, it is a masculine ethic that some women have used to advance the interests of women in society.

In her psychological research, Carol Gilligan detected a noted difference between how females think about morality and how males think about morality. Psychological theorists before Gilligan (such as Freud and Kohlberg) had noticed that there were differences in how men and women think about ethics. But after noticing the difference, it was common for psychological theorists to then describe female moral reasoning as *inferior* to male moral reasoning, or *deficient*, simply because female moral reasoning was less likely to focus on rights, rules, and principles. Gilligan, by contrast, argued that a feminine view of ethics (ethics of care), although different, is just as legitimate as the male view of ethics (see Figure 7.2). She titled her book *In a Different Voice* (1982). For Gilligan, "in the different voice of women lies the truth of an ethic of care" (Gilligan 1982: 173).

The popular book by John Gray about how men and women communicate with each other, *Men Are from Mars, Women Are from Venus* (1992), memorably captures the notion that male and female styles of thinking can be very different.

Figure 7.2

1. Male moral reasoning is more likely to focus on rights, rules, and principles.
2. Female moral reasoning is less likely to focus on rights, rules, and principles.

---

3. Therefore, there is a noted difference between how females think about morality and how males think about morality.
4. *Different* does not mean *inferior* or *deficient*.

---

5. Therefore, female moral reasoning although *different*, is not *inferior/deficient*, as compared to male moral reasoning.

7.6 Care Ethics: Relativist or Universalist?

The problem of relativism is a very large and abstract issue that focuses on whether, in general, there are any ethical values, standards, or principles that are universal or whether all ethical values, standards, and principles are relative to a particular culture or era. Comparatively speaking, ethical universalism does not think context is as significant as ethical relativism says it is. Ethical relativism says that ethics is entirely determined by context, while universalism says that a context – a culture – is only the place where universal values and standards are put into practice.

Because of how care ethics emphasizes the concrete relationships people are in, at first glance care ethics might seem like a version of relativist ethics. Overall, though, care ethics endorses universalism as the solution to the problem of relativism. Let's look at why this is the case. At the beginning of the chapter we noted that care ethics is in the tradition that says ethics has more to do with feelings than rationality. The kinds of feelings that form the foundation for care ethics are due to the kind of biological nature humans beings possess. Nel Noddings says that ethical caring arises out of natural caring, which is a primitive biological urge; and that care ethics is based on the natural sympathy human beings feel for each other. For Noddings, all human beings feel the pain and joy of others to some degree; and she says that for one who feels nothing, directly or by remembrance, we must prescribe re-education. Noddings explains:

> One either feels a sort of pain in response to the pain of others, or one does not feel it. If he does feel it, he does not need to be told that causing pain is wrong. If he does not feel it in a particular case, he may remember the feeling ... and allow himself to be moved by this remembrance of feeling. For one who feels nothing, directly or by remembrance, we must prescribe re-education or exile. Thus, at the foundation of moral behavior – as we have already pointed out – is feeling or sentiment. (Noddings 1984: 92)

Underpinning moral behavior, then, is feeling or sentiment. Because of the universality of feelings for others, there is a fundamental universality recognized in care ethics.

Another important aspect of care ethics, as we have already seen, is its observation that humans are relational beings. It is part of our human nature to be related and connected to others. Being naturally related to others provides the context for feelings of love. Since it is a universal feature of human beings that they are relational creatures, care ethics endorses a universalist, instead of a relativist, ethic. In sum, to say that generally speaking there are some values that are universal is not disagreeable to care ethicists. After all, we saw above that Nel Noddings describes the feminine as something that all humanity can participate in. There are certain aspects of care ethics, then, that indicate how it is a universalist ethic, one that stands opposed to ethical relativism.

Even though there are good reasons to regard care ethics as universalist rather than relativist, we must remember that care ethics still rejects the principle of universality, which is the centerpiece of Kant's deontological ethics. Care ethicists acknowledge that certain feelings and attitudes are universal, which causes them to disagree with ethical relativism, but care ethics does not endorse a set of universalizable moral judgments.

Here we must note the difference between ethical universalism and the principle of universality. The easy way to make the distinction between the two is to keep in mind that the principle of universality is a practical principle to use when making a decision about how to act; it is offered by deontologists as a solution to the problem of conduct. By contrast, ethical universalism, a theory about the nature of ethics, is a solution to the more theoretical problems in ethics: the problem of relativism and the problem of the origins of ethics. Care ethicists disagree with universality when it is put to work as a practical principle to use when deciding how to live. In other words, care ethicists do not think that the principle of universality is an adequate solution to the problem of conduct. Universalizability, they say, is much too abstract to use when thinking about how to live one's life. From the perspective of care ethics, the solution to the problem of conduct is not to be found in abstract principles. One ought not to think of abstract principles when deciding how to live. For care ethicists, the best solution to the problem of conduct focuses on the concrete needs of those with whom we are in close personal relationship.

7.7 Care Ethics Applications

One of the unique features of a care ethics solution to the problem of conduct, as opposed to the other solutions we have surveyed, is that a care ethics solution promotes caring for those with whom we are in close relation as the mark of an ethical life. Care ethicists solve the problem of conduct by saying we should evaluate actions as right or wrong depending upon how deeply they are rooted in caring. A care ethicist would ask if the action was a genuine response to the perceived needs of others.

The obvious and most straightforward way of applying care ethics is using it to examine our own behavior toward our family and friends. Are we attending to the needs of those with whom we are in close relationship? Are we putting efforts into nurturing the natural relationships we are in? But consider a slightly more complicated example offered by Virginia Held. Let's say there is a teacher who has special skill in helping troubled young children succeed academically, and the teacher is also the father of a young child. Applying the principle of utility would seem to imply that the teacher should devote more time to his students, since that would have greater utility for all concerned. Applying a deontological approach, we might reason that the teacher's duty not to neglect his students outweighs his duty not to neglect his child. Virginia Held maintains that this kind of example illustrates how care ethics is different. She claims that, "the moral demands of care suggest to him that he should spend more time with his child" (Held 2006: 98). Applying care ethics, the fact that there is a relationship between the father and his child is highly significant. The father would reason that, "his relationship with his child is of enormous and irreplaceable value. He thinks that out of concern for this particular relationship he should spend more time with his child" (Held 2006: 99).

Some proponents of care ethics, such as Virginia Held in her book *The Ethics of Care: Personal, Political, and Global* (2006), describe how care ethics has social and political implications. Care ethics was originally conceived as an ethic that defined living an ethical life as caring for those with whom we are in close relationship. For Virginia Held, though, care as a practice and as a value can and should be extended beyond this early formulation. She argues that care ethics should not be limited to the household or the family. In her view, care ethics has much to offer society at large because care is badly needed in the public domain. A caring society, she claims, would reorder its social roles and transform its practices. She discusses the implications of care ethics in unsurprising areas such as child care, education, and health care; but she also argues that care ethics applies to the realm of law, the economy, and international affairs (see Figure 7.3).

In order to extend the application of care ethics from the private and personal realm into public issues, Virginia Held introduces the notion of degrees of care. Care giving at the personal level is the most intense, while care extended into the public domain has less intensity, but it is caring nonetheless. It is only in the family and among friends that we find the deepest and most compelling forms of care, but in her view caring is even relevant to law, for example, because in a caring society "the realm of law would shrink" (Held 2006: 130). Care ethics applies to economic issues in that, "An ethic of care can provide the basis for asserting the relevant values that the market ignores" (Held 2006: 123). "From the perspective of care," she says, "markets should be limited rather than ever more pervasive, as they undermine the caring relations in which persons and the relations between them are valued for their own sakes" (Held 2006: 159).

Care ethics is also relevant to international affairs. Care ethics acknowledges that violent conflict is often part of family life, and that it persists in societies, and between groups and states. In the face of such conflict, though, care ethics upholds standards of care. "At the level of groups and states," she argues, "the ethics of care would promote the exploration of nonviolent alternatives to the use of military force"

Figure 7.3

1. Care is badly needed in the public domain.
2. Care ethics has much to offer society at large.

---

3. Therefore, care as a practice and as a value can and should be extended beyond the household or the family.

(Held 2006: 139). Moreover, care ethics is relevant to international affairs because of its view of relational human nature. Care ethics "understands how our ties to various social groups and our historical embeddedness are also part of what makes us who we are" (Held 2006: 156–7). The nature of who we are has to do with the cluster of relationships in which we live: family, friends, and fellow citizens. These are not abstract relationships discovered by reason, but they are emotional bonds of partiality.

7.8 Conclusion

Care ethics is an example of an ethical theory with a short history. Universal ethics, relative ethics, and virtue ethics have notable places in ancient ethical thought. And natural law ethics has a notable place in medieval ethical thought. Social contract ethics, deontological ethics, and utilitarian ethics are known as modern ethical theories. But ethics of care as a distinct moral theory only made its appearance in the late twentieth century. It has taken a long time for the flowering of a distinctly feminine ethic. Care ethics emerged as a feminine response to the common masculine ways of characterizing ethics. The "different voice" we have been considering in this chapter is a woman's perspective on ethics, a voice that has not been heard or taken seriously in the field of ethics until the twentieth century.

A few concerns cause some ethical theorists to be hesitant about embracing care ethics. One concern has to do with whether care ethics is a fully comprehensive ethic. Perhaps care ethics is only for dealing with those who are personally close to us. Does a care ethic properly apply to issues beyond those that impact our immediate family and friends, such as public policy issues? Another hesitation about accepting care ethics stems from its generalization about female ethics and masculine ethics. The worry is not only that the generalizations are sweeping and perhaps oversimplified, but that in the past one of the sexes has used such conceptual divisions to justify the oppression of the other sex.

As a developed ethical theory, care ethics offers solutions to all four problems in ethics. Its solution to the problem of human nature emphasizes that humans are feeling creatures and relational beings whose lives are inextricably bound up in concrete personal relationships with others. The feelings that bind people together are ultimately what form the foundations of ethics. Care ethics' solution to the problem of the origins of ethics, then, is that ethical standards are ultimately based on feelings, feelings that have their roots in a universal human nature.

Care ethics' insistence on a universal human nature naturally leads it to a universalist solution to the problem of relativism. Since all humans have basic needs and all exist in concrete relationships, it makes sense that ethics is not something wholly determined by the folkways of a society; care ethics thus rejects ethical relativism. Due to a universality of feelings for others, there is a fundamental universality recognized in care ethics.

Care ethics also has a solution to the problem of conduct. The solution to this practical problem is not to be found in abstract principles, it claims. One ought not to think of abstract principles when deciding how to live. The best solution to the problem of conduct focuses on the concrete needs of those with whom we are in close personal relationship. Care ethics sees the mark of an ethical life as caring for those with whom we are in close relation. Care ethicists solve the problem of conduct by saying we should evaluate actions as right or wrong depending upon how deeply they are rooted in caring. A care ethicist would ask if the action was a genuine response to the perceived needs of others. In one sense, care ethics is similar to utilitarianism because it emphasizes that feelings are significant in ethics. In another sense, care ethics is like virtue ethics because it de-emphasizes using principles in deciding how one should act. It has a unique feature, though, in its attention to the concrete personal relationships that humans live in. It emphasizes that a fundamental fact about human beings is that they are immersed in relationships. Relational beings are beings that are embedded in relationships, and attached to other beings. Feelings and emotions are the glue that attaches people to one another; consequently, a feminine ethic involves "feeling with," that is, receiving what others are feeling.

Concepts, Principles, Theories, and Traditions Introduced in Chapter 7

Concepts

Care – Attending to the needs of those with whom we are in close relationship.

Cared-for – The person being cared for.

Feminine ethic – An ethic rooted in receptivity, relatedness, and responsiveness.

Feminism, feminist – Feminism consists in various efforts and initiatives to advance the interests of women in society. A feminist promotes such efforts.

Joy – In care ethics, a good feeling that comes through our interactions and personal relationships with others. In some religious ethics, joy is a spiritual pleasure that does not depend on a point of contact with a physical object.

Love – In care ethics, the bonding feeling between those in close personal relationship. In Christianity, love (charity) is the most important virtue.

One-caring – The care giver; the care provider.

Partiality – Impartiality is a position of neutral detachment that shows an equal regard for all concerned. Partiality is giving special regard to those who are close to us.

Relationships – Concrete bonds, ties, attachments between people.

Principles

None. (Care ethics does not see ethical principles as primary.)

Theories/Traditions

Care Ethics (Ethics of Care) – The theory and tradition that views caring as the key ethical ideal: to live an ethical life is to care for those with whom we are in close relationship.

Deism – The tradition that says human beings cannot enter into personal relationships with God, even though God does exist.

Theism – The tradition that holds that humans can have personal relationships with God.

For Further Reading

Darwall, Stephen. 1998. *Philosophical Ethics*. Boulder, CO: Westview. Discusses care ethics alongside deontological ethics and utilitarian ethics (chapter 19).

Levin, Michael. 2000. "Is There a Female Morality?" in James Fieser (ed.), *Metaethics, Normative Ethics, and Applied Ethics: Historical and Contemporary Readings*. Belmont, CA: Wadsworth. pp. 361–8. A view critical of care ethics.

Lindemann, Hilde. 2006. *An Invitation to Feminist Ethics*. New York, NY: McGraw-Hill. A short introduction to feminist ethics. Offers a feminist critique of prevailing ethical traditions (chapter 4).

Noddings, Nel. 2010. *The Maternal Factor: Two Paths to Morality*. Berkeley, CA: University of California Press. Noddings continues to explain and defend care ethics and situates it within an evolutionary framework.

Rudnick, Abraham. 2001. "A Meta-Ethical Critique of Care Ethics," *Theoretical Medicine and Bioethics* 22: 505–17. A view critical of care ethics.

Slote, Michael. 2001. *Morals from Motives*. New York: Oxford University Press. Develops a version of virtue ethics that seeks to incorporate care as a central element.

Wollstonecraft, Mary. [1792] 1986. *Vindication of the Rights of Woman*. New York: Penguin Books. An example of an early feminist who sought to advance the interests of women in society by offering rights-based arguments.

Online Resources

Mary Wollstonecraft's *A Vindication of the Rights of Woman* (1792), http://www.earlymoderntexts.com/assets/pdfs/wollstonecraft1792.pdf Accessed October 12, 2016.

Carol Gilligan's "In a Different Voice: Women's Conceptions of Self and of Morality" (1985), http://sfonline.barnard.edu/sfxxx/documents/gilligan.pdf Accessed October 12, 2016.

Nel Nodding's *Caring: A Feminine Approach to Ethics & Moral Education*, chapter 1, (1984), http://blogs.baruch.cuny.edu/english2150cwrowe/files/2015/08/Caring_A_Feminine_Approach_to_Ethics_and_Moral-Education_Chapter-1.pdf Accessed October 12, 2016.

Review Questions

1. How is Care Ethics similar to Utilitarian Ethics? In what ways are they different?
2. Do you agree that humans are relational beings? Do you think it is a fact that has significant ethical implications?
3. What kind of drawbacks with ethical principles do care ethicists detect?
4. How is Care Ethics similar to Virtue Ethics? In what ways are they different?
5. Do you think that all humanity can participate in a feminine Care Ethics?
6. Do you think Care Ethics can be applied beyond immediate family and friends, to public policy issues?

Discussion Questions

1. Deontological Ethics is commonly applied to issues in medical ethics pertaining to the doctor/patient relationship. Patients are not to be treated as means by doctors; patients are said to have rights because they are autonomous beings and doctors need to obtain the patient's voluntary informed consent before administering various treatments to the patient. Because of patients' rights, doctors have duties. Explain how Care Ethics might critique this conception of the doctor/patient relationship. What do you think Care Ethics would offer in place of the deontological model? Which model do you think is most effective and appropriate? (In your answer, underline each care ethics concept and deontological concept and principle you mention.)
2. In the biblical story of the lost son, also known as the prodigal son (Luke 15:11–32), Jesus describes the relationship between a father and his two sons. The younger son asked his father for his share of his inheritance. The father gave it to him and his son set off to a distant country. He wastefully spent his entire inheritance (he was prodigal with his money). When he is penniless, he takes a job at a farm tending to pigs. He is so hungry that he is half-inclined to eat the pigs' food. It occurs to him that his father's hired workers have plenty of food. He decides to go back to his father, confess he was wrong, and ask to be treated as a hired worker. When the son returned, the father, filled with compassion, embraced and kissed his son. The father decided to celebrate the return of his son with a feast. The older son, who was working in the field, was surprised to find the celebration. In anger, he said to his father: "I have served you for years and yet when your irresponsible son returns, you lavish him with a feast!" But the father responded: "We must celebrate because your brother was lost and has been found." Explain how the father displays Care Ethics. Explain how the older brother seems to be thinking along the lines of an ethics of principle. How would the father have acted if he had followed an ethics of principle? (In your answer, underline each care ethics concept and ethics of principle concept and principle you mention.)
3. According to the World Bank, in 2012 12.7 percent of the world's population lived at or below the poverty line (living on less than $1.90 a day), which is 895 million people. This level of poverty is hard for citizens of the industrial world to comprehend. In 2007, development aid from the "Group of 8" industrialized nations

amounted to $62 billion. By the standards of Care Ethics, explain whether the developed world needs to do more to help the world's most vulnerable people. (In your answer, underline each care ethics concept you mention.)

4. If developments and discoveries in the field of genetics continue, with the aid of medical professionals parents could decide what kinds of characteristics their children might have. Parents who are deaf, blind, or dwarfs can decide whether their children will or won't have the same characteristics that they do. There is some evidence to suggest, for example, that some deaf parents might decide that they want their children to be deaf, while other deaf parents would decide that they want their children not to be deaf. Is there anything wrong with parents deciding that their children have the same characteristics that they have? Apply Care Ethics. (In your answer, underline each care ethics concept you mention.)
5. Some Care Ethicists argue that Care Ethics can be applied to public policy issues. Use Care Ethics to work out a position on the ethics of pornography. (In your answer, underline each care ethics concept you mention.)

Chapter 8

Conclusion: Using the Tools of Ethics

In this book we have looked at four core philosophical problems in ethics – the problem of the origins of ethics, the problem of relativism, the problem of human nature, and the problem of conduct. We have also considered a variety of solutions to these problems. The book has provided an introduction to many of the necessary conceptual tools you will need for working out your own solutions to them.

Because you are living a life right now, you have no choice but to deal with the main ethical problem, the problem of conduct. You have no choice but to attempt to answer the ethical questions that give rise to this problem, questions such as: How should you live your life? What counts as a life lived well? What kind of person should you become? What makes an action morally right or wrong? How should you determine the right thing to do? You will likely find that, in attempting to work out a solution to the practical problem of conduct, you will be led to thinking about solutions to the other three problems.

The ethical concepts, principles, theories, and traditions outlined in this book are useful tools when we are trying to deal with these ethical questions and various other ethical issues that confront us. We should conceive of them as tools that help us to understand a range of ethical categories – categories such as ethical behavior, ethical motivation, ethical questions, ethical dilemmas, ethical issues, ethical discussions, ethical deliberations, ethical analyses, ethical traditions, and ethical positions. As we can see from this list, these ethical tools have wide applications.

In any thinking that we do (about ethics or anything else), we use concepts. Think about anything right now, ethical or non-ethical. Can you do it without using concepts? If I'm thinking about my car, I'm using the concept "car." If I'm thinking about my country, I'm using the

Ethics: The Basics, Second Edition. John Mizzoni.

concept "country." If I'm thinking about the US economy, I'm using the concept "economy." As thinking beings, concepts are inescapable for us. At this point in the book, having reviewed many different ethical tools, we must ask ourselves which ethical concepts we personally use when we deal with ethical issues.

When we draw logical conclusions and make logical judgments, we unconsciously use principles and theories. Similarly, when we draw ethical conclusions and make ethical judgments, we unconsciously use principles and theories. For instance, in Chapter 6 when looking at the principle of universality version of the categorical imperative, which says to act only from those personal rules that you can at the same time will to be universal moral laws, we encountered the notion of a personal rule. In order to apply the principle of universality, you first have to ask yourself what personal rule you are following, or considering following. In that chapter we considered several examples of personal rules: the personal rule to live an irrational life, the personal rule to tell the truth to my family and friends but no one else, the personal rule to live a happy life, etc. Just as we can ask ourselves what ethical concepts we personally use when we deal with ethical issues, we can also ask ourselves what ethical principles and rules of thumb we personally use when we normally deal with ethical issues.

It is likely that we have developed habitual ways of thinking ethically. We may find ourselves constantly going back to the same set of ethical concepts and principles. For example, we may evaluate a situation by asking: What is just? What is in my self-interest? What feels right? What makes me happy? What are my responsibilities? Or perhaps: What do my loved ones need? We may then find that we are operating with a particular ethical theory or in a particular ethical tradition, possibly something like deontological ethics, utilitarian ethics, or natural law ethics. Using the wide range of ethical tools available can aid us in broadening the ways we think about ethical issues. This book has asked you to think like a relativist, a universalist, a virtue ethicist, a utilitarian, a deontologist, etc. In taking a range of ethical theories and traditions seriously, we sharpen our awareness of ethical issues and become more comfortable with consciously using the ethical tools available. Also, in considering ethical views that are different from our own, we learn not only about others, but about ourselves. Additionally, when we understand ethical views that are different from our own, we are in a better position to engage in constructive ethical discussion with others.

In this concluding chapter, I will not introduce any new concepts, principles, theories, or traditions. I will simply illustrate how the concepts, principles, theories, and traditions described in the earlier chapters can be used both separately and jointly in contemporary issues, whether in personal ethics (doing the right thing, living a good life) or in social ethics (what is good for society? what will contribute to the common good?). In the process of working through the illustrations below, and reviewing all of the ethical concepts, principles, theories, and traditions, we gain a deeper understanding of how the ethical tools operate. The task for you in this process is to try to develop the best solution you can to the problem of conduct. (Although, as I said above, in doing so you will likely be led to the other ethical problems as well.)

8.1 Living Ethical Concepts, Principles, Theories, and Traditions

As an example of how diverse fields of interest currently use many of the materials in this book, consider the field of business ethics (see Figure 8.1). Some theorists have taken virtue ethics and applied it to ethical issues in business; others have applied deontological ethics; yet others have used social contract ethics. Beyond business ethics, there are other fields of applied ethics such as criminal justice ethics, bioethics, medical ethics, computer ethics, engineering ethics, environmental

Figure 8.1

Examples of books that apply an ethical theory to ethical issues in **business**:

1. **Virtue Ethics**: *Ethics and Excellence: Cooperation and Integrity in Business*. Robert C. Solomon. Oxford University Press, 1992.
2. **Virtue Ethics**: *If Aristotle Ran General Motors*. Tom Morris. Owl Books, 1998.
3. **Deontological Ethics**: *Business Ethics: A Kantian Perspective*. Norman E. Bowie. Blackwell, 1999.
4. **Social Contract Ethics**: *Corporations* and *Morality*. Thomas Donaldson. Prentice-Hall, 1982.
5. **Social Contract Ethics**: *Ties That Bind: A Social Contracts Approach to Business Ethics*. Thomas Donaldson and Thomas W. Dunfee. Harvard Business School Press, 1999.

ethics, communication ethics, etc. There are many, many examples in each of these fields of applied ethics where ethical theorists have used many of the materials in this book as tools to assist with understanding, sorting out, and coping with an assortment of ethical issues that practitioners in each of those fields face.

8.2 Ethical Issues, Both Private and Public

The various ethical issues we have looked at in this book roughly fall into private (personal) domains, and public (social, societal) domains. When we look back over them, they seem to be a hodge-podge of examples. But again, this only indicates the wide application that these ethical tools have.

Here are the issues from previous chapters that are clearly public in scope: international human rights and tolerance between cultures (Chapter 1); civil disobedience, segregation, and voting rights (Chapter 4); war, the equality of men and women, and the ethical status of non-human animals (Chapter 5); and feminism (Chapter 7). The following issues, on the other hand, have more to do with one's private life: What is my understanding of the good life? What virtues do I want to develop in myself? (Chapter 2); Is it morally permissible to kill in self-defense? Or be sterilized? (Chapter 3); Are elaborate funerals or robbery ever morally justified? (Chapter 5); Should I always tell the truth to everyone? Is suicide morally wrong? (Chapter 6); Am I a good caregiver? (Chapter 7).

There is of course much overlap between the private and the public. Rights, for instance, have personal as well as public dimensions. The same is true of the ethical treatment of non-human animals, killing in self-defense, sterilization, and care giving (according to care ethicists like Virginia Held). However, there is enough difference between public and private issues that we can separate them to help focus our thinking.

8.3 Useful Ethical Concepts, Principles, Theories, and Traditions

Let us begin with a public issue. Consider the case of Stanley "Tookie" Williams. He was a co-founder of the Crips gang and the state sentenced him to death for being involved in several murders. When the time came for his execution, some people asserted that since he killed four people in the past, he therefore deserved death. This is a position often justified along the lines of deontological ethics. When a person knowingly and freely commits an act, we believe it is only just to hold that person fully responsible for the action. In deontological terms, we are respecting that person's autonomy. Since Tookie Williams knew what he was doing and he knew the penalty for such actions, then he deserved death. Deontological ethics, as an ethic of freedom and rationality, justifies state execution.

Others, however, saw the issue differently. While Tookie Williams was in prison, he worked on anti-gang children's books, and those books seem to have had a positive impact on future children's lives. Some people then asserted that putting off his execution and keeping him alive would likely have more good effects than executing him, because he would continue to do work that discourages children from getting involved in gangs. This position, in emphasizing the good effects of keeping him alive, sounds like a utilitarian position.

Let us go further with this and try to look at the death penalty from the perspective of other ethical theories. What can the virtue ethics tradition contribute to an analysis of the issue? Let us consider the kinds of questions and concerns virtue ethics would highlight about this issue. We perhaps could start by asking what habits and traits of character Tookie had when he committed those crimes. Was he involved in criminal behavior because he had not mastered control over his feelings; that is, he had not developed the virtues of self-control or courage? In his youth, did he have role models who exhibited virtuous behavior? What vision of the good life did he have when he was involved in gang behavior? Although his environment may have negatively influenced him, he is still responsible for the character he developed. After he was incarcerated, however, Tookie had the chance in prison to develop other character traits. He attempted to model positive behavior for young people who face pressures to join gangs. Are we as a society exhibiting virtuous behavior when we execute criminals, especially after they attempt to redeem themselves and give back to society? How do *we* control our feelings?

To apply natural law ethics, we should first consider the main principle of natural law ethics: We ought to perform those actions that promote the values specified by the natural inclinations of human beings. To directly contradict our natural inclination to preserve ourselves is wrong, so Tookie was correct in trying to avoid his execution. However, other human beings have natural inclinations to preserve themselves, also. According to the golden rule, then, we ought not to take the life of another person, so Tookie has committed moral wrongs by killing others. If it is morally wrong to take the life of a human being, then is the state morally wrong in executing criminals? Natural law ethics has two principles to use in unclear moral situations. The Pauline principle encourages us to think in terms of ends and means. We might say, then, that the state is doing an evil (executing a human being), in order to bring about a greater good (a safer society). If so, that would contradict the Pauline principle and would thus be morally wrong. What would the principle of double effect imply? We would have to consider whether executing a criminal has two effects, one good and one evil, and we are only intending to bring about the good end. For, if we are directly intending to destroy a life, then we are not acting in accord with the natural law. Did the action of executing Tookie simultaneously have a good effect and a bad effect? The bad effect was his death; that is clear. But, did executing a convict have a good effect on society? Traditional natural law theorists, like Aquinas, believed that it does, and therefore concluded that the state could protect the citizens by executing criminals.

According to social contract ethics, people – as rational beings – will agree to follow a set of rules (a contract) only if they believe they stand a good chance of benefiting themselves. Perhaps Tookie reasoned that if he followed the rules and laws of America (which include a law against killing), he would not benefit, thus he became involved in criminal activity. But we must ask if a rule/law against killing other human beings is a reasonable rule for rational and selfish beings to follow. A rule is reasonable when it benefits an individual, not only in the short run. We are talking about the rules that are necessary to have a reasonably organized and stable society where people can exercise the most amount of freedom without that freedom bringing down the whole framework. A rule against killing other humans seems very basic, and perhaps Tookie, while in prison, realized this himself and consequently became involved in trying to help young people see it. But again, is it just for the state to take a human life? We must consider the moral status of *that* law/rule. Is having capital punishment in your society a benefit to you as an individual? There can be differences in a social contract analysis of the death penalty because the answer will depend on the expected consequences of having that kind of rule. Some people do believe there are benefits to them as individuals. They will say that society is safer for them because capital punishment deters some criminals from committing violent crimes and they will say that in executing criminals then those individuals do not have an opportunity to pose a danger to society anymore. Others, though, will say that there are *not* benefits to me as an individual in having capital punishment; therefore, such a rule is not what a reasonable, rational, and enlightened person would want as part of his or her society's laws/rules.

In none of the ethical applications so far have we considered if Tookie were related to us, as a brother or a son. Care ethics would, of course, try to bring out that dimension. How would we feel about the situation if he were our friend, brother, or son? One reason why the issue is difficult is that we must also empathize with the victims and the victims' families. In addition to the personal dimension, care ethics could treat the issue as having larger, public, dimensions. Even though Tookie is not your friend or family member, care ethics would still have implications for how you ought to respond to this issue, for we are related to him as fellow citizens. Would a caring society have capital punishment? It seems unlikely. Which course of action would be living up to standards of care ethics, a violent policy that condoned execution or a non-violent one that promoted rehabilitation and compensation to the victims? Obviously, with care ethics, non-violent alternatives are preferred over violent ones. Care ethics takes relationships seriously, so in looking at this issue care ethics will not focus attention on the offender. Care ethics will look at the concrete relationships that are at stake: the offender and his relations, the victims and the victims' families, and the communities in which these crimes occurred. A caring society perhaps would have the offender confront the victims' families and provide compensation. In many ways, then, it seems care ethics would favor keeping Tookie alive instead of executing him.

8.4 Ethical Tools Are Not Mechanical Tools

In using the tools of ethics, we must bear in mind that applying an ethical principle or theory will not generate an answer for us in a mechanical way. Think back to a point mentioned in Chapter 2 about Aristotle's observation concerning imprecision in ethics. Aristotle recommends that we should not seek the same degree of exactness in all kinds of reasoning, and we should not expect more precision than the subject matter would allow. The point for us is that we should not expect ethics to be as precise as science or math. In Aristotle's opinion, this is not a cop-out, but a realistic assessment of the complexity and richness of human experience. A virtue ethics approach will strive to take that into account.

Secondly, think back to a situation we encountered in Chapter 6 in the discussion of deontological ethics and animal rights. Depending on how deontological ethics is used, we may end up with the position that animals do not have rights (Kant's conclusion). Alternatively, we may end up with the position that animals *do* have rights (Regan's position). A similar ambiguity in deontological ethics exists in the case of Tookie Williams, because there are some who argue that since he has a right to life, the state has a duty not to take that away from him. Others who take a deontological approach will emphasize that he is an autonomous rational being who must pay the ultimate punishment for the free and willful choices he made.

Furthermore, in looking at utilitarian ethics in Chapter 5, we noticed that it too has a degree of indeterminacy in that the morality of an action always depends on the consequences. Normally, we are not in a good position to weigh all consequences of our actions. Hence, although a utilitarian approach attempts to make ethical decision making straightforward by characterizing it as simply a matter of weighing the bad consequences against the good, and determining if the action has more good than bad in its favor, the process will not be as precise as we might want it to be. Many of the ethical issues discussed in this book have the same level of indeterminacy. The ethical materials presented in this book only offer assistance; they do not replace doing the ethical deliberation that is required in working toward ethical solutions, responses, and resolutions.

8.5 How to Use Ethical Tools

In this section, we will illustrate how to bring to bear on a single issue the whole arsenal of concepts and principles that fall under a given theory/tradition. By applying each theory to the same issue, we will be in a better position to compare and contrast the different solutions to the problem of conduct. To facilitate comparisons between the theories, I have listed in Appendix 1 all the ethical concepts, principles, theories, and traditions introduced in this book. In Appendix 2, I have listed only the ethical principles.

We will focus on an issue that has both public and private dimensions, fetal alcohol syndrome. If a pregnant woman drinks alcoholic beverages while she is pregnant, there is a chance that the drinking could cause her baby to be born prematurely or with birth defects. The birth defects could be low birth weight, facial deformity, hearing and vision problems, motor-skill problems, hyperactivity, memory or attention problems, or language problems.

As a way of analyzing this issue with the ethical tools, we will consider what each of the entries under each theory/tradition seems to imply about this issue. We will begin with relative ethics and universal ethics.

Recall from Chapter 1 that both **ethical relativism** and **ethical universalism** primarily address the basic question "What is ethics?" and do not focus on the more practical questions of ethics such as "How should I live my life?" In other words, these two theories have the most to say about the three theoretical ethical problems – the problem of the origins of ethics, the problem of relativism, and the problem of human nature – and have the least to say about the practical problem of conduct.

In general, relative ethics says that **right and wrong are relative**, thus in this case the ethical issues surrounding fetal alcohol syndrome are seen as entirely relative. Second, ethical relativism implies that the values at stake in this issue are **relative values** that are only meaningful because of their being valued in particular **folkways**. That is, if our society sees that it is ethically wrong for mothers to drink alcoholic drinks during pregnancy that cause their babies to be born with birth defects, that is only because of the value that our society – in our folkways – puts on newborns. If, perhaps, there is a society that does not look at the issue in this way, and sees nothing unethical with mothers causing their babies to be born with birth defects through their alcohol consumption, that is only because that society has different values that have historically developed through different folkways. Further, if our society asserts that unborn fetuses have the right not to be harmed by their mothers' alcohol consumption, **such a right is relative** to our society's values. Therefore, defenders of ethical relativism will state that we must be **tolerant** of other societies' folkways. **Cultural relativism** implies that, in fact, different societies and cultures will look at the morality of this issue differently; and each society and culture has a different **list of virtues** that it holds in high regard. **Ethical relativism** implies the stronger claim that *all* ethical standards are relative, to the degree that there are no permanent, universal, objective values or standards – including the ones that are at stake in the issue of fetal alcohol syndrome.

Ethical universalism is the view that there are at least some **objective and universal values and principles**. Even though ethical universalists concede that there is disagreement about the morality of this issue (that is, they concede that cultural relativism accurately describes what goes on in the world), they will still claim that there are some values and standards that are not relative. In this case they will likely point to the fact that fetuses are utterly innocent, and they in no way deserve to suffer with physiological defects. Thus through her alcohol consumption, the pregnant woman violates the universal standard that one ought not to harm an innocent human being.

Ethical universalists may appeal to **universal reason** to justify this position. They might say that anyone who uses their **reason** to think about whether an innocent human being should needlessly be harmed would reach the same conclusion. In addition, ethical universalists may seek to justify their position by appealing to the fact that there is a **universal human nature** that is shared by both adults and fetuses alike; and just as it would be wrong to harm an innocent adult, it is likewise wrong to harm an innocent fetus.

In terms of rights, an ethical universalist maintains that some **rights are universal**. Even though, as we saw above, ethical relativists could endorse the view that unborn fetuses have the right not to be harmed by their mothers' alcohol consumption, they would say such a right is purely relative to our society's values. An ethical universalist, by contrast, could assert that an innocent human being has the right not to be harmed, regardless of what a particular society believes.

An ethical universalist will charge that ethical relativism is inconsistent regarding **tolerance**, for if there is a society that has intolerance ingrained into its folkways, then intolerance will be the right thing to do. Ethical universalists will contend that to demand tolerance at all times to all societies is to uphold tolerance as a universal value. In this case, an ethical universalist could counsel that we ought to be tolerant of others when they violate universal human values, but that does not mean that we must condone fetal alcohol syndrome.

In turning now to **virtue ethics**, we can refer back to the basic notion of a virtue. A **virtue** is a **character** trait that is good for a person to have: it is an **excellent** character trait. A moral virtue is the result of **habitual** actions. One's character is the product of one's habitual actions. If so, then it would not make much sense to talk about the virtues or character of a fetus, for it has not performed many actions, if any. Concerning this issue, then, our focus will again be on the pregnant woman.

Which virtue seems most relevant to the issue at hand? The virtue of temperance seems very relevant. Temperance, as a moral virtue, has to do with how we handle our desires. By using the **principle of the golden mean,** we can get a handle on what the virtue of temperance consists in. According to the golden mean, a moral virtue is a mean between two extremes. If a pregnant woman lets her desires for alcoholic beverages control her, then she is intemperate and she drinks alcoholic drinks excessively for someone who is pregnant. At the other extreme, if she totally denies her desire for alcoholic beverages, then that also seems extreme, for why not only have one drink? In this case, however, what temperance will require for a pregnant woman who wishes to drink alcoholic beverages will depend on the facts about fetal alcohol syndrome. If any alcohol consumption whatsoever puts the fetus at risk, then it is temperate for her to abstain from *any* alcohol consumption. The excellence is controlling one's desires to the *proper* degree.

More important than using the principle of the golden mean to determine the particular nature of a virtue, the virtue ethics tradition views **role models** as highly influential in communicating and transmitting the ideals of virtuous behavior, for much of what we learn is by imitating others. A woman may be in the habit of consuming alcohol, a pattern of behavior she developed because of her role models. Becoming pregnant and needing to restrain her alcohol consumption may pose quite a challenge.

According to virtue ethics, the reason we ought to develop virtues is to bring about our own **happiness**, that is, well-being. Is temperance a trait that will contribute to human flourishing/happiness? If a pregnant woman is intemperate and drinks alcohol excessively during pregnancy and her baby is born with fetal alcohol syndrome, will that enhance and contribute to her well-being? Probably not; so we see that the fetus's happiness and well-being is not the only factor that is relevant here.

Intemperance is a **vice**, a bad habit, a habit that detracts from achieving happiness, well-being, and **the good life**. We could expand our analysis of this issue by considering many other relevant virtues. We may want to look over the sample **lists of virtues** in Figure 2.4, to get some ideas.

Shifting now to **natural law ethics**, we should recall that the natural law tradition distinguishes different kinds of laws: eternal, divine, natural, and human. With regard to fetal alcohol syndrome, since **eternal law** exists only in the mind of God, we would obviously not be able to apply it to this issue. **Divine law** refers to Holy Scriptures, so if the religious tradition we belong to contains Holy Scriptures concerning alcohol consumption, then we could apply it here. Natural law ethics views divine law as necessary for achieving **supernatural happiness**.

Are there **human laws** that our society has enacted regarding this issue? Some US states have extended child endangerment laws to cover fetuses. In those states, then, a pregnant woman has a legal responsibility to not put her fetus at risk. So far, legal cases have applied to situations where the woman's use of cocaine, heroin, and amphetamines caused harm to her fetus. In the future, though, perhaps states may modify such laws to include pregnant women's use of cigarettes or alcohol, since those substances – although legal – have had more widespread negative effects on fetuses.

According to natural law ethics, however, the **natural law** is a rational creature's participation in the eternal law. Natural law ethics is a form of **universalism** because it understands that there are some universal ethical values and standards. The main **principle of natural law** says that we ought to promote those actions that promote the values specified by the natural inclinations of human beings. The primary analysis of this issue from the natural law perspective, then, will involve determining if drinking alcoholic beverages during pregnancy promotes the values specified by the natural inclinations of human beings. The natural law tradition reasons that individuals have the **natural inclination** to preserve their own lives and life is a **human good**. Then, following the **principle of the golden rule** – do unto others as you would have them do to you – we realize that others have the same inclination that we do, to protect our own lives. If so, then it is wrong to take or endanger the life of another; so we would reach the conclusion that a pregnant woman ought not to act in ways that would put her fetus in danger. The natural law tradition emphasizes the **Pauline principle** – it is not morally permissible to do evil so that good may come. This is not a case where someone is tempted to do an evil action for a future greater good. But the **principle of double effect** does seem to be relevant. The principle of double effect says that it is morally permissible to perform an action that has two effects, one good and the other bad, if certain conditions are met. In this case, the action in question is drinking alcoholic beverages. Consuming alcohol in moderation does not seem to contradict the natural inclination to promote one's life. And presumably the pregnant woman is intending the good effect (a pleasant experience) and not the bad effect (fetal alcohol syndrome). If she were intending for her fetus to be born with fetal alcohol syndrome then that would clearly violate the principle and be immoral. The action also seems to meet the third condition, because the woman does not pursue the evil effect (the fetus acquiring fetal alcohol syndrome) to bring about the good effect (a pleasant drinking experience).

The fourth condition, however, seems to show that it would be an impermissible action for the pregnant woman to consume alcohol. In order to perform the action, which we foresee to have bad effects, there must be a grave reason for doing so. Fetal alcohol syndrome is a serious health condition, since the baby could be born with birth defects that will probably scar it for life. Is there a grave reason for a pregnant woman to drink alcoholic beverages while pregnant? Compared to the effects that could befall the baby, the drinking is not as important. Since the principle of double effect does not justify this action that has one good and one bad effect, natural law ethics would judge the action to be morally wrong.

How would **social contract ethics** frame the issue? With social contract thinking, it is helpful to remember that the concept of **state of nature** is always in the background. In the state of nature, each person would have unlimited **freedom**. Out of their egoistic tendencies, people would agree to leave the state of nature (thereby giving up some of their freedom) and enter into a **social contract**. They would seek to gain something in return – a **reciprocity** – for abiding by the terms of the contract. In this tradition, not only are people thought to be selfish by their human nature (**psychological egoism**), but they are advised to act selfishly (**ethical egoism**), because acting selfishly is the most rational course of action. The **principle of the social contract** advises people to agree to participate in social contracts. In doing so, people would seek to have **equal** standing with everyone else in the contract, and be regarded fairly under the **law**. When the social contract is a fair exchange between freedoms given up and social benefits gained, then the contract is **just**. In order to judge whether a contract is just, we must gauge whether there are good **consequences** for the participants who enter into the contract.

In terms of application to the fetal alcohol issue, social contract ethics does not provide a great deal of guidance, but there are a few useful aspects. The **principle of self-interest** sums up the general orientation of social contract ethics; it says we ought always to do whatever is in our best interest. If I am a pregnant woman, is it a good idea for me to drink alcoholic beverages? Is it in my best interest? Social contract ethics would seem to reach the same conclusion as virtue ethics: if my baby is born with fetal alcohol syndrome will that be in my best interest? Probably not. As a rational egoist, then, a pregnant woman should refrain from consuming alcohol while pregnant.

Social contract ethics incorporates the **principle of the golden rule**, but gives it an egoistic slant: I should treat others decently, because *I* want others to treat me decently. Using this principle, then, we could reason in the following way: If I were a fetus, would I want my mother to drink alcohol while she is pregnant with me? The background premise of egoism would tell us that the fetus, while growing in the womb, would also be self-interested, and would not want its mother to expose it to the toxins of alcohol.

Moving on to **utilitarian ethics**, we note that the utilitarian ethical tradition also incorporates the **principle of the golden rule,** but supports it for different reasons. The main reason to treat others as you wish to be treated is that you are no different from others. Utilitarian ethics emphasizes **equality**, and the **principle of equality** says that you and others deserve equal consideration. Like the social contract tradition, then, a utilitarian ethic would recommend for the pregnant woman to treat the fetus as she wishes to be treated, and give it equal consideration. If she were a fetus, would she want her mother to drink alcohol while she is pregnant with her? In utilitarian ethics, there is a background premise of **altruism**. For the utilitarian, you have an innate feeling of sympathy and **sentiment** for others, even for non-human **sentient** creatures (**non-anthropocentrism**).

A pregnant woman knows that her fetus is a sentient being and may experience suffering if born with fetal alcohol syndrome. The **principle of utility** says to do what will have the most **utility** in bringing about **happiness** for all concerned. Even though she, as a drinker of alcoholic beverages, may enjoy the experience, nevertheless, her actions affect another sentient being. The early utilitarians thought they could define happiness in terms of **pleasure**, a view known as **hedonism**. As a **consequentialist** ethic, utilitarian ethics advises that we measure the morality of an action by what consequences it has. If drinking during pregnancy has overall more negative consequences than positive consequences, then by utilitarian standards it is an immoral action. Even if it has been common practice for women to consume alcohol during pregnancy, that in itself does not justify continuing the practice. We cannot derive an **ought** from an **is**.

Let us now consider what **deontological ethics** can offer. Does a pregnant woman have a **duty** to refrain from drinking alcohol while she is pregnant? Is it her **obligation** and **responsibility**? Duties correlate with **rights**; do fetuses have rights that pregnant women must respect? The traditional way to determine if a being has rights is to check to see if that being is **autonomous**, capable of **freedom**. The **principle of autonomy** version of the **categorical imperative** has the concept "**person**" in it – act in regard to all *persons* in ways that treat them as ends in themselves and never simply as means to accomplish the ends of others. It is a *categorical* principle in that it is not saying that *if* you *desire* to be ethical then you ought to treat persons with respect, for that would be a **hypothetical imperative**. The categorical imperative takes the form of an **imperative**; it is a **command**. A categorical imperative commands you to treat persons with respect, regardless of whether you desire to or not. Although Kant maintains that the categorical imperative is a command of reason, **divine command ethics** is a religious version of deontological ethics. Both versions assert that human persons have **dignity** and we should regard them as having **equal** moral standing. The deontological tradition also incorporates the **Pauline principle** that says it is not morally permissible to do evil so that good may come. It is not morally permissible to violate the dignity of a human person (an evil) in order to bring about some kind of greater good. Deontological ethics is thus a form of **non-consequentialism**. As we said in the context of natural law ethics above, though, the Pauline principle does not seem to apply to this particular situation.

Let us consider the other form of the categorical imperative, **the principle of universality** version. It says to act only from those personal rules that you can at the same time will to be universal moral laws. The personal rule in question would be a pregnant woman's decision to follow the practice of drinking alcohol while pregnant. Can she will that her practice be elevated to the status of a universal moral **law**? Here is where we see a similarity to **the principle of the golden rule**. We again would be asking whether a pregnant woman could will that not only *she* drink alcohol while pregnant but *everyone*, including her own mother. Could she consistently will that *she herself* would be subject to the very real possibility of fetal alcohol syndrome? Probably not, since she is looking to benefit herself (by enjoying an alcoholic beverage), rather than harm herself. Another way to put the point is to say that drinking alcohol while pregnant does not pass the **universalizability** test.

Leaving deontological ethics, we finish our analysis with the tools of **care ethics**. When a pregnant woman drinks alcoholic beverages, is she exhibiting **care** for those with whom she is in close relationship? Is she attending to their needs? Our initial response might be that she is most certainly in a close relationship with her fetus, yet she is engaging in a practice that is harmful to the fetus. Although physical connectedness is something that care ethicists point to when they describe humans as relational beings, their conception of a **relationship** is a bit more complicated. We might think that if we are talking about concrete and close relationships, how can a relationship get any closer than a mother/fetus relationship, where the fetus's lifeblood is literally entwined with the mother's?

But care ethicists are not talking merely about physical connectedness; what is more important in this ethical tradition is emotional connectedness. Care ethics is in the tradition that sees ethics as based on feelings. According to Nel Noddings, an advocate of care ethics who discusses the mother/fetus relationship in the context of discussing abortion: "It is not a question of when life begins but of when relation begins" (Noddings 1984: 88). In Noddings' thinking, it is possible that there is *not* a personal relationship between the pregnant woman and the fetus, one in which the pregnant woman cares for her fetus. On the other hand, there *could* be a personal relationship between the pregnant woman and her fetus. In her version of care ethics, whether there is a personal relationship depends not on a *physical* connection but an emotional connection.

With regard to fetal alcohol syndrome, then, the issue is not as straightforward as we would think. Nevertheless, since in applying care ethics we should evaluate actions as right or wrong depending upon how deeply they are rooted in caring, drinking alcohol while pregnant still does not seem to be an ethical practice. A care ethicist would ask if the action was a genuine response to the perceived needs of the others. Drinking alcohol while pregnant is not a response to the needs of others. We are not dealing with a situation where a **one-caring** is in relationship with a **cared-for**; unless, that is, the pregnant woman feels **love** for her fetus and wishes to take care of it by not partaking in alcoholic beverages. She may even experience feelings of **joy** as she feels the movement of her fetus inside her. Such considerations, in fact, seem to be the kind of example that **feminist** philosophers would have in mind when they describe care ethics as a **feminine ethic**, one that deliberately attempts to give voice to unique female experiences, such as feeling a fetus move inside one's womb. One would think that the emotional bond of **partiality** would prompt a mother to do whatever she can to care for her fetus, and not harm it by drinking alcohol during pregnancy. Again, since care ethics emphasizes **altruism** rather than egoism as the ethical ideal, we would think that a woman living out of a care ethic would give up alcohol for the time while she is pregnant.

8.6 Pitfalls and Practice

Since ethical tools are not mechanical tools, applying them is not always a straightforward undertaking. In this section, I will mention several common pitfalls we should try to avoid when evaluating and applying the tools of ethics.

First, recall that relative ethics and universal ethics primarily address the question, "What is ethics?" and the theoretical problems in ethics, rather than the practical question, "What should I do?" or "How should I live?," which are the main questions in the problem of conduct. This is why in Appendix 2, where I have listed the ethical principles outlined in this book, you will not find principles from Chapter 1, because Chapter 1 focuses on relative ethics and universal ethics.

Second, in the list of ethical principles in Appendix 2 you should notice that the principle of the golden mean is unique among the ethical principles listed. The reason for this stems from the fact that virtue ethics is essentially a theory about ethical persons, not ethical actions. The principle of the golden mean helps us to understand what a particular virtue consists in – it is an aid for understanding, not a direct aid for deciding on an action. Conceiving of a moral virtue as a mean between two extremes helps us to see not only what the virtue is, but also why it is an excellence. We see its excellence by contrasting it with two associated vices – one of excess and one of deficiency.

Third – and related to virtue ethics as uniquely focused on a person's character rather than right action – is that in Appendix 2 there are no ethical principles associated with care ethics. Since care ethics bears similarities to virtue ethics, it should come as no surprise that care ethics also avoids principles that focus on actions. The fact that some feminist philosophers have characterized most ethical principles as masculine principles again gives us reason to suspect as much.

Fourth, we must be careful not to confuse the categorical imperative (whether in the form of the principle of autonomy or the principle of universality) with a consequentialist principle. Although the categorical imperative is a deontological principle and the central insight of a non-consequentialist ethic, we may find ourselves inadvertently transforming it into a consequentialist principle. For instance, a consequentialist formulation of the principle of autonomy would go something like this: *if I do not want to be treated as a means then I ought not to treat you as a means*. When we formulate the principle in this way, it seems that we ought not to treat others as means because of the negative consequences it will have. This, however, is consequentialist ethical reasoning. We have distorted Kant's ethical principle.

An inadvertent transformation of the principle of universality into a consequentialist principle would go something like this: *this personal rule would bring about a world in which I would not want to live; therefore I ought not to act on such a personal rule*. This way of ethical reasoning is consequentialist, since it locates the wrongness of the action in the negative consequences that will come about because of the action. However, if we put the emphasis on consequences then we are not really using the categorical imperative any more. In applying deontological ethics, we need to bear in mind that it is a non-consequentialist ethical theory, one that denies that determining the morality of an action, rule, policy, or law is a matter of weighing the consequences that the action, rule, or policy will have.

Fifth, we should not think that all concepts, principles, and theories apply equally well in all contexts. I have tried to show this in the previous section that focused on the ethical issues surrounding fetal alcohol syndrome. Different theories seem to be appropriate for particular contexts. We should treat this as a very important concern when attempting to fashion a reasonable solution to the problem of conduct. We may take it as a mark against an ethical theory, for example, if the theory seems to have limited contexts in which it applies. For more perspectives on how to evaluate and apply the various ethical concepts, principles, and theories, consider the suggested readings listed at the end of this chapter.

Sixth, there is not a sharp distinction between an ethical theory and an ethical tradition. Part of the difference between an ethical theory and an ethical tradition is that over time a theory may be changed and modified. For instance, the virtue ethics approach of Confucius is different from Aristotle's, which is different from Benjamin Franklin's. Similarly, the utilitarian approach of Bentham is different from Mill's, which is different from Singer's; so there is not *one* utilitarian or virtue theory, but rather, there is a utilitarian ethical tradition and a virtue ethics tradition.

The best way to avoid the pitfalls of applying the tools of ethics is simply through practice. Work with them, try out different ways of using them, become familiar with them, and increase your comfort level with them.

8.7 Wrap Up

From the building blocks of ethics – ethical concepts – to centuries-old ethical traditions, and many ethical principles and theories in between, we have looked at what ethics has to offer. The ethical materials provided in this book are ethical tools that present a framework for approaching four central philosophical problems in ethics. Ethical concepts, principles, theories, and traditions are inescapable. We need only to look at our own everyday ethics and see where we fit. Doing so requires reflection. Deep and serious reflection includes critical self-reflection: it requires going further than simply identifying the everyday ethical habits we have developed in ourselves over the years. Serious ethical reflection about philosophical problems in ethics involves challenging ourselves and asking ourselves whether the ethical habits we have are the ones that we *should* have, and whether we are living up to the standards of the kind of person we want to be. It also involves asking whether our ethical standards themselves are adequately justified.

In our personal lives and as public citizens, we face a raft of ethical issues. As a way to confront these issues, I invite you to explore how the ethical tools in this book can aid you, not only in *understanding* ethics, but also in *living* a fulfilling ethical life. Equipped with a range of ethical tools, and having worked at developing solutions to the four ethical problems, we can face ethical issues with a little more confidence. Yet – bearing in mind Aristotle's doctrine of the golden mean – not too much confidence.

For Further Reading

Fisher, Andrew, and Simon Kirchin (eds.). 2006. *Arguing About Metaethics*. New York: Routledge. An anthology that solely consists of *metaethical* selections. Theorists who work with ethical theories such as virtue ethics, natural law ethics, social contract ethics, deontological ethics, utilitarian ethics, and care ethics attempt to articulate and defend principles that people can use in a practical way in deliberating about specific ethical actions. Because of the emphasis on a practical question (What should I do? What kind of person should I be? How should I live my life?), these theories are called *normative* ethical theories. In other words, normative ethical theories are preoccupied with the problem of conduct. Whereas normative ethical theories provide guidance about what we ought to do or what kind of persons we ought to become, there are other kinds of ethical theories known as *metaethical* theories, which are not practical, action-guiding theories. Examples of metaethical theories are ethical relativism and ethical universalism, among many others. Metaethical theories are more concerned with the problem of the origins of ethics, the problem of relativism, and the problem of human nature. For further discussion of metaethics, see Appendix 4.

LaFollette, Hugh (ed.). 2002. *Ethics in Practice: An Anthology*, 2nd edition. Oxford: Blackwell Publishers. A collection of 64 essays on a wide range of ethical issues, both private and public.

Weston, Anthony. 2001. *A 21st Century Ethical Toolbox*. New York, NY: Oxford University Press. Offers a much more pragmatic approach regarding the tools of ethics, an approach that is not premised upon standard ethical concepts, principles, theories, or traditions.

Review Questions

1. When you deal with ethical issues, which particular ethical concepts do you personally use? Which ethical principles do you personally use? Do you find that you operate with a particular ethical theory or in a particular ethical tradition? Explain. (In your answer, underline each ethical concept, principle, theory, or tradition you mention.)
2. Can you think of an alternative way in which to apply one of the ethical theories to the issue of the death penalty? (In your answer, underline each ethical concept, principle, theory, or tradition you mention.)
3. What are some ethical questions that cluster together to form the philosophical problem of the origins of ethics? Which ethical questions form the philosophical problem of relativism? Which ethical questions form the philosophical problem of human nature? Which ethical questions form the philosophical problem of conduct?
4. In your estimation, what is the best solution to each of the following four problems: the problem of the origins of ethics, the problem of relativism, the problem of human nature, and the problem of conduct? What kinds of considerations led to your conclusions?

Discussion Questions

In your answers to each of the following questions, underline each ethical concept, principle, theory, and tradition you mention.

1. Focus on one ethical theory/tradition and apply it to one of the following *personal issues*: academic cheating, choice of career, donating blood, drug and alcohol use, gambling, marital infidelity, or sexuality.
2. Focus on one ethical theory/tradition and apply it to one of the following *public issues*: abortion, affirmative action, euthanasia, global warming, human rights abuses, taxes, terrorism, or world hunger/poverty.
3. There have been several cases of mass cheating on standardized tests, and in a national survey of 25,000 high school students from

2001 to 2008, more than 90 percent said they had cheated in one way or another. Analyze the ethics of academic cheating by using three approaches to ethics. Does this comparison help to bring out the strengths or weaknesses of these ethical approaches?

4. Analyze the ethics of drunk driving by using the tools of ethics.
5. The Zika virus is carried by mosquitoes and people, but is usually spread by mosquitoes. Unborn babies are most at risk from the Zika virus; when pregnant women are infected with Zika, their babies can be born with birth defects. There have been many travel-linked cases of Zika in the US. Identify some of the personal and public ethical issues involved. Use the tools of ethics to clarify those ethical issues.

Appendix 1: Ethical Concepts, Principles, Theories, and Traditions

Relative Ethics

cultural relativism The theory that, as a matter of fact, different cultures have different practices, standards, and values.

ethical relativism (relative ethics) The theory that *all* ethical standards are relative, to the degree that there are no permanent, universal, objective values or standards.

folkways The concept that customs are developed by average people (folk) over long periods of time.

relative values The concept that values are always relative to a context.

relativism A tradition of thought that holds that matters of knowledge, truth, value, and ethics are always relative to a context.

right/wrong is relative The concept that matters of right and wrong are always relative to a context.

rights are relative The concept that rights (whether moral, legal, or contractual) are always relative to a context.

tolerance The concept that we should tolerate, accept, and not criticize others who have different values and ways of living than we do.

Universal Ethics

ethical universalism (universal ethics) The theory that at least some ethical values, rules, and standards are universal.

Ethics: The Basics, Second Edition. John Mizzoni.

objective, universal values and principles The concept that some values and principles obtain independently of whether human beings believe in them or not.

rights are universal The concept that there are certain rights that all human beings have, no matter what culture or society they belong to.

tolerance The concept that we should tolerate, accept, and not criticize others who have different values and ways of living than we do.

universal human nature The concept that human beings have a shared, universal, set of essential characteristics.

universal reason/rationality The concept that human beings have a shared, universal, capacity for thinking and reasoning.

universalism A tradition of thought that holds that matters of knowledge, truth, value, and ethics admit of universal standards.

Virtue Ethics

character The concept that each person possesses a distinctive grouping of traits (traits such as generosity, integrity, honesty, and kindness).

excellence The concept that a virtue is a perfection, a perfected trait, an excellent trait.

good life, the A life of happiness, well-being, and flourishing. (A concept.)

habit The concept that repeated actions eventually become second nature, because over time repeated actions will require less effort. A moral virtue is a good habit.

happiness For Aristotle, happiness is that which all human beings seek. It is a condition of well-being and flourishing in which one has developed one's full potential. (A concept.)

lists of virtues The concept that different individuals, societies, and cultures have assembled different lists of what they believe are the appropriate and necessary character traits (virtues) for living a good life. For examples, see Figure 2.4.

principle of the golden mean The principle that says a moral virtue is a mean between two extreme vices, the vice of excess and the vice of deficiency.

role models One of the natural ways human beings learn is by imitating others. The concept of a role model is a person who possesses and thus displays developed character traits.

vice A character trait that stands in the way of one's flourishing. (A concept.)

virtue A character trait that contributes to one's flourishing; examples include generosity, integrity, honesty, and patience. (A concept.)

virtue ethics The ethical theory and tradition that focuses on discovering which character traits are most important for living an ethically good life.

Natural Law Ethics

divine law The revealed word of God that provides guidance as to how human beings can achieve eternal salvation. (A concept.)

eternal law God's plan as God understands it. (A concept.)

human goods Aquinas identifies four categories of fundamental human goods: life, procreation, sociability, and knowledge. (A concept.)

human law Laws that are designed, proposed, passed, and enacted by humans. (A concept.)

natural inclinations The concept that human nature directs human beings toward certain fundamental goods, which human beings then naturally value.

natural law The rational creature's participation in and (limited) understanding of the eternal law. (A concept.)

natural law ethics The theory and tradition that says there are universal ethical standards discoverable through human reflection on human natural inclinations.

Pauline principle The ethical principle that says it is not morally permissible to do evil so that good may follow (the end does not justify the means).

principle of double effect The ethical principle that says it is morally permissible to perform an action that has two effects, one good and the other bad, if certain conditions are met.

principle of natural law The ethical principle that says we ought to perform those actions that promote the values specified by the natural inclinations of human beings.

principle of the golden rule The ethical principle that says you ought to do unto others as you would have them do unto you.

supernatural happiness Happiness in the afterlife; eternal salvation. (A concept.)

universalism A tradition of thought that holds that matters of knowledge, truth, value, and ethics admit of universal standards.

Social Contract Ethics

consequentialism The theory that an action (or rule or law) is determined to be ethically right or wrong depending on the consequences it brings to people.

equality In social contract ethics, each person entering the contract has the same status, due to his or her rational ability to enter the contract in the first place. (A concept.)

ethical egoism The theory and tradition that says individuals ought always to do whatever is in their best interest.

justice The ethical concept that sums up whether a social contract is a good contract (a just one) or a bad contract (an unjust one).

law A law is a standard enacted by human beings through a social contract. (A concept.)

liberty, freedom In the state of nature, human beings possess unlimited freedom; there are no legitimate laws that can constrain their behavior. (A concept.)

principle of self-interest The ethical principle that says one ought always to do whatever is in one's best interest.

principle of the golden rule The ethical principle that says you ought to do unto others as you would have them do unto you.

principle of the social contract The ethical principle that says one ought to agree to participate in social contracts.

psychological egoism The theory and tradition that says all human behavior is, as a matter of fact, motivated self-interest.

rational egoism The theory that humans are rational and selfish beings.

reciprocity The concept that in a contractual arrangement a person gives something up in order to get something in return.

rule-egoism The theory that says people should follow a set of rules (a contract) that will yield for them the best consequences.

social contract An agreement between people, whether implicit or explicit, to follow a set of mutually beneficial rules. (A concept.)

social contract ethics The theory and tradition that says ethical standards are, and should be, the products of a social contract.

state of nature, state of war The state of nature is a condition, hypothetical or actual, in which there is no human law, no government, no police, no infrastructure, no civilization, and no society. Since in this condition human beings will experience continual conflict and strife, it is appropriate to think of it as a state of war. (A concept.)

Utilitarian Ethics

altruism The view that people can be genuinely motivated for the sake of others. (A concept.)

consequences Outcomes; effects; results. (A concept.)

consequentialism The theory that an action (or rule or law) is determined to be ethically right or wrong depending on the consequences it brings to people.

egalitarianism The tradition that views everyone as having equal ethical standing.

equality In utilitarian ethics, my happiness, suffering, well-being, pleasure, and pain are not more important than yours. (A concept.)

happiness In classical utilitarian ethics, happiness is pleasure. (A concept.)

hedonism The theory and tradition that says "good" should be understood in terms of pleasure.

is vs. ought The statement that *one cannot derive an ought from an is*, in addition to being a shorthand way that Hume recaps his theory of moral sentiments, has also become a handy way to distinguish the ethical realm from the non-ethical realm. (Concepts.)

non-anthropocentrism An anthropocentric value system centers on human beings as having ethical importance. A *non*-anthropocentric value system takes the focus off the human species and views non-humans (such as animals and other species) as having ethical importance. (A concept.)

pleasure The experience of good feelings. (A concept.)

principle of equality The ethical principle that says the interests of every being affected by an action are to be taken into account and given the same weight as the like interests of any other being.

principle of the golden rule The ethical principle that says you ought to do unto others as you would have them do unto you.

principle of utility The ethical principle that says one ought always to do whatever will have the most utility in bringing about happiness for all concerned.

sentience The ability to feel; a sentient creature has the capacity to experience pleasure and pain. (A concept.)

sentiment A feeling; an emotion. (A concept.)

utilitarian ethics The theory and tradition that says actions (or rules or laws or standards) ought to be judged to be ethically right or wrong depending on the consequences they will have on all who will be affected.

utility Usefulness. In utilitarian ethics, an action, for example, has utility if it is useful in bringing about happiness. (A concept.)

Deontological Ethics

autonomy The freedom and independence that rational beings possess. (A concept.)

categorical imperative An absolute and unconditional moral command. (A concept.)

categorical imperative (principle of autonomy) The ethical principle that says we ought to act in regard to all persons in ways that treat them as ends in themselves and never simply as means to accomplish the ends of others.

categorical imperative (principle of universality) The ethical principle that says we ought to act only from those personal rules that we can at the same time will to be universal moral laws.

command An order that directs us to perform an action; a prescription that prescribes what we ought to do. (A concept.)

deontological ethics The theory and tradition that focuses on ethical duties and says that actions are ethically right or wrong depending on whether they are in accord with one's ethical duties.

dignity The value that a person has by simply being a person; a person's value, which ought to be respected by others. (A concept.)

divine command ethics The tradition that views ethical duties as ultimately derived from God's commands.

duty Something one is required to do; a responsibility; an obligation. (A concept.)

equality In deontological ethics, all autonomous beings deserve the same respect. (A concept.)

freedom Independence; autonomy. (A concept.)

hypothetical imperative A command that is not absolute, but conditional, and premised on one's desires. (A concept.)

imperative A command. (A concept.)

law The collection of God's commands can be thought of as God's law. The collection of moral imperatives can be thought of as the moral law. As (scientific) laws of nature apply universally, so does the moral law. (A concept.)

non-consequentialism The theory that an action is determined to be ethically right or wrong not because of its consequences, but because of other factors, such as the person's intention.

obligation Something one is required to do; a responsibility; a duty. (A concept.)

Pauline principle The ethical principle that says it is not morally permissible to do evil so that good may follow (the end does not justify the means).

person A rational, autonomous being. (A concept.)

principle of the golden rule The ethical principle that says you ought to do unto others as you would have them do unto you.

responsibility Something one is required to do; a duty; an obligation. (A concept.)

rights Rights are legitimate claims that limit others' freedom. Rights correlate with duties: if I have a legitimate right, then you have a duty to respect that right. (A concept.)

universalizability A personal rule possesses universalizability – is universalizable – if it could consistently be willed to become a universal rule or law that everyone, everywhere, for all times, ought to follow. (A concept.)

Care Ethics

altruism The view that people can be genuinely motivated for the sake of others. (A concept.)

care Attending to the needs of those with whom we are in close relationship. (A concept.)

care ethics (ethics of care) The theory and tradition that views caring as the key ethical ideal: to live an ethical life is to care for those with whom we are in close relationship.

cared-for The person being cared for. (A concept.)

deism The tradition that says human beings cannot enter into personal relationships with God, even though God does exist.

feminine ethic An ethic rooted in receptivity, relatedness, and responsiveness. (A concept.)

feminism, feminist Feminism consists in various efforts and initiatives to advance the interests of women in society. A feminist promotes such efforts. (Concepts.)

joy In care ethics, a good feeling that comes through our interactions and personal relationships with others. (A concept.)

love In care ethics, the bonding feeling between those in close personal relationship. (A concept.)

one-caring The care giver; the care provider. (A concept.)

partiality Impartiality is a position of neutral detachment that shows an equal regard for all concerned. Partiality is giving special regard to those who are close to us. (A concept.)

relationships Concrete bonds, ties, attachments between people. (A concept.)

theism The tradition that holds that humans can have personal relationships with God.

Appendix 2: Ethical Principles

Chapter 2. Virtue Ethics

Principle of the Golden Mean: A moral virtue is a mean between two extreme vices (the vice of excess and the vice of deficiency).

Chapter 3. Natural Law Ethics

Principle of Natural Law: We ought to perform those actions that promote the values specified by the natural inclinations of human beings.

Principle of Double Effect: It is morally permissible to perform an action that has two effects, one good and the other bad, if certain conditions are met.

Pauline Principle: It is not morally permissible to do evil so that good may follow. (The end does not justify the means.)

Principle of the Golden Rule: Do unto others as you would have them do unto you.

Chapter 4. Social Contract Ethics

Principle of Self-Interest: One ought always to do whatever is in one's best interest.

Principle of the Social Contract: One ought to agree to participate in social contracts.

Ethics: The Basics, Second Edition. John Mizzoni.

Chapter 5. Utilitarian Ethics

Principle of Utility (*Greatest Happiness Principle*): One ought always to do whatever will have the most utility in bringing about happiness for all concerned.

Principle of Equality: The interests of every being affected by an action are to be taken into account and given the same weight as the like interests of any other being.

Chapter 6. Deontological Ethics

Categorical Imperative: Act in regard to all persons in ways that treat them as ends in themselves and never simply as means to accomplish the ends of others. (*Principle of Respect for Autonomy*)

Categorical Imperative: Act only from those personal rules that you can at the same time will to be universal moral laws. (*Principle of Universality*)

Appendix 3: Notes on Sources

Chapter 1. Relative Ethics or Universal Ethics?

The sociologist Sumner (1906) and anthropologist Benedict (1934) are examples of social scientists from the first half of the twentieth century who have defended both cultural and ethical relativism. The folkways notion is from Sumner. Wilson (1978), Ruse and Wilson (1986), and Ruse (1998) are evolutionists who explicitly oppose ethical relativism. Abbott (1966a; 1966b) and encyclicals of Pope John Paul II (1993; 1998) are theological writings that engage with the relative ethics/universal ethics issue.

The information about child labor was obtained from *Lost Futures: The Problem of Child Labor* (Item No. 300, American Federation of Teachers). For information on breast ironing see Barns (2015). Female circumcision is discussed in Khazan (2015); and chapter 20 of Moser & Carson (2000).

Chapter 2. Virtue Ethics

The road rage example is from "Driving Instructor Resigns Over Incident of Road Rage," *The New York Times*, October 17, 1997. The anger management statistics are from *HMS Exchange* (West Chester, PA: Human Management Services, Inc., 2004). Socrates' ethical probing appears in Plato's *Apology* (380 BCE). Aristotle (337 BCE) offers a systematic analysis of virtue ethics. Gupta (2002, part IV) contains both Western and non-Western examples of virtue ethics. For more on

Ethics: The Basics, Second Edition. John Mizzoni.

Confucian ethics see Chan (1963). For the connection between (virtue) ethics and literature see Pojman (2004) and Rosenstand (2000). Aristotle's statement of the principle of the golden mean appears in (337 BCE: bk 2, ch. 6, lines 1106b15); his comment that virtue and vice are voluntary and up to us is in (337 BCE, bk 3, ch. 5, lines 1113b5); his comment that moral virtue comes about as the result of habit is in (337 BCE: bk 2, ch. 1, lines 1103a15); his statement about precision in ethics is in (337 BCE: bk 1, ch. 3, lines 1094b12). The suggestion that Aristotle's life of contemplation is a life of retirement is in van Hooft (2006). Williams distinguishes thin ethical concepts from thick ethical concepts in (1985: 129). For charity as the main Christian virtue, see Pinckaers (2001: 20). Kyte (2004) is the author who claims that hospitality is the central Franciscan virtue. Hume describes justice and benevolence as the two main virtues in (1751: 16). For how virtue ethics can be coupled with either ethical relativism or ethical universalism see Nussbaum (1988). The objection that virtue ethics falls short in justifying a moral obligation to have concern for human beings generally is from Slote (2001: vii–viii). Andrew Weil's comment about doctors and hospitals is from Weil (2006). Aristotle's point about righteous indignation appears in (337 BCE: bk 4, ch. 5, lines 1126a5). DesJardins (2009: 152) discusses "gatekeepers" in business.

Chapter 3. Natural Law Ethics

Aquinas's *Summa Theologiae* (1270) is enormous and divided into three main parts, the middle part focuses on ethics. The part about different kinds of law is in the first half of the middle part, which scholars customarily refer to as I-II, "the first part of the second part." St. Paul uses the concept of natural law in his Letter to the Romans (2:14–15). The Pauline principle is in Romans (3:8). Aquinas's discussion of the four categories of goods connected in with the four natural inclinations is in (1270: I-II, Question 94, section 2). Aquinas on self-defense is in (1270: II-II, Qu. 64, sect. 7). Aquinas says intention is important for moral action in (1270: I-II, Qu. 72, sect. 1; II-II, Qu. 64, sect. 7). Aquinas describes the process of acquiring the theological virtues in (1270: I-II, Qu. 62). Aristotle mentions natural law in (Aristotle 350 BCE: Bk I, Chapter 12: 1373b2-10).

The story of St. Gianna is from Baldwin (2004). For how Catholic theologians incorporate natural law ethics, see Pope Paul VI's *Humanae Vitae* (1968).

Chapter 4. Social Contract Ethics

Thomas Hobbes's masterpiece is *Leviathan* (1651), which he divides into four parts; the first two have been the most influential. In the first part, he describes his theory of human nature and the human mind, and in the second part, he describes his views about the nature and structure of a commonwealth (civilized society). Hobbes's claim that the golden rule sums up the social contract is in (1651, ch. 15). The story of the wolf of Gubbio is more of a peace-making parable. Francis of Assisi demonstrates that to make peace between different parties one must first identify the source of the tension and then find ways to solve the problem; see Blow (2003, ch. 9). The free-rider concept is in Gauthier (1986: 96, 152, 201). For the story of Jerry Bowles see Gates (2016). For contracts and ancient trade agreements, see Ridley (1996, ch. 10). For an explanation and defense of common-sense morality, see Gert (2004).

Chapter 5. Utilitarian Ethics

Hume's powerful argument to prove that ethics rests on sentiment not rationality is in (1739, Book 3, part 1, sect. 1) and his is/ought point is the concluding statement at the end of the same section. R. M. Hare dubs Hume's is/ought point "Hume's Law" in (1963: 108). Hume's claim that reason is, and ought to be, the slave of the passions, is in (1739, Book 2, part 3, sect. 3). For the Freudian view that the decisions we make are not simply the result of our conscious thinking, see Hall (1954). The story about Chef Trotter and foie gras is from Downes (2005) and Davey (2006).

Bentham introduces the principle of utility in (1789, chapter 1). Singer (1975, chapter 1) discusses the principle of equality. Mill says the golden rule sums up the spirit of utilitarian ethics in (1861, chapter 2). The man who killed his wife who was suffering from Alzheimer's was reported in "Italian Shoots Wife in Hospital," *BBC News*, December 2, 2007. The example of Jim and the Indians is from Williams & Smart (1973: 98–9).

Chapter 6. Deontological Ethics

We can compare an inquiry into duty with an inquiry into virtue. In introducing virtue ethics, we can first identify some easy examples of virtues; it makes sense to consider that there are some virtues that are especially important for certain roles, as workers, as parents, as citizens, etc. Then, asking the question about *why* we need to develop the virtues, we venture into a philosophical analysis of virtue. The same basic outline of introduction applies to duty-centered ethics. First, we think about straightforward examples of duties that we have, perhaps with regard to our particular roles, then, we venture into a philosophical analysis of duty. A traditional starting point for a philosophical analysis of duty is to think about divinely ordained duties. Kant draws the hypothetical/categorical distinction in (1785, second section); and he discusses the different versions of the categorical imperative as well as their applications to different examples in (1785, second section). Kant discusses animals in (1780: 239–41). The ancient Indian book *The Bhagavad Gita*, a sacred text of Hinduism, is actually a long poem; Barbara Stoller Miller (1986) provides a good English translation of it. The quotations in the text are from: ch. 2, lines 31, 47; ch. 9, line 3; and ch. 18, line 47. Regan (1983) offers a 400-page defense of rights, both human and non-human.

Chapter 7. Care Ethics

Carol Gilligan sketches out the notion of a care ethics in her book, *In a Different Voice* (1982). Nel Noddings gives a book-length treatment to care ethics in *Caring* (1984). The story of Abraham and Isaac is from Genesis: 22. Noddings discusses the story in (1984: 43–4). Virginia Held further develops care ethics and applies it to global issues in *Ethics of Care* (2006).

An example of a religious ethic that makes joy a central component is Pinckaers (2001). Pinckaers describes the difference between feelings of pleasure and feelings of joy, as the difference between physical pleasures and spiritual pleasures. In Plato's dialogue, *Euthyphro* (380 BCE), Socrates converses with Euthyphro, a religious expert, about the logical puzzles that emerge when we conceive of a caring relationship between God and humans.

The point about the brain size of an infant is from Arnhart (1998: 108). The world poverty statistic is from http://www.worldbank.org/en/topic/poverty/overview. The breast cancer statistic is from http://www.breastcancer.org/symptoms/understand_bc/statistics. The literacy statistic is from http://www.unesco.org/new/en/education/themes/education-building-blocks/literacy/resources/statistics. The concern about the traditional use of generalizations about female ethics and masculine ethics in justifying the oppression of one of the sexes is in Grimshaw (1991: 495). Figure about development aid is from "An Even Poorer World," *The New York Times*, September 2, 2008.

Chapter 8. Conclusion: Using the Tools of Ethics

The case of Tookie Williams is described at http://www.biography.com/people/stanley-tookie-williams-476676. Aquinas discusses the difference between a public authority killing a criminal and a private person killing a criminal (1270: II-II, Qu. 64, sect. 3). Pollock (2007, chapter 2) applies care ethics to criminal justice issues. The information about fetal alcohol syndrome is from The Centers for Disease Control and Prevention, http://www.cdc.gov/ncbddd/fasd/.

Although there is not a sharp distinction between an ethical theory and an ethical tradition, it still remains helpful to distinguish the two. The notion of an ethical tradition captures the sense that when a view of ethics (a theory) persists through multiple generations, it is the property of more than one philosopher. We are then invited to ask ourselves if we are part of that tradition, perhaps without even realizing it. For example, though we might not be consciously "following" the philosopher J. S. Mill (say), own way of thinking about ethics may nevertheless situate us in the utilitarian ethical tradition.

Further, the notion of an ethical tradition has a significant and legitimate place in contemporary moral philosophy: MacIntyre (1984: 221–3, 276–7; 1988: 335, 349–403; 1990; 1998: 1–4); Kekes (1989); Singer (1991: x). Fieser (2001: 202–6) discusses the utilitarian ethical tradition and Kymlicka (1991: 186–96) discusses the social contract ethical tradition. For the natural law ethics tradition, see Simon (1965); Schneewind (1990: Part I, 65–198); and Boyle (1992: 4).

Appendix 4: Metaethics

The Status of Ethics

Metaethics is a branch of ethical theory that inquires into the ultimate nature of ethics. Definitions of metaethics, like this one, are often too general to be helpful. This is partly because of the abstractness of the subject matter and partly due to the fact that the boundary line between metaethics and normative ethics is sometimes blurry. The purpose of this appendix is to describe the fundamentals of metaethics and how they relate to the ethical theories discussed in this book.

The field of contemporary metaethics is a wide-ranging and extremely vibrant area of research. Important developments in metaethics have occurred in the last few decades. The number of new articles and books published in this area is remarkable. First and foremost, the field of metaethics deals with the issue of the status of ethics. The main philosophical question here is: what is the status of ethics? In other words, are ethics merely social inventions? Is ethics a product of human invention? Are the rules of morality merely conventional? Are claims about morality just statements of a society's standards or an individual's opinion? Or do claims about ethics involve more than expressions of our individual emotions, and more than our society's standards? Where do our ethical principles ultimately come from?

These questions and this issue of the status of ethics should sound familiar. It is obvious that the problem of the origins of ethics and the problem of relativism as discussed in this book are metaethical problems concerning the status of ethics. The theory of ethical relativism that we looked at is a theory about the status of ethics, not a theory

Ethics: The Basics, Second Edition. John Mizzoni.

about which values people should have. Ethical universalism, the theory we looked at that contradicts ethical relativism, is also a theory about the status of ethics. Those two theories disagree about the status of ethics. All of Chapter 1, "Relative Ethics or Universal Ethics?" dealt with metaethics and the issue of the status of ethics. In Chapters 2 through 7, we saw how virtue ethics, natural law ethics, social contract ethics, utilitarian ethics, deontological ethics, and care ethics also deal with the status of ethics by dealing with the problem of the origins of ethics and the problem of relativism.

Another common metaethical issue concerning the status of ethics and the origins of ethics is the issue of the relationship between ethics and God or religion. The philosophical questions here would be: Does ethics depend on God or religion? Is God the ultimate origin of ethics? Or is ethics something that can exist independently from God and religion? We have seen that some ethical theories affirm that ethics is ultimately dependent on God. Natural law ethics, for instance, sees ethics as ultimately dependent on God's will, and so does divine command ethics. Other ethical theories, though, like Aristotle's virtue ethics, Hobbes's social contract ethics, utilitarian ethics, Kantian deontological ethics, and care ethics view ethics as existing independently of God and religion. Because all of these theories take positions about the status of ethics, they thus have metaethical dimensions.

In metaethics, another common way to distinguish different views about the status of ethics is with the terms *objective* and *subjective.* Consider the following philosophical question about ethics: Is there any such thing as an ethic's being objectively correct? With this question we are asking if an ethic can have an objective status. To say that something is objectively correct would mean that it persists in being correct regardless of whether people *think* it is correct. An objective ethic would be correct independently of people's beliefs about it. Its being correct would not be a function of people's opinions about it; it would be correct whether people believed it or not. For shorthand, we can use the term *objectivism* to designate the view that ethics possesses an objective status.

Some of the ethical theorists we looked at in this book believe that ethics has an objective status: Aristotle, Aquinas, and Mill, for instance. And surely Kant believed that the categorical imperative had an objective status. To substantiate the view that ethics has an objective status, we would have to show how an ethic could have this status, and how we could know about it, especially since if we believe it is objective, it is supposed to be correct independently of human opinion.

If we do not think an ethic can be objectively correct and have an objective status, we might still think it is possible for an ethic to be correct. We might think it is subjectively correct, and has a subjective status. This would mean that it is correct only because people (subjects) have certain beliefs about it, namely, beliefs that it is correct. For shorthand, we can use the term *subjectivism* to designate the view that ethics has a subjective status.

It is easy to think of scientific claims that are regarded as having an objective status, claims that are correct regardless of what people think about them. The science of astronomy, for instance, says that the earth orbits the sun. We take this as objectively correct even though not everyone has always thought it was objectively correct. Its correctness is thought to be independent of people's beliefs about it. But maybe ethics is not at all like science; maybe ethics does not consist of objective claims. Maybe ethics is subjective, like art and beauty, for instance. The view that beauty is subjective is summed up in the common expression, beauty is in the eye of the beholder. In this view, beauty depends on a beholder, a subject who perceives something. Art critics say the *Mona Lisa*, the portrait painted by Leonardo da Vinci in the sixteenth century, is beautiful. Someone of the opinion that beauty is subjective would say that although the portrait indeed has objective qualities – it is objectively a portrait of a woman, with dark hair, her eyes open, her holds folded, wearing dark clothes – the portrait's beauty, on the other hand, is a matter of subjectivity. A subjectivist about beauty would say the portrait does not objectively possess beauty; so, if someone deems the portrait beautiful, that judgment really has more to do with the subject (the viewer) than the object (the portrait).

In the same way, some theorists hold that ethics has a subjective status. An ethic, or something's being morally right or wrong, depends on a subject, a person who holds those beliefs. A consistently subjectivist view of ethics would have to say that ethics depends on the beliefs and opinions of individual subjects. Subjectivism in ethics bears a close resemblance to ethical relativism. Ethical relativism says that *all* ethical standards are relative, to the degree that there are no permanent, universal, objective values or standards. When subjectivists say that ethics has only subjective status, they might then mean that all ethical standards are relative to individual subjects, which would imply that there are no permanent, universal, objective ethical standards.

A different version of subjectivism was put forward by Hume. As we saw in Section 5.5, "Utilitarianism: Relativist or Universalist?," Hume explained that ethics is grounded in human sentiment. In order to know that something is wrong, one must feel it, he argues. But, even though ethics is subjective in this sense, Hume maintained that that does not mean ethics is subjective in a relativist way. Hume viewed ethics as subjective, but not as relative. He observed that by and large and for the most part, all human beings have the same types of feelings and sentiments, such as anger, envy, fear, guilt, indignation, joy, love, pity, sadness, and shame. Because human beings have similar enough emotional responses, ethical relativism will seem implausible. In short, Hume's view of human nature prevents his subjectivism from collapsing into relativism. Hume's metaethical theory is an example of a subtle metaethical position: it is subjectivist and universalist without being objectivist or relativist. Contemporary metaethics today is filled with subtle metaethical positions like this one. And Hume's subjectivism, in particular, has been very influential in contemporary metaethics.

Just as there are varieties of subjectivism, there are also varieties of objectivism. In Chapter 6 when looking at Kant's deontological ethics, we saw how he develops a theory that views ethics as having an objective status. Kant's is a strongly objectivist view, since in his theory ethical duties are absolute and categorical. Above, I also mentioned Aristotle and Mill as examples of other theorists who view ethics as having an objective status. Their ethical theories, though, do not portray ethics as being as strongly objective as Kant's theory does because Aristotle and Mill do not characterize ethics as being absolute and categorical. They view ethics as objective, to be sure, but in contrast to an absolutist kind of objectivity, their ethical theories characterize ethics as more moderately objectivist.

When I first introduced objectivism above I said that to substantiate it we would have to show how an ethic could have objective status and how we gain knowledge about it. Consider what these demands require of subjectivism. What would it mean to say that we would have to show how an ethic could have subjective status? For one thing, when people ordinarily state their position about a serious ethical matter, do they regard what they are claiming as having subjective status or objective status? When someone says that the serial killer Jeffrey Dahmer committed horribly unethical acts by murdering and dismembering 17 people, it is usually meant as an objective statement: what Dahmer did was wrong, objectively. A subjectivist will need to explain how it is that people regularly regard their ethical claims as objective, when, according to the subjectivist, all ethical claims are really subjective. With regard to moral knowledge, a subjectivist will need to explain if moral knowledge is at all possible, since, according to subjectivism, an ethic is only correct because people subjectively believe it to be correct. Is belief sufficient for knowledge, though? Just because I believe something, does that mean it is a piece of knowledge? Philosophers who work with theories of knowledge (the branch of philosophy called epistemology), usually claim that more than mere belief is necessary in order to justifiably regard something as knowledge.

For more on the issue of the status of ethics, see Shafer-Landau (2004), which is a short and engaging introduction to metaethics, or Harman & Thomson (1996), a rigorous interchange between two philosophers who take opposing views on the status of ethics.

Moral Psychology

Beyond the issue of the status of ethics, another large area of metaethical concern is known as moral psychology. In this area of inquiry, theorists attempt to determine what the connection is between our psychological makeup and what it is to make moral judgments, reach ethical conclusions, and be ethical. As we saw in the previous section of this appendix, the problem of the origins of ethics and the problem of relativism are metaethical problems concerning the status of ethics. The problem of human nature, as we have been treating it in this book, is also a metaethical problem.

When we talk about human nature in the context of discussing ethics, what aspects of human nature would be most relevant? The blood type of human beings? The number of chromosomes they have? The average number of hair follicles on a human body? No, the aspects of human nature that would be most relevant have to do with human actions and motivation for action. Also, the human capacities for emotional experiences and rational thinking would be highly relevant. It is not surprising, then, that theorists working in metaethics have chosen to use the phrase "moral psychology" when discussing human nature and ethics, for when discussing ethics, all of the most significant aspects of human nature concern human psychology.

As an essential part of metaethics, a theory of moral psychology must describe what human moral agents are like and what capacities and abilities they possess. Theories that deal with the issue of the status of ethics, and theories of moral psychology are metaethical because they are not the kind of theories that give practical advice about what people should do and how people should act. If one is interested in a practical ethical theory that helps one decide how to act, one needs to turn to normative ethical theories such as virtue ethics, natural law ethics, social contract ethics, utilitarian ethics, deontological ethics, or care ethics. Even normative theorists, though, as we have seen in this book, make some assumptions about moral psychology and offer solutions to the problem of human nature as part of what is involved in substantiating their normative ethical theories.

Here are a few examples of moral psychology discussed in previous chapters. Aristotle, when he characterizes human beings as rational animals with passions and desires who can do things voluntarily, is dealing in moral psychology. The theory of psychological egoism, clearly, is an example of a theory of moral psychology. Theorists who maintain that human beings are not wholly selfish but are naturally altruistic – defenders of utilitarian ethics and care ethics, for example – would also be working in moral psychology. The view that human beings are always and only motivated by emotion and never by reason alone (Hume's theory of moral sentiments), is obviously a moral psychological view. Kant's response to Hume that human beings *can* be moved by reason alone is an example of how Kant engages in moral psychology. The issue of whether human beings are motivated only to seek pleasure and happiness, which is a classical utilitarian view, is part of moral psychology. Every solution to the problem of human nature we have looked at in earlier chapters, in fact, is about moral psychology.

For more on moral psychology and how it relates to metaethics and normative ethics, see Jacobs (2002).

Naturalism and Non-Naturalism

A further area of metaethical concern is the question of how moral values relate to the rest of what there is in the world. To see how this set of issues arises, let us again turn to a parallel case about artworks. Da Vinci's *Mona Lisa* has various objective qualities – it is objectively a portrait of a woman, with dark hair, her eyes open, her holds folded, and wearing dark clothes. The beauty of the painting, on the other hand, seems to be a different kind of quality. To say that the painting is beautiful, or ugly, or a great piece of art, or a masterpiece, is much different than saying the painting has several shades of brown in it, there are mountains in the background, and the woman depicted is wearing a veil. Calling the painting beautiful or great is making a value claim about the painting, while saying the painting is of a woman, with her hands folded, wearing dark clothes, etc., is simply making claims about simple facts. We see, then, that value claims are different from factual claims. And the same distinction carries over into ethics: moral values are of a different quality than non-moral facts about the natural world. The metaethical question here is: how do moral values relate and connect to non-moral facts about the world?

We have seen the distinction between value claims and factual claims before, in previous chapters. In Chapter 5, on utilitarian ethics, for instance, I mentioned that Hume's statement that one cannot derive an *ought* from an *is*, in addition to being a shorthand way that Hume recaps his theory of moral sentiments, has also become a handy way to distinguish the ethical realm from the non-ethical realm – *is* differs from *ought*. *Is* refers to facts and *ought* refers to values. Even theorists who disagree with Hume's theory of moral sentiments still believe that the *is/ought* distinction is important, because it captures the difference between facts and values. In Chapter 4, on social contract ethics, we saw that the *is/ought* distinction was implicitly used in distinguishing between psychological egoism and ethical egoism. Psychological egoism, a theory about human nature, is put forward as a factual theory, a statement of *is*. Ethical egoism, in contrast, is put forward as a thesis about *ought*; it recommends what we ought to do, should do, and what has value, morally. But, making the distinction between facts and values is one thing; actually explaining how values connect to facts is another, more difficult, task.

The metaethical challenge of explaining how values (in general) connect to facts (in general) has significance for all normative ethical theories. Let's look at an obvious example. At the end of Chapter 3, on natural law ethics, I mentioned that today many moral theorists are skeptical about any kind of reasoning that proceeds from observations about human natural inclinations to moral conclusions. This is because observations about human natural inclinations are about facts (is) while moral conclusions are about values (ought).

In metaethics the view known as *naturalism* says that values and moral claims are just special kinds of natural facts. Naturalism further asserts that if value claims are just a special kind of factual claim then, in principle, we should be able to spell out how values connect to facts. In principle, we should be able to define moral concepts like "good" by using purely factual terms like "natural." Naturalists have worked out various ways of attempting to show this. For some theorists, though, the divide between natural facts and moral values is unbridgeable. The early twentieth-century philosopher G. E. Moore, for instance, famously said: "it is ... always an open question whether anything that is natural is good" (1903: 44). This is known as Moore's open question argument, and it is used to challenge any and all forms of naturalism. The argument is a formidable challenge to naturalism because if Moore is correct that it is always an open question whether anything that is natural is good, then any naturalistic definition one offers for moral goodness will always be open and never settled. And this means that the connection between "good" and "natural" can never be assured.

Because Moore did not believe moral terms like "good" could be defined in factual terms, how did he think moral terms should be defined? Moore said:

> If I am asked "What is good?" my answer is that good is good, and that is the end of the matter. Or if I am asked "How is good to be defined?" my answer is that it cannot be defined, and that is all I have to say about it. (Moore 1903: 6)

While naturalism, then, is the view that values and moral claims are just special kinds of natural facts and we should in principle be able to spell out how values connect to facts, Moore's view, which denies naturalism, has been dubbed *non-naturalism*. Moore says "good" is indefinable, and so any attempt to define it in terms other than "good" therefore commits a mistake in reasoning, a fallacy. Moore called this mistake that he believes naturalists commit, the naturalistic fallacy.

In metaethics today, there are multiple varieties of both naturalism and non-naturalism. Both of these metaethical traditions attempt to answer the metaethical question about the correct way to conceive of how moral values relate to non-moral facts about the world.

Metaethics as a Bird's-Eye View of Ethics

While naturalism and non-naturalism are broad categories of metaethical theories, in this section we will look at more specific examples of metaethical theories in order to get a sense of the range of metaethical positions that have recently been developed on the issue of the status of ethics.

Metaethics is quite abstract; it takes a bird's-eye view of ethics. Let's take that analogy literally for a moment. Imagine two friends, Gary and Orlando, sitting on a park bench on a bright, sunny day. A light breeze cools them, birds are chirping, and the park's greenery surrounds them as they enjoy a beautiful spring afternoon. The two friends are discussing the ethics of capital punishment. Both Gary and Orlando reside in one of the 32 states in the USA that employs the death penalty. Gary tells Orlando that it is morally wrong for the state they live in to perform executions. Orlando disagrees and asserts that execution is the only morally deserving punishment for those who commit terrible crimes.

As Gary and Orlando debate the ethics of capital punishment, suppose a bird is circling above them. And further suppose that the bird has the intelligence to know what the two friends are saying, but does not have an opinion on the matter, since it cares nothing about human criminal law. From a bird's-eye perspective, what are the friends doing when they put forth their opinions, make ethical claims, offer arguments, and reach ethical conclusions about capital punishment?

This is a *metaethical* question. The *ethical* question at hand is whether capital punishment is morally right or wrong. It is a metaethical question, though, to ask what someone is doing when he or she is sincerely answering the ethical question and making an ethical claim. Asking a question about a question takes us one level removed from the issue. This is what metaethics is about: looking at ethics from a different level.

Different metaethical theories will differently describe what Gary and Orlando are doing. From the intelligent bird's perspective, it may seem that the two friends are simply expressing their emotions about capital punishment. The metaethical theory of *expressivism* takes this approach; this view is also known as *emotivism*, and it obviously derives from Hume's analysis of the nature of moral judgments that we looked at in Chapter 5, on utilitarian ethics. Or from the bird's perspective it may seem that the two friends are doing more than simply expressing their emotions. The bird may detect that the two friends are really prescribing to each other what the other should believe and do. This is how the metaethical theory known as *prescriptivism* characterizes the situation. When Gary makes an ethical claim, prescriptivism says he is prescribing what ought to be done, not only expressing his feelings.

But maybe the language and forms of reasoning that Gary and Orlando use lead the observing bird to think the debaters are actually stating facts about capital punishment when one of them asserts it is right and the other asserts it is wrong. Gary, for instance, declares that capital punishment is morally wrong; and he seems to be asserting it as a fact, a true declarative statement. It seems that Gary is attributing the property of moral wrongness to this policy. Perhaps *moral realism*, then, the view that some ethical statements are true and that there are such things as moral facts and properties, more accurately characterizes what Gary is doing.

Should we simply ask Gary what he is doing when he declares that capital punishment is morally wrong? Should we ask him if he means to be making a declarative true statement, or if he means to be prescribing, or expressing, or emoting? Will that be a reliable way to get to the bottom of things? Metaethicists don't think so, since people can be mistaken about their own conception of what they are doing. Even if Gary confides in us that he sincerely means to be making a declarative claim that capital punishment is morally wrong, and he insists that his claim is true, the theory of *ethical relativism* will respond, "That's what they all say." Moral truth is relative, says the theory of ethical relativism, for Orlando has also confided in us that he is sincerely setting forth true ethical claims when he asserts that capital punishment is morally acceptable. Lastly, a metaethical *error theory* says that although people like Gary and Orlando commonly believe there can be objectively true moral claims, that assumption is false, for there are no objectively true moral statements. Anyone who believes that moral statements can be objectively true is in error.

But metaethical theorists can be mistaken as well. The proper way to characterize moral statements and moral judgments thus remains an unsettled metaethical issue. The metaethical theories of expressivism, emotivism, prescriptivism, moral realism, ethical relativism, and error theory are all examples of theories about the status of ethics, for they each offer an account of the status of ethical claims.

For more on these topics see Miller (2003), a rigorous examination of contemporary metaethics. The following are anthologies that solely consist of metaethical selections: Darwall, Gibbard, & Railton (1997), Fisher & Kirchin (2006), and Shafer-Landau & Cuneo (2007).

Metaethics and Other Branches of Philosophy

Metaethical issues intersect with many other branches of philosophy. These other branches of philosophy include: metaphysics (inquiry into ultimate reality), aesthetics (inquiry into art and beauty), philosophy of mind (inquiry into the nature of mind and consciousness), epistemology (inquiry into knowledge and truth), philosophy of language (inquiry into the nature of language and meaning), logic (the study of reasoning), and the philosophy of science (inquiry into the nature of science).

When doing metaphysics, we inquire into the general nature of reality. So in metaethics when we face questions about the general nature of value and how values connect with the world, we are also engaged with metaphysics. Also, in metaethics when we inquire into the nature of moral qualities, moral properties, and moral facts, these are metaphysical pursuits. In aesthetics, we are interested in aesthetic value and how it connects to the world. As we saw above, in the section on subjectivity, objectivity, and the status of ethics, figuring out how value connects with the world is also a metaethical concern. Metaethics and the philosophy of mind obviously cross paths on the topics of moral judgments and moral psychology.

Metaethics and epistemology overlap when we attempt to figure out how we come to know ethical concepts, principles, and values. The topics of moral truth, moral knowledge, and moral justification are so extensive that some theorists use the term *moral epistemology* to refer to this domain of intersection. Metaethics and the philosophy of language overlap in the pursuit of the meaning of moral statements and moral assertions. The study of logic and language themselves overlap, and metaethical issues arise concerning the role of moral assertions in logical arguments, as well as identifying legitimate and illegitimate forms of moral reasoning. Finally, the philosophy of science has offered ethical naturalists many ideas about how to define and/or reduce moral terms to non-moral terms.

Philosophical Ethics

I began this appendix by saying that metaethics is a branch of ethical theory that inquires into the ultimate nature of ethics. Such a simple definition of metaethics falls flat and masks the knotty philosophical issues and problems that complicate the extensive terrain of metaethics. If one requires a quick definition of metaethics, it is more enlightening, therefore, to contrast metaethics with normative ethics. Normative ethical theories are theories that aim to provide practical guidance about how to act and what kind of person to be, and metaethical theories are purely theoretical ethical theories that aim to enlighten our understanding of ethics but not to provide practical guidance for action.

Simply put, normative ethical theories deal with the philosophical problem of conduct, and metaethical theories deal with the problem of the origins of ethics, the problem of relativism, and the problem of human nature.

The main solutions we looked at to the practical problem of conduct were virtue ethics, natural law ethics, social contract ethics, utilitarian ethics, and care ethics. As developed normative ethical theories, though, these theories also engage with the problem of the origins of ethics, the problem of relativism, and the problem of human nature. At the outset of this appendix I also said that the boundaries between metaethics and normative ethics are sometimes blurry. The contemporary moral philosopher Stephen Darwall uses the term *philosophical ethics* to describe the integrated treatment of normative ethics and metaethics (Darwall 1998: 9). Darwall points out that in the works of the great figures in the history of ethics, we rarely find a clear separation between metaethics and normative ethics. Thinkers such as Aristotle, Hobbes, Kant, and Mill, Darwall says, all attempt to *integrate* metaethics and normative theory into a coherent systematic view (Darwall 1998: 12). Shelly Kagan, too, another contemporary moral philosopher, makes a similar claim. Kagan says that metaethics and normative ethics are not so independent from each other, and instead of a sharp line between metaethics and normative there is a continuum (Kagan 1998: 5). In the main text of this book I have remained true to the venerable tradition of integrating normative ethics and metaethics, and have only emphasized the separation between them in this appendix, which serves as an introduction to the main signposts, labels, and terminology in contemporary metaethics for those readers who wish to pursue ethics at a more theoretical level.

The following are three anthologies that have some selections on metaethics and some selections on normative ethics: LaFollette (2000), Fieser (2000), and Shafer-Landau (2007).

Appendix 5: References

Abbott, Walter M. (ed.). 1966a. "Declaration on the Relationship of the Church to Non-Christian Religions (Nostra Aetate)," in *The Documents of Vatican II*. New York: Guild Press, pp. 660–8.

Abbott, Walter M. (ed.). 1966b. "Decree on Ecumenism (Unitatis Redintegratio)," in *The Documents of Vatican II*. New York: Guild Press, pp. 341–2.

Ackrill, J. L. (ed.). 1987. *A New Aristotle Reader*. Princeton, NJ: Princeton University Press.

Anscombe, G. E. M. 1958. "Modern Moral Philosophy," *Philosophy* 33: 1–19.

Aquinas, St. Thomas. [1270] 1989. *Summa Theologiae*, trans. T. McDermott. Allen, TX: Christian Classics.

Arendt, Hannah. 1963. *Eichmann in Jerusalem*. New York: Penguin Books.

Aristotle. [350 BCE] 1954. *Rhetoric*, trans. W.R. Roberts. In *Rhetoric and Poetics of Aristotle*. Toronto, Canada: Random House.

Aristotle. [337 BCE] 1985. *Nicomachean Ethics*, trans. T. Irwin. Indianapolis, IN: Hackett Publishing Co.

Arnhart, Larry. 1998. *Darwinian Natural Right: The Biological Ethics of Human Nature*. Albany, NY: State University of New York Press.

Arnhart, Larry. 2001. "Thomistic Natural Law as Darwinian Natural Right," in E. F. Paul, F. D. Miller, and J. Paul (eds.), *Natural Law and Modern Moral Philosophy*. Cambridge: Cambridge University Press, pp. 1–33.

Baldwin, Lou. 2004. "Gianna Beretta Molla," *The Catholic Standard and Times*, May 6, 2004.

Barcalow, Emmett. [1994] 2006. "Problems for Natural Law Theory," in Mark Timmons (ed.), *Conduct and Character: Readings in Moral Theory*, 5th edition. Belmont, CA: Thompson, pp. 84–7.

Barns, Sarah. 2015. "The Terrifying Rise of Breast Ironing," *Daily Mail*, October 13, 2015.

Baron, Marcia W., Philip Pettit, and Michael Slote. 1997. *Three Methods of Ethics: A Debate*. Oxford: Blackwell Publishers.

Ethics: The Basics, Second Edition. John Mizzoni.

Benedict, Ruth. 1934. *Patterns of Culture*. Boston, MA: Houghton Mifflin Company.

Bentham, Jeremy. [1789] 1988. *The Principles of Morals and Legislation*. Amherst, NY: Prometheus Books.

Blow, Thomas. 2003. *Build With Living Stones: Formation for Franciscan Life and Work*, 3rd edition. St. Bonaventure, NY: The Franciscan Institute.

Bowie, Norman E. 1999. *Business Ethics: A Kantian Perspective*. Oxford: Blackwell Publishers.

Boyd, Craig A. 2007. *Shared Morality: A Narrative Defense of Natural Law Ethics*. Ada, MI: Brazos Press.

Boyle, Joseph M. Jr. 1980. "Toward Understanding the Principle of Double Effect," *Ethics* 90: 527–38.

Boyle, Joseph M. Jr. 1984. "The Principle of Double Effect: Good Actions Entangled in Evil," in *Moral Theology Today: Certitudes and Doubts*. St. Louis, MO: The Pope John Center, pp. 243–60.

Boyle, Joseph M. Jr. 1992. "Natural Law and the Ethics of Traditions," in R. P. George (ed.), *Natural Law Theory: Contemporary Essays*. New York: Oxford University Press, pp. 3–30.

Buber, Martin. [1923] 1970. *I and Thou*, trans. W. Kaufmann. New York, NY: Scribners.

Chan, Wing-Tsit (ed.). 1963. *A Source Book in Chinese Philosophy*. Princeton, NJ: Princeton University Press.

Cicero. 52 BCE. *Treatise on the Laws*. http://oll.libertyfund.org/titles/cicero-treatise-on-the-laws Accessed October 10, 2016

Comte-Sponville, Andre. 2001. *A Small Treatise on the Great Virtues*. New York: Henry Holt & Company.

Confucius. [450 BCE] 1938. *The Analects of Confucius*, trans. A. Waley. New York: Vintage.

Covey, Stephen R. 1989. *The Seven Habits of Highly Effective People: Restoring the Character Ethic*. New York: Simon and Schuster.

Crisp, Roger. 1996. *How Should One Live? Essays on the Virtues*. New York: Oxford University Press.

Crisp, Roger, and Michael Slote (eds.). 1997. *Virtue Ethics*. New York: Oxford University Press.

Dancy, Jonathan. 1993. *Moral Reasons*. Oxford: Blackwell Publishers.

Darwall, Stephen. 1998. *Philosophical Ethics*. Boulder, CO: Westview.

Darwall, Stephen, Allan Gibbard, and Peter Railton (eds.). 1997. *Moral Discourse & Practice: Some Philosophical Approaches*. New York: Oxford University Press.

Davey, Monica. 2006. "Defying Law, a Foie Gras Feast in Chicago," *The New York Times*, August 23, 2006.

DesJardins, Joseph. 2009. *An Introduction to Business Ethics*, 3rd edition. Boston, MA: McGraw-Hill.

Donaldson, Thomas. 1982. *Corporations and Morality*. Englewood Cliffs, NJ: Prentice-Hall.

Donaldson, Thomas, and Thomas W. Dunfee. 1999. *Ties That Bind: A Social Contracts Approach to Business Ethics*. Boston, MA: Harvard Business School Press.

Downes, Lawrence. 2005. "One Man's Liver …," *The New York Times*, April 4, 2005.

Fieser, James (ed.). 2000. *Metaethics, Normative Ethics, and Applied Ethics: Historical and Contemporary Readings*. Belmont, CA: Wadsworth.

Fieser, James. 2001. *Moral Philosophy through the Ages*. Mountain View, CA: Mayfield Publishing Co.

Fisher, Andrew, and Simon Kirchin (eds.). 2006. *Arguing About Metaethics*. New York: Routledge.

Foot, Philippa. [1967] 2007. "The Problem of Abortion and the Doctrine of the Double Effect," in Russ Shafer-Landau (ed.), *Ethical Theory: An Anthology*. Oxford: Blackwell Publishers, pp. 582–9.

Gardiner, Stephen M. (ed.) 2005. *Virtue Ethics: Old and New*. Ithaca: Cornell University Press.

Gates, Lisa Uzzle. 2016. "Mississippi Volunteer to Receive National Honor," *Methodist Rehabilitation Center*.

Gauthier, David. 1986. *Morals by Agreement*. New York: Oxford University Press.

Gert, Bernard. 2004. *Common Morality: Deciding What To Do*. New York: Oxford University Press.

Gilligan, Carol. 1982. *In a Different Voice: Psychological Theory and Women's Development*. Cambridge, MA: Harvard University Press.

Gomez-Lobo, Alfonso. 2001. *Morality and the Human Goods: An Introduction to Natural Law Ethics*. Washington, DC: Georgetown University Press.

Gray, John. 1992. *Men Are from Mars: Women Are from Venus: A Practical Guide for Improving Communication and Getting What You Want in Your Relationships*. New York, NY: HarperCollins Publishers.

Grimshaw, Jean. 1991. "The Idea of a Female Ethic," in Peter Singer (ed.), *A Companion to Ethics*. Oxford: Blackwell Publishers, pp. 491–9.

Gupta, Bina (ed.). 2002. *Ethical Questions: East and West*. Lanham, MD: Rowman & Littlefield.

Hall, Calvin S. 1954. *A Primer of Freudian Psychology*. New York: Mentor Books.

Hare, R. M. 1963. *Freedom and Reason*. New York: Oxford University Press.

Harman, Gilbert. [1975] 2007. "Moral Relativism Defended," in Shafer-Landau, R. and Cuneo, T. (eds.) *Foundations of Ethics: An Anthology*. Oxford: Blackwell, pp. 84–92.

Harman, Gilbert. 1984. "Is There A Single True Morality?" In D. Copp & D. Zimmerman, eds. *Morality, Reason and Truth: New Essays on the Foundations of Ethics*. Totowa, NJ: Rowman & Allanheld, pp. 27–48.

Harman, Gilbert, and Judith Jarvis Thomson. 1996. *Moral Relativism and Moral Objectivity*. Oxford: Blackwell Publishers.

Held, Virginia. 2006. *The Ethics of Care: Personal, Political, and Global*. New York: Oxford University Press.

Helm, Paul (ed.). 1981. *Divine Commands and Morality*. New York: Oxford University Press.

Hobbes, Thomas. [1651] 1962. *Leviathan*, ed. M. Oakeshott. Introduction by R. S. Peters. New York: Collier Books.

van Hooft, Stan. 2006. *Understanding Virtue Ethics*. Chesham, Bucks: Acumen Publishing Limited.

Hume, David. [1739] 1989. *A Treatise of Human Nature*. Oxford: Oxford University Press.

Hume, David. [1751] 1983. *An Enquiry Concerning the Principles of Morals*. Indianapolis, IN: Hackett Publishing Company.

Jacobs, Jonathan. 2002. *Dimensions of Moral Theory: An Introduction to Metaethics and Moral Psychology*. Oxford: Blackwell Publishers.

Kagan, Shelly. 1998. *Normative Ethics*. Boulder, CO: Westview Press.

Kahane, Howard. 1995. *Contract Ethics*. Lanham, MD: Rowman & Littlefield.

Kant, Immanuel. [1780] 1979. *Lectures on Ethics*, trans. L. Infield. Indianapolis, IN: Hackett Publishing Co.

Kant, Immanuel. [1785] 1981. *Grounding for the Metaphysics of Morals*, trans. J. W. Ellington. Indianapolis, IN: Hackett Publishing Co.

Kant, Immanuel. [1790] 1959. *The Science of Right*, trans. W. Hastie. In C. Morris (ed.), *The Great Legal Philosophers*. Philadelphia: University of Pennsylvania Press, pp. 239–60.

Kekes, John. 1989. *Moral Tradition and Individuality*. Princeton, NJ: Princeton University Press.

Khazan, Olga. 2015. "Why Some Women Choose To Get Circumcised," *The Atlantic*, April 8, 2015.

Krausz, Michael (ed.) 1989. *Relativism: Interpretation and Confrontation*. Notre Dame, IN: University of Notre Dame Press.

Krausz, M. and J. W. Meiland (eds.) 1982. *Relativism: Cognitive and Moral*. Notre Dame, IN: University of Notre Dame Press.

Kymlicka, Will. 1991. "The Social Contract Tradition," in Peter Singer (ed.), *A Companion to Ethics*. Oxford: Blackwell Publishers, pp. 186–96.

Kyte, Richard. 2004. "Hospitality in the Franciscan Tradition," *The AFCU Journal: A Franciscan Perspective on Higher Education* 1: 10–22.

LaFollette, Hugh (ed.). 2000. *The Blackwell Guide to Ethical Theory*. Oxford: Blackwell Publishers.

LaFollette, Hugh (ed.). 2002. *Ethics in Practice: An Anthology*, 2nd edition. Oxford: Blackwell Publishers.

Laing, Jacqueline A. and Russell Wilcox. 2014. *The Natural Law Reader*. Oxford: Wiley-Blackwell.

Levin, Michael. 2000. "Is There a Female Morality?," in James Fieser (ed.), *Metaethics, Normative Ethics, and Applied Ethics: Historical and Contemporary Readings*. Belmont, CA: Wadsworth. pp. 361–8.

Levy, Neil. 2002. *Moral Relativism: A Short Introduction*. Oxford: Oneworld.

Lindemann, Hilde. 2006. *An Invitation to Feminist Ethics*. New York, NY: McGraw-Hill.

Locke, John. [1689] 1980. *Second Treatise of Government*. Indianapolis, IN: Hackett Publishing Co.

MacIntyre, Alasdair. 1984. *After Virtue: A Study of Moral Theory*, 2nd edition. Notre Dame, IN: University of Notre Dame Press.

MacIntyre, Alasdair. 1988. *Whose Justice? Which Rationality?* Notre Dame, IN: University of Notre Dame Press.

MacIntyre, Alasdair. 1990. *Three Rival Versions of Moral Enquiry: Encyclopaedia, Genealogy, and Tradition*. Notre Dame, IN: University of Notre Dame Press.

MacIntyre, Alasdair. 1998. *A Short History of Ethics: A History of Moral Philosophy from the Homeric Age to the Twentieth Century*, 2nd edition. Notre Dame, IN: University of Notre Dame Press.

McInerny, Ralph. 1982. *Ethica Thomistica: The Moral Philosophy of Thomas Aquinas*. Washington, DC: The Catholic University of America Press.

Mill, John Stuart. [1861] 1979. *Utilitarianism*. Indianapolis, IN: Hackett Publishing Co.

Mill, John Stuart. [1869] 1997. *The Subjection of Women*. Mineola, NY: Dover Books.

Miller, Alexander. 2003. *An Introduction to Contemporary Metaethics*. Oxford: Polity Press.

Miller, Barbara Stoller (trans.). [100 BCE] 1986. *The Bhagavad-Gita: Krishna's Counsel in Time of War*. New York, NY: Bantam Books.

Moore, G. E. [1903] 1991. *Principia Ethica*. Cambridge: Cambridge University Press.

Morris, Tom. 1998. *If Aristotle Ran General Motors*. New York: Owl Books.

Moser, Paul K., and Thomas L. Carson (eds.). 2001. *Moral Relativism: A Reader*. New York: Oxford University Press.

Noddings, Nel. 1984. *Caring: A Feminine Approach to Ethics & Moral Education*. Berkeley, CA: University of California Press.

Noddings, Nel. 2010. *The Maternal Factor: Two Paths to Morality*. Berkeley, CA: University of California Press.

Nussbaum, Martha. [1988] 2007. "Non-Relative Virtues: An Aristotelian Approach," in Russ Shafer-Landau, *Ethical Theory: An Anthology*. Oxford: Blackwell Publishers, pp. 684–700.

O'Connor, D. J. 1967. *Aquinas and Natural Law*. London: Macmillan.

Olen, Jeffrey, and Vincent Barry (eds.). 1999. *Applying Ethics*, 6th edition. Belmont, CA: Wadsworth.

Pinckaers, Servais. 2001. *Morality: The Catholic View*, trans. M. Sherwin. South Bend, IN: St. Augustine's Press.

Plato. [380 BCE] 1975. "Apology," in *The Trial and Death of Socrates*, trans. G. M. A. Grube. Indianapolis, IN: Hackett Publishing Co., pp. 21–42.

Plato. [380 BCE] 1975. "Euthyphro," in *The Trial and Death of Socrates*, trans. G. M. A. Grube. Indianapolis, IN: Hackett Publishing Co., pp. 3–20.

Plato. [380 BCE] 1976. *Meno*, trans. G. M. A. Grube. Indianapolis, IN: Hackett Publishing Co.

Pojman, Louis P. (ed.). 2004. *The Moral Life: An Introductory Reader in Ethics and Literature*, 2nd edition. New York: Oxford University Press.

Pollock, Joycelyn M. 2007. *Ethical Dilemmas and Decisions in Criminal Justice*, 5th edition. Belmont, CA: Thomson Wadsworth.

Pope John Paul II. 1993. *The Splendor of Truth* (*Veritatis Splendor*). Boston, MA: St. Paul Books & Media.

Pope John Paul II. 1998. *Faith and Reason* (*Fides et Ratio*). Boston, MA: St. Paul Books & Media.

Pope Paul VI. 1968. *Of Human Life* (*Humanae Vitae*). Boston, MA: Pauline Books & Media.

Rawls, John. 1971. *A Theory of Justice*. Cambridge, MA: Harvard University Press.

Regan, Tom. 1983. *The Case for Animal Rights*. Berkeley, CA: University of California Press.

Ridley, Matt. 1996. *The Origins of Virtue*. New York: Penguin Books.

Rodin, David. 2004. "Terrorism without Intention," *Ethics* 114: 752–71.

Rosenstand, Nina. 2000. *The Moral of the Story: An Introduction to Ethics*, 3rd edition. Mountain View, CA: Mayfield Publishing Co.

Rudnick, Abraham. 2001. "A Meta-Ethical Critique of Care Ethics," *Theoretical Medicine and Bioethics* 22: 505–17.

Ruse, Michael. 1998. *Taking Darwin Seriously*. Amherst, NY: Prometheus Books.

Ruse, Michael, and Edward O. Wilson. 1986. "Moral Philosophy as Applied Science," *Philosophy* 61: 173–92.

Scanlon, T. M. 1998. *What We Owe to Each Other*. Cambridge, MA: Harvard University Press.

Schneewind, J. B. (ed.). 1990. *Moral Philosophy from Montaigne to Kant: An Anthology, Volume 1*. Cambridge: Cambridge University Press.

Shafer-Landau, Russ. 2004. *Whatever Happened to Good and Evil?* New York: Oxford University Press.

Shafer-Landau, Russ (ed.). 2007. *Ethical Theory: An Anthology*. Oxford: Blackwell Publishers.

Shafer-Landau, Russ, and Terence Cuneo (eds.). 2007. *Foundations of Ethics: An Anthology*. Oxford: Blackwell Publishers.

Shaw, William H. 1999. *Contemporary Ethics: Taking Account of Utilitarianism*. Oxford: Blackwell Publishers.

Sigmund. P. E. (ed.). 1988. *St. Thomas Aquinas on Politics and Ethics*. New York: W. W. Norton & Company.

Simon, Yves. 1965. *The Tradition of Natural Law*. New York: Fordham University Press.

Singer, Peter. [1975] 1990. *Animal Liberation*, new revised edition. New York: Avon Books.

Singer, Peter (ed.). 1986. *Applied Ethics*. New York: Oxford University Press.

Singer, Peter (ed.). 1991. *A Companion to Ethics*. Oxford: Blackwell Publishers.

Slote, Michael. 2001. *Morals from Motives*. New York: Oxford University Press.

Solomon, Robert C. 1992. *Ethics and Excellence: Cooperation and Integrity in Business*. New York: Oxford University Press.

Sumner, William G. 1906. *Folkways*. Boston: Ginn & Company.

Timmons, Mark. (ed.) 2006. *Conduct and Character: Readings in Moral Theory*, 5th edition. Belmont, CA: Thompson.

Weil, Andrew. 2006. "Surgery With a Side of Fries," *The New York Times*, July 6, 2006.

Weston, Anthony. 2001. *A 21st Century Ethical Toolbox*. New York, NY: Oxford University Press.

Williams, Bernard. 1985. *Ethics and the Limits of Philosophy*. Cambridge, MA: Harvard University Press.

Williams, Bernard, and J. J. C. Smart. 1973. *Utilitarianism: For & Against*. Cambridge: Cambridge University Press.

Wilson, Edward O. 1978. *On Human Nature*. Cambridge, MA: Harvard University Press.

Wollstonecraft, Mary. [1792] 1986. *Vindication of the Rights of Woman*. New York: Penguin Books.

Wong, David B. 1991. "Relativism." In P. Singer, ed. *A Companion to Ethics*. Oxford: Blackwell, pp. 442–50.

Wong, David B. 2006. *Natural Moralities: A Defense of Pluralistic Relativism*. New York: Oxford University Press.

Woodward, P. A. (ed.). 2001. *The Doctrine of Double Effect: Philosophers Debate a Controversial Moral Principle*. Notre Dame, IN: University of Notre Dame Press.

Index

Ethics: The Basics, Second Edition. John Mizzoni.